the Legend of La-Z-Boy

the Legend
of
La-Z-Boy

Jeffrey L. Rodengen & Richard F. Hubbard

Edited by Heather Deeley
Design and layout by Wendy Iverson

For Bill Hatch—
No one ever looked better in a La-Z-Boy.
Keep those hooks sharpened.

Write Stuff Enterprises, Inc.
1001 South Andrews Avenue
Second Floor
Fort Lauderdale, FL 33316
1-800-900-Book (1-800-900-2665)
(954) 462-6657
www.writestuffbooks.com

Publisher's Cataloging in Publication

Rodengen, Jeffrey L.
    The Legend of La-Z-Boy/ Jeffrey L.
Rodengen & Richard F. Hubbard. — 1st ed.
    p. cm.
    LCCN 2002115059
    ISBN 0-945903-93-6

    1. La-Z-Boy (Firm)—History 2. Furniture industry and trade — United States — History. I. Hubbard, Richard F. II. Title.

    HD9773.U7L39 2003   338.7'6841'00973
                                                      QBI03-200222

Library of Congress
Catalog Card Number 00-132978

    ISBN 0-945903-93-6

Completely produced in the
United States of America
10 9 8 7 6 5 4 3 2 1

Also by Jeffrey L. Rodengen

The Legend of Chris-Craft

IRON FIST: The Lives of Carl Kiekhaefer

Evinrude-Johnson and The Legend of OMC

Serving the Silent Service: The Legend of Electric Boat

The Legend of Dr Pepper/Seven-Up

The Legend of Honeywell

The Legend of Briggs & Stratton

The Legend of Ingersoll-Rand

The Legend of Stanley: 150 Years of The Stanley Works

The MicroAge Way

The Legend of Halliburton

The Legend of York International

The Legend of Nucor Corporation

The Legend of Goodyear: The First 100 Years

The Legend of AMP

The Legend of Cessna

The Legend of VF Corporation

The Spirit of AMD

The Legend of Rowan

New Horizons: The Story of Ashland Inc.

The History of American Standard

The Legend of Mercury Marine

The Legend of Federal-Mogul

Against the Odds: Inter-Tel—The First 30 Years

State of the Heart: The Practical Guide to Your Heart and Heart Surgery with Larry W. Stephenson, M.D.

The Legend of Pfizer

The Legend of Worthington Industries

The Legend of Trinity Industries, Inc.

The Legend of IBP, Inc.

The Legend of Cornelius Vanderbilt Whitney

The Legend of Amdahl

The Legend of Litton Industries

The Legend of Gulfstream

The Legend of Bertram with David A. Patten

The Legend of Ritchie Bros. Auctioneers

The Legend of ALLTEL with David A. Patten

The Yes, you can of Invacare Corporation with Anthony L. Wall

The Ship in the Balloon: The Story of Boston Scientific and the Development of Less-Invasive Medicine

The Legend of Day & Zimmermann

The Legend of Noble Drilling

Fifty Years of Innovation: Kulicke & Soffa

Biomet—From Warsaw to the World with Richard F. Hubbard

NRA: An American Legend

The Heritage and Values of RPM, Inc.

The Legend of Grainger

The Legend of The Titan Corporation

The Marmon Group: The First Fifty Years

The Legend of HealthSouth

The Legend of Discount Tire Co. with Richard F. Hubbard

TABLE OF CONTENTS

INTRODUCTION

L A-Z-BOY'S STORY BEGINS ON the eve of the Great Depression, when Edwin Shoemaker and Edward Knabusch introduced what would become an American icon: the recliner. The two cousins from Monroe, Michigan, were natural partners. Shoemaker was a brilliant mechanic, and Knabusch was a gifted woodworker and salesman. Before their recliner invention, the two men spent their free time tinkering in the Knabusch family garage creating end tables, magazine racks, doll furniture, and other small items. Some who knew them would affectionately claim "either one without the other probably would have starved," a testament to how well they worked together.

In 1927 the cousins decided to turn their hobby into a future and founded the Kna-Shoe Manufacturing Company, which was later renamed Floral City Furniture. A year later, they introduced what would become the first La-Z-Boy® recliner—a wood-slat porch chair they upholstered on the advice of a furniture buyer from Toledo, Ohio. La-Z-Boy, today a household name and admired trademark, was not the only moniker considered. Other contenders in Floral City Furniture's naming contest included the "Sit-N-Snooze" and the "Slackback." The employee who came up with the winning name of "La-Z-Boy" took home $25.

Like most Americans, Shoemaker and Knabusch struggled through the Great Depression years. In the hard times they accepted wheat, corn, coal, and farm animals in exchange for furniture. By 1933, sales had grown enough to open the company's first retail store and to hold its first annual furniture show.

In the show's debut year, Shoemaker and Knabusch gave each attendee a flowering shrub, an appropriate gift considering the name of their store. By the second year, the show was so popular that the founders rented a circus tent and displayed the furniture outside. Always looking to fill customers' needs, they even set up a mouse circus to entertain children so the parents could shop without distraction.

In 1940, the partners formed the La-Z-Boy Chair Company to manufacture furniture, but the plant soon was converted to war production, which occupied 85 percent of workers' time. The postwar buying frenzy put the company back on its feet.

The 1960s brought many changes. La-Z-Boy paid more attention to style, and its advertising began to include celebrities, such as Bing Crosby. Knabusch stepped down as president, passing the baton to his son, Charles. Then the 1970s brought expansion and growth with new plants in Tennessee and Arkansas.

The company's focus on the needs of its consumers and dealers strengthened in 1981 when Chairman Patrick Norton brought his wealth of experience—20 years with furniture giant Ethan Allen—to La-Z-Boy. Norton stabilized and energized La-Z-Boy and developed a unique and efficient distribution system that remains a retail industry model today. It supports a vast network of stand-alone La-Z-Boy Furniture Galleries and La-Z-Boy in-store galleries that add up to nearly 9 million square feet of retail floor space dedicated exclusively to selling La-Z-Boy® products and brands.

Seventy-five years after its inception, La-Z-Boy Incorporated is still headquartered in the small town where it was founded, but the company has grown to enormous proportions. With some 18,000 employees and annual sales in excess of $2 billion, its manufacturing operations can be found in nine states and in Canada, Mexico, the United Kingdom, and Thailand.

La-Z-Boy enjoys two unique marketing advantages: the power of its brand name and its proprietary distribution system. The La-Z-Boy brand name is synonymous with comfort and quality, and its marketing power is unparalleled in the industry. After all, La-Z-Boy is the best-known furniture brand among American consumers.

The Legend of La-Z-Boy celebrates 75 years of building comfortable furniture for America's families and commemorates the integrity and innovation of this icon of American industry. Even with a strong reputation as one of the fastest-growing and best-managed companies in the world, the La-Z-Boy team won't be reclining anytime soon.

ACKNOWLEDGMENTS

A GREAT NUMBER OF PEOPLE ASSISTED in the research, preparation, and publication of *The Legend of La-Z-Boy.*

The principal research and assembly of the narrative time line was accomplished by our gifted research assistant and indexer Barbara Koch. Her efforts went a long way toward making this book a success. Heather Deeley, associate editor, did a superb job of overseeing the text and photos from beginning to end. Art Director Wendy Iverson's graphic design brought the story to vivid life.

This book would not have been possible without the forthright recollections of Patrick Norton, chairman; Gerald Kiser, president and CEO; John Case, senior vice president and president, Upholstery Group; and Kurt Darrow, president, La-Z-Boy Residential. The organization and insight of Judy Carr, museum director, was invaluable to us. Richard Micka, vice president, corporate administration, was helpful in providing us with photos. Marsha Oberleiter, marketing projects supervisor, served as our tireless and resourceful liaison. Kathi Stiefel provided archival financial information, and photographer Joel Blohm provided us with photos promptly. We also wish to thank the families of Edwin Shoemaker and Edward Knabusch for providing photos and family stories. The late photographer Everette Payette took many of the early photos in this book.

Many other La-Z-Boy executives, employees, retirees, friends, and family members greatly enriched the book by discussing their experiences. The authors extend particular gratitude to these men and women for their candid recollections and anecdotes: Ed Breunig Jr., Ed Breunig III, Mary Bruce, Doug Collier, Rodney England, Bill Gallagher, Gene Hardy, Fritz Jackson, Steve Kincaid, Larry LaPointe, Courtney Leckler, Rocque Lipford, Steve Matlock, Charles McIntyre III, Paul Opfermann, John Quinn, Dale Shoemaker, Mark Stegeman, Alice Vagt, Marc Valentine, Jim Waltz, John Weaver, Betty Lou White, Gregory White, Lloyd White, Kaye Lani Wilson, and Caroline Zarend.

As always, special thanks are extended to the dedicated staff at Write Stuff Enterprises, Inc.: Jon VanZile, executive editor; Melody Maysonet, senior editor; Bonnie Freeman, copyeditor; Mary Aaron, transcriptionist; Barbara Koch, indexer; Sandy Cruz, senior art director; Rachelle Donley and Dennis Shockley, art directors; Bruce Borich, production manager; Marianne Roberts, vice president of administration; Sherry Hasso, bookkeeper; Linda Edell, executive assistant to Jeffrey L. Rodengen; Lars Jessen, director of worldwide marketing; Irena Xanthos, sales and promotions manager; Rory Schmer, distribution supervisor; and Jennifer Walter, administrative assistant.

The interest Edwin Shoemaker (left) and Edward Knabusch shared in furniture making led the cousins to form a partnership in 1927.

CHAPTER ONE

ANYTHING BUT LAZY

1900–1929

*Their abilities complemented one another beautifully. If there was a
little lack in one side, why, the other would make up for it.*

—Herman Gertz, a longtime store manager, 1986

RURAL MONROE COUNTY, Michigan, was a pleasant place to grow up during the early 20th century. Many of the county's 37,000 residents were hardworking farmers who grew corn, soybeans, vegetables, and fruit. The area's many nurseries produced trees, shrubs, and flowers, earning Monroe the nickname Floral City.

Monroe residents attended church functions, fished and swam in Lake Erie, and enjoyed picnics beside the River Raisin. They took pride in the area's history. Schoolchildren learned about the lives sacrificed in the county during the War of 1812. Residents passing through Monroe's Loranger Square gazed up at a larger-than-life statue of General George Armstrong Custer, who had lived in Monroe as a young man and married in the city's Presbyterian Church. President William Howard Taft had dedicated the statue in 1910.[1]

Young boys growing up on Monroe farms were expected to quit school at the age of 12 or 13 to join their fathers on their family farms. Some eventually left the farms to work at paper mills along the River Raisin. Others traveled to nearby Detroit or Toledo to take jobs in the budding automotive industry. Two Monroe County youngsters, Edward Knabusch (pronounced Kuh-NAY-bush), born in 1900, and his cousin Edwin Shoemaker, born in 1907, did what was expected of them and quit school after completing the eighth grade. They worked on their families' farms, but both dreamed of someday leaving agriculture to pursue other interests.[2]

Knabusch the Woodworker

Edward Knabusch was the son of John and Ida Knabusch. The young Knabusch loved the outdoors, but he disliked farming. He was more interested in woodworking, and at the age of 12, he made a three-piece bedroom suite for his mother.[3] Woodworking remained a hobby throughout Knabusch's youth, and at the age of 19, he set out to find a job away from the farm. He worked for six months at Monroe Auto Equipment Company before injuring his finger in a punch press accident. After recovering from the injury, he took a job as a machinist at Weis Manufacturing Company, a manufacturer of wood desks and other office furniture.[4]

Working an eight-hour shift was a new experience for Knabusch, who was used to the long hours he had been putting in on the farm. In 1952, Knabusch told *Inside Michigan* magazine that an 8 A.M. to 4 P.M. shift "made you feel you were only putting in a half day's work."[5] So when Knabusch

---

In its early years, Floral City Furniture Company specialized in novelty furniture such as this sewing cabinet.

returned home at 4 P.M., he retreated to his workshop, located in a small building he'd put up at the back of the property, beside the River Raisin. There he would make and repair furniture until midnight. He earned little money on the enterprise and spent what he had on used machinery.[6]

His first machine was a combination band saw, table saw, jointer, shaper, and boring machine. They all worked simultaneously; when one was on, they were all on.[7] Later, Knabusch purchased individual machines that ran on what he called a "one-lung" gasoline engine and line shaft. The roaring engine elicited complaints when he operated it long after the neighbors' bedtimes. To silence the engine, he shoved the exhaust pipe into the sewer. But exhaust fumes seeping through adjacent plumbing drew more complaints from neighbors, who smelled fumes wafting into their homes. Knabusch finally borrowed money to buy an electric motor.[8]

Shoemaker the Mechanic

A few miles away, Knabusch's young cousin Edwin Shoemaker was also getting restless on his family's farm. The Shoemakers had no automated machinery, and young Ed hated the grueling work, especially the long days of harvesting corn in the fall.

Like his cousin, Shoemaker liked to tinker. At 11, he made a 2-foot-high cabinet for his sister out of cigar boxes and orange crates. His meager tools included a hammer, an old screwdriver, a saw, a jackknife, and sandpaper. Because he couldn't afford to buy nails, he reused the nails from the boxes to secure the cabinet.[9]

Shoemaker eventually set up a workshop in the loft of his family's barn. He made a lathe and other tools. At 15, he bought his first drill press for $4.75 from the Montgomery Ward catalog.[10] In 1925, at age 18, Shoemaker set out to build a cabinet for a crystal radio he had made. The only wood

he had, a piece of yellow pine, was too thick. He heard that his cousin had a planer, so he drove his father's Model T to the Knabusch home in Monroe. The planer wasn't suitable for the job, but the young men's mutual interest in woodworking and their distaste for farming formed the foundation for a close friendship.[11]

Shoemaker examined his cousin's tools and found that some of them didn't work properly. Knabusch pointed out that his saw didn't cut square. Shoemaker rebabbitted the bearings and realigned the saw, correcting the trouble. He went on to repair the other tools as well.[12]

Shoemaker spent as much time as he could in Knabusch's workshop. Shoemaker's father, Louis Shoemaker, was disappointed with his son's lack of interest in farming. "Dad would only let me come to work with Ed when he didn't need me,"[13] Shoemaker said. "My father wanted me to take on the family farm, but I was much more interested in what Ed was coming up with in his family garage."[14]

Edwin Shoemaker honed his mechanical skills in this makeshift workshop in a barn loft. The drill press was purchased in 1922 from the Montgomery Ward catalog for $4.75. It was later used in the Floral City Furniture shop.

Shoemaker had promised his dad he would stay on the farm. But, he said, "I just couldn't get interested."

Combining Talents

"I would say they each had their talents," said Edwin Shoemaker's son, Dale. "Either one without the other probably would have starved."[15]

Shoemaker's mechanical ability complemented Knabusch's woodworking skills. When the proper tools weren't available, Shoemaker made his own. In 1925, while working at Weis, Knabusch came up with an idea for guiding a band saw without having to mark the wood. He described the idea to Shoemaker, who fashioned the device, and the young entrepreneurs obtained their first patent. Shoemaker spent more and more time at Knabusch's workshop, and the two cousins began making and repairing furniture together.[16] The entrepreneurs made end tables, magazine racks, framed mirrors, and other small items. Within a year, when Knabusch was 26 and Shoemaker was 19, Knabusch quit his job at Weis, and the two young men made plans to formalize and expand their business.

Because they had outgrown their makeshift workshop, their first task was to purchase land on which to build a larger facility. They chose a 2.5-acre field one mile north of Monroe. The land fronted a wagon trail known as Nelson's Lane.[17] Knabusch's previous run-ins with neighbors would not be a problem here; the nearest neighbors were a mile away on a pig farm. The land was almost inaccessible, but the foresighted partners had heard that a state highway was to be built over the wagon trail. Within a year, the anticipated highway was built and named Telegraph Road. It extended from Detroit to Toledo and soon became one of the most traveled routes in Michigan.[18]

A Partnership of Minds

On March 24, 1927, Shoemaker and Knabusch formed a partnership. John Knabusch and Louis Shoemaker accompanied their sons to the office of attorney Oliver J. Golden, where the partnership papers were signed. Louis signed for Edwin, who at 19 was too young to enter into

In 1925, Shoemaker and Knabusch obtained their first patent: this band saw guide, which they used to make end tables, magazine racks, framed mirrors, and other small items.

legal agreements. Edward put money he had saved from his job at Weis into the business. Louis Shoemaker mortgaged his farm to loan his son the money for an equal share in the partnership. Each partner contributed $5,600.

The cousins named their business Kna-Shoe Manufacturing Company. The name didn't last long, however. A few months after forming the partnership, Knabusch went to pick up a freight order and was turned away by an agent who told him the shipment was for the "New Shoe Company" on Telegraph Road. An angry Knabusch convinced the agent the order was his. This inconvenience would lead Knabusch and Shoemaker to change the name of their business to Floral City Furniture Company.[19]

The day after signing the partnership document, Knabusch and Shoemaker began building their new shop. With help from Knabusch's brother, William, who provided a team of horses and a board scraper, they dug the basement and sewers.[20] They mixed the cement, laid the foundation, and built the walls. The only tradesmen hired to help were two masons.

When the exterior of the building was completed, on August 10, 1927, the partners found themselves "fresh out of money," according to Shoemaker. They borrowed $3,000 from a friend to finish the building's interior.[21]

The 40-by-60-foot building was outfitted with the tools Knabusch and Shoemaker had used in their former workshops. Unable to buy more, the cousins built additional equipment and tools themselves, including an elevator. Metal and maintenance departments were located in the basement. Woodworking machinery was on the first floor. The second floor was used for finishing and storage.[22]

The *Monroe Evening News* described the completed building.

From sewer and basement to chimney and roof the factory was built by their own hands. The only help required was a couple of men to act as [masons]. Machinery and other essential equipment was purchased, assembled, and installed without seeking advice from experts. Several castings were designed by the men; two or three machines were designed and constructed by them; a safety device for a particular need was invented by the two minds and a patent was granted for it in face of competition from some of the greatest companies in the country. There are many interesting details about Monroe's newest factory which will win both admiration and praise from those who visit the concern.[23]

The building was situated a distance from the road. On the same land, fronting Telegraph Road, Knabusch built a house for himself and his young wife, Henrietta, whom he married on August 11, 1927. Shoemaker was his cousin's best man.

Knabusch felt optimism for the success of the new business, reported a *Monroe Evening News* article.

"We do not like to boast," Knabusch remarked as he paused for a moment in his labors. "But we think we have a splendid layout and we look for a very big business within the next few months. We have a fine line, an efficient, economical plant, and all the pep and enthusiasm that any enterprise could possibly want. All we need now is more hard work and a continuation of the cheerful goodwill that our friends and customers have given us."[24]

After settling into their new building, the partners continued to make and repair furniture. They worked 16 hours a day and earned little money. They paid themselves $5 a week and returned the rest of their earnings to the business.[25]

A 1928 advertisement in the *Monroe Evening News* described some of Floral City Furniture's myriad services.

Did you know that it is possible and practicable to take a fine old piece of furniture that has outlived its usefulness but that you still prize highly, and rebuild it into a table, desk, or chest of drawers that is attractive and useful? You retain the sentiment attached to the piece and still have it of real use. Did you know that you can have a chair, dresser, buffet or any other piece made to make a suite complete?

For instance, we recently rebuilt a prized old organ into a handsome buffet. An old-fashioned washstand of solid walnut was made into an attractive chest of drawers. A dilapidated old table (a Civil War trophy) was remade into a graceful desk. For another party a graceful old side chair was duplicated to complete a pair.[26]

Knabusch and Shoemaker created their own furniture designs for end tables, plant stands, radio cabinets, magazine racks, framed mirrors, and sewing cabinets. One of their most successful designs was called the Gossiper, a telephone stand that one could sit on while talking on the phone. A telephone book fit into a small rack built into the stand.[27]

Despite the success of the Gossiper, Knabusch and Shoemaker experienced keen frustration during these early days.

"We made all kinds of novelty furniture," Knabusch said. "I loaded the car and went to Detroit and peddled the stuff. When we came back for second and third orders, we'd find that some large furniture manufacturer had copied our design and because of larger, more economical production, could undersell us so much we couldn't get the business. So we would have to design something new. Many a time I remarked to Mr. Shoemaker

Edward Knabusch's mother, Ida, and his dog, Toodles, atop a smoker table, pose outside the Floral City Furniture building on a 2.5-acre field one mile north of Monroe, Michigan.

that we would have to get something that we could protect by patents."[28]

A Momentous Event in Relaxation

In the spring of 1928, the partners came up with a new product: a reclining porch chair. The seat of the wood-slat chair moved forward as the back reclined. By now, Shoemaker had taken a mail order drafting course, and he worked out the chair's mechanical device using a makeshift drafting board consisting of a square of plywood and a yardstick.[29]

"The secret of the whole thing was getting the linkages right," Shoemaker recalled. "We tried to avoid any sliding elements because of friction problems. A link that would swing would not rub on anything and would always work easily, so we stuck to that principle."[30]

The men made 12 wood-slat chairs. In May, Knabusch took six of the chairs to Lion Department Store in Toledo, where buyer Arthur Richardson commented on the seasonality of the chair.

"Well, I don't know if you noticed or not, but we bought all of our summer furniture last October, and we're buying winter furniture now," Richardson said.[31] He suggested Floral City Furniture create an upholstered version of the chair that would sell year-round.[32]

Knabusch and Shoemaker knew nothing about upholstery.

"I didn't know velour from tapestry and mohair," Knabusch said. But they set to work creating a recliner suitable for a living room. They'd made little progress by September, when they took time off to prepare for the upcoming Christmas season, for which they made 5,000 sets of doll furniture and 100 Gossiper telephone stands.[33] The doll furniture was produced in cooperation with two Toledo, Ohio, entrepreneurs, who supplied Floral City Furniture with discontinued upholstery purchased from automotive companies. Floral City Furniture hired 12 men to make frames and 15 women to upholster the pieces. The three-piece sets consisted of a rocker, a chair, and a davenport. The Toledo men sold the sets on Detroit and Toledo street corners.[34] The sets were also advertised at $2.50 in the *Monroe Evening News*.[35]

The doll furniture sold well, and just before Christmas, Shoemaker and Knabusch again turned their attention to the upholstered reclining chair. On December 15, they employed the help of an upholsterer, George Welker, from Fort Wayne, Indiana. Welker was the father-in-law of a local minister and a friend of Knabusch.[36] He wasn't convinced an upholstered version of the reclining porch chair would work, but with his help, Knabusch and Shoemaker produced two chairs during Christmas week.

"Until George came, we didn't know very much about upholstery," Shoemaker recalled. "He worked at a mattress company there in Fort Wayne, but he was a skilled upholsterer. He could take quality antiques and reupholster them using horsehair . . . Spanish moss, and flax straw, which was called tow."[37]

The Sit-N-Snooze?

Local buyers were enthusiastic about the new chair. Knabusch and Shoemaker believed their design would sell if produced in quantity. To protect the mechanics, Shoemaker borrowed $146 from his father and applied for a patent.[38]

The December 31, 1928, *Monroe Evening News* reported that Floral City Furniture was preparing to produce its automatic adjustable chair for the national market. "We have applied for a patent on this chair, plan to incorporate, increase our capital, and expand our working force to accommodate

what we expect to be a great demand for our special product," Knabusch told the *News*.[39]

The unusual thing about this chair is that it will give the occupant any position—sitting, semi-reclining, or entirely reclining—without touching a lever or regulator of any kind. The action of the seat automatically regulates that of the back and vice versa. A child weighing 50 pounds can as easily change from a sitting to a lying position as can a man weighing 200 pounds.[40]

Knabusch continued, "There's at least one thing I want to make clear. When we start on production with these chairs, we shall not sacrifice quality."[41]

Knabusch asked workers in Floral City Furniture's shop and office to name the chair. A number of ideas were submitted, including Sit-N-Snooze, Slackback, and Comfort Carrier. But one, La-Z-Boy, stood out among the entries. The winner, whose name is lost to history, earned $25 for the suggestion.[42]

Knabusch and Shoemaker contracted with a Toledo upholsterer to make La-Z-Boy® chairs and

Opposite: A reclining wood-slat porch chair preceded the upholstered La-Z-Boy chair in the spring of 1928. The seat of the chair moved forward as the back reclined.

Right: A December 31, 1928, article in the *Monroe Evening News* described Floral City Furniture's automatic adjustable chair.

Below: Shoemaker and Knabusch applied for a patent on the La-Z-Boy chair in 1929 to protect its mechanics.

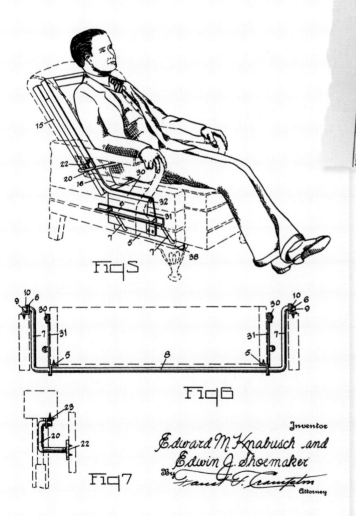

Jan. 20, 1931.   E. M. KNABUSCH ET AL   1,789,337

RECLINING CHAIR

Filed Jan. 24, 1929   3 Sheets-Sheet 3

MONDAY, DECEMBER 31, 1928.

FURNITURE COMPANY EXPANDING RAPIDLY IN LOCAL FACTORY

A New Industry Rises Here

Edward Knabusch and Edwin Shoemaker Have Perfected an Adjustable Chair

THEY BUILD A PLANT WITHOUT ASSISTANCE

Specialty Business Has Grown Rapidly in Single Year of Production

EDWARD KNABUSCH   EDWIN SHOEMAKER

—*Photos By Beck.*

matching ottomans using frames and mechanics supplied by Floral City Furniture. They hired Everett Richardson, son of the Lion Department Store buyer who had suggested upholstering the recliner, as a salesman. He traveled through Ontario, Canada, with the chair, making 64 sales calls, and 62 dealers placed orders.[43] A 1929 price list stated, "We fully guarantee all mechanical parts on La-Z-Boy Chairs and stand ready to replace them free of charge."[44]

Although they believed they had a winner, Knabusch and Shoemaker envisioned the chair as just one component of their furniture manufacturing business. Knabusch told the *Monroe Evening News*, "For the first time, we are going to make living room suites and a full line of upholstered articles this year. This adjustable chair belongs in a living room set, and we figure that now is a logical time to branch out into that general type of furniture making. Though the manufacture of living room suites will be a specialty of our business in 1929, we can say now that we expect a great demand for our radio cabinets, also."[45]

Becoming Incorporated

In April 1929, Floral City Furniture Company was incorporated. Edward Knabusch was named president and general manager; Attorney Oliver J. Golden became vice president; Howard M. Comstock, a Monroe County pharmacist, was named secretary; and Edwin Shoemaker became treasurer. Knabusch and Shoemaker each contributed $10,000, which they had already invested in the business. Golden and Comstock each invested $5,000.[46]

Howard Comstock, 40, was a graduate of the University of Michigan.[47] He took little interest in the daily operations of Floral City Furniture. Golden, however, kept close tabs on the company's finances.

"He couldn't figure out why we couldn't determine at the end of every workday how much money we had made that day," Shoemaker recalled. "He always criticized Ed [Knabusch] quite a bit because Ed was too optimistic for him."[48]

Encouraged by Richardson's success selling the chairs, Knabusch made plans to display the La-Z-Boy® chair at the Grand Rapids Furniture Show in May 1929. One night after work, Knabusch and Richardson loaded 13 chairs on Floral City Furniture's truck and set out. Grand Rapids, Michigan, 175 miles northwest of Monroe County, was the country's furniture manufacturing capital during the early 20th century. Twice a year, thousands of salesmen, buyers, and reporters attended the furniture market in showrooms throughout the city.

The duo drove all night to get to the market, then unloaded the chairs and arranged them in a

---

Edward Knabusch installed the platform and racks on a 1925 Chevrolet truck chassis and cab to make this delivery truck for Floral City Furniture Company. Toodles rests in the cab.

display. Knabusch later recalled, "All the dealers got a big laugh when they saw the owner of the factory muscling the chairs off the truck."[49] But they didn't laugh long. The chair attracted a lot of attention—and orders.

The market newsletter described the La-Z-Boy chair.

Take the weight off of the seat, and presto, a perfectly comfortable, upholstered chair becomes a reclining chair without any effort whatever. This is the bombshell sensation that the Floral City Furniture Company of Monroe, Michigan, is introducing to buyers in this market. In appearance, the chair looks no different from any other. When one sits solidly in it, it is motionless. But throw back the head, and take the weight off of the seat slightly, and the back slides to a horizontal position, the seat comes up, and you have the most comfortable easy chair imaginable. The clothing is pulled in no way during the process, and one

may recline and sit up again and again without causing a wrinkle in coat or skirt.[50]

Knabusch left the market with his pockets bulging with orders. His and Shoemaker's youthful optimism and hard work appeared to be drawing them closer to their dream. The *Monroe Evening News* noted, "It is quite improbable that Monroe will ever attain such prominence in the furniture industry as Grand Rapids has built for itself. But if the hopes and dreams of two Monroe men come true, this city will be the home of a significant and far-reaching furniture industry."[51]

The two entrepreneurs hoped they could ride to success on their reclining chair. But they were faced with an immediate challenge. Their small facility did not have the capacity to fill all the La-Z-Boy orders from the Grand Rapids show. Already in debt, they had no hope of borrowing money to expand. Shoemaker and Knabusch would have to find a way to make large quantities of La-Z-Boy chairs.

These 1935 Frigidaire refrigerators made up a display at Floral City Furniture. Money was tight during the 1930s, and one farmer paid for a refrigerator with a cow.

CHAPTER TWO

BY THE SEAT OF THEIR PANTS

1930–1941

We welcome competition because if there's more on a team letting the people know about the chairs, the quicker the market will expand.

—Edward Knabusch, co-founder

EDWARD KNABUSCH AND ED-win Shoemaker had a winning formula—not only for their reclining La-Z-Boy® chair but for their growing business. Although neither was formally educated, their natural talents provided the ingredients for a successful furniture enterprise.

Knabusch was a natural businessman and salesman with lots of ideas. He impressed everyone he met with his personal magnetism. He traveled the region meeting with dealers and suppliers, and he directed Floral City Furniture's administrative and marketing efforts. Shoemaker preferred to remain in the background, putting his mechanical genius to work on the drawing board and in the shop. His metalworking skills complemented Knabusch's woodworking knowledge. Both men had a reputation for integrity and honesty.[1]

Knabusch and Shoemaker had to make a big decision about the influx of orders for La-Z-Boy chairs at the 1929 Grand Rapids Furniture Show. Because they could not fill all the orders from their small shop, they would have to either expand their operation or find another furniture manufacturer to make the chairs. With little capital available for expansion, the two Eds, as they were known, decided to seek an established company to produce the chair on a royalty basis.

When Ed Knabusch approached Kroehler Manufacturing Company, one of the largest manufacturers of living room furniture in the country,

the Chicago company rejected his offer. Knabusch's search eventually led him to Michigan Chair Company, in Grand Rapids, Michigan, and a two-year agreement was signed on October 5, 1929. The agreement called for Floral City Furniture to provide mechanical fixtures for La-Z-Boy chairs, which would be manufactured and sold by Michigan Chair on a royalty basis. Michigan Chair would pay Floral City $2 per chair. The licensing agreement covered the entire United States, except Monroe County, Michigan, where Floral City Furniture could continue to make and sell La-Z-Boy chairs.

"We always kept in touch with the chair," Shoemaker said. "We wouldn't let go of it."[2]

Floral City signed a similar licensing agreement with Deluxe Upholstering Company, in Kitchener, Ontario, for manufacture and sale of La-Z-Boy chairs in Canada.

Patent Pressures

Shoemaker traveled to Michigan Chair to help set up its shop and train workers to make the mechanical chair. But soon after production began,

---

Licensees produced La-Z-Boy chairs between 1930 and 1939. This chair was made by the Aulsbrook Company, in Detroit.

Knabusch got a disturbing telephone call from Pete Kroehler, owner of Kroehler Manufacturing. Kroehler was a giant of the furniture industry and was credited with many manufacturing, retailing, and distribution innovations.[3]

"You don't know me," the voice on the phone said, "but I'm Pete Kroehler from Chicago and I understand that the Michigan Chair Company is making your La-Z-Boy chair under your patent."

"Yes, what about it?" Knabusch responded.

Kroehler informed Knabusch that he had just bought Michigan Chair Company, and he said, "I don't pay royalties. I either buy it or throw it out." Kroehler summoned Knabusch to Chicago to work out an agreement.[4]

Kroehler initially tried to whittle the royalty down from $2 to 35 cents per chair.[5] When Knabusch refused that proposal, Kroehler offered to buy the La-Z-Boy® chair patent, which was still pending. Knabusch walked out of many discussions with Kroehler because he didn't think he was being offered a fair price. "We were determined not to give it away even though we weren't in any bargaining

position. We didn't have a dime, and he had millions," Knabusch recalled.[6]

In a negotiating session in Grand Rapids, John Knabusch accompanied his son to the meeting. When the two men entered Kroehler's office, Kroehler asked who the elderly man was. When he was told, he ordered John Knabusch out of the room.

When the meeting began, Ed Knabusch thus found himself alone, facing nearly 30 men from Kroehler Manufacturing. Pete Kroehler told Knabusch to buy back the license he had sold to Deluxe Upholstering in Canada since Kroehler intended to buy the license. Knabusch, who had previously rejected an offer from Kroehler for $25,000, said, "What are you ordering me to do this for? We haven't agreed on a price yet."

Kroehler responded, "You are embarrassing me in front of all these people. I thought the price was agreed upon for $25,000, but I will give you $35,000." Knabusch walked out yet again.[7]

Two weeks later, Kroehler invited Knabusch and the rest of the Floral City board of directors to a meeting in Chicago. Shoemaker recalled an icy day in February 1930 when he, Knabusch, Oliver Golden, and Howard Comstock drove to Chicago to meet with Kroehler.

"We went to his office and he had the whole bottom floor of the American Furniture Mart for his displays," Shoemaker said. "He had about 15 plants at that time and they were making upholstered furniture of every description. Of course, he had to show us all of what he was doing, which we were glad to see, and then he got talking about our deal." The men finally agreed to a price of $50,000.

Kroehler was ready to write a check, but the men from Floral City pointed out that the patent hadn't been issued yet. The two parties decided that the patent would be sold on an option that would come due in 90 days, on May 7, 1930.

"How much do you want down?" Kroehler asked. The Floral City board met privately to discuss the amount of the down payment.

Golden didn't believe a large payment was necessary. Kroehler was a respected executive in the furniture industry. "I trust that man to the hilt.

I know he'll keep his word," Golden told the other three men.

But Shoemaker insisted that they should obtain a down payment, and the board members agreed on the sum of $5,000.

When they returned to Kroehler's office, he asked about their decision. Nobody spoke up.

"Would $1,000 be all right?" Kroehler asked.

"Oh sure," Golden replied.

Kroehler gave them a personal check, which was placed in escrow at a local bank. The four men celebrated with dinner and a vaudeville show before returning to Monroe the next day.[8]

Face-Off

Floral City returned to making furniture in its small shop, waiting for the day when Kroehler would pay the balance on the patent agreement. On May 6, the day before the option expired, Kroehler called Floral City and asked Knabusch to return to Chicago for another meeting.

Opposite: A worker stains wood chair arms in 1939.

Right: La-Z-Boy Chair Company began producing its own chairs again in 1939. Chairs were sold with matching ottomans.

"There's no reason to come to Chicago," Knabusch replied. "All you've got to do is pay the other $49,000 and that's it."

But Kroehler's firm was suffering the effects of the Depression. Some of his company's 15 plants were closing, and he chose not to exercise his option to purchase the La-Z-Boy patent. The option expired, and Floral City retained its patent.[9]

With revenge in mind, Kroehler stopped production of La-Z-Boy® chairs in his Grand Rapids factory.

"We had dealings with him after that," Shoemaker said, noting how close the cousins came to losing the rights to the famous La-Z-Boy chair. "I guess it made him so mad that he started infringing on our patent. We reduced the royalty . . . to get away from the exclusive arrangement so we could go out and get other [U.S.] manufacturers . After we cautioned him about infringing, he said, 'Well, I'll break you somehow.'"

When Floral City's patent attorney, Arthur Durand, threatened Kroehler with a lawsuit, he backed off.[10]

Knabusch and Shoemaker had won the fight to retain their patent, but their immediate future was not very promising. With production halted in Grand Rapids, Floral City's only income was custom furniture sales and La-Z-Boy sales in Monroe County and Canada. The company was losing money. Oliver Golden carefully examined the company's finances and helped develop a recovery plan.

In September 1930, Floral City mortgaged its property and assets for $10,000. The company issued stock to the mortgagees—Golden, Louis Shoemaker, and John and Ida Knabusch. Once again, Shoemaker's and Knabusch's parents were backing their sons financially. Shoemaker's and Knabusch's salaries were put on hold, and the company's expenses were watched carefully.[11]

In October 1931, the licensing agreement with Michigan Chair Company expired, and Floral City was once again free to find a manufacturer for the La-Z-Boy chair. The company signed a new licensing agreement for U.S. production and sales with

E. Wiener & Company, Milwaukee, marketed La-Z-Boy chairs as a healthy way to refresh oneself. The company originated the slogan "Recline, Relax, Recuperate."

E. Wiener & Company in Milwaukee, Wisconsin. Wiener paid Floral City $10,000 for the exclusive U.S. right to manufacture the La-Z-Boy chair for two years. Floral City received $416 per month, which Golden insisted be used to pay off the mortgage.[12]

Production reached 1,200 a month in 1932, then fell in 1933 as the Depression deepened. In a way, the country's economic crisis had little effect on Floral City Furniture.[13] As a new business, it had little to lose. One morning in 1933, John Knabusch rushed to Floral City with a warning for his son.

"You better go downtown and draw your money out of the bank," he said. "They're standing in line."

"What money?" Ed Knabusch responded.

"We didn't have any money, so we never got excited about it," Shoemaker recalled.[14]

Behind the Wheel

Floral City continued making specialty furniture, fixtures for its Canadian licensee, and

La-Z-Boy chairs for Monroe County. Eager for new sources of income, Shoemaker and Knabusch also continued to develop new products. They believed they could adapt the La-Z-Boy chair fixture for use in cars, buses, Pullman cars, and airplanes.[15]

In 1934, they obtained a patent for an adjustable car seat mounted on four springs. When the car stopped suddenly, the seat moved forward slightly, absorbing some of the shock. The seat moved back when the car started. The seat back reclined slightly.

"It had a shock absorber as well as a reclining mechanism and a bed position," Shoemaker said. When Floral City tried to interest the automotive companies in its invention, the automakers declined.[16]

"It was too expensive to [manufacture]," Shoemaker said, "especially during those years when [automakers] were looking for something simple. We had the thing designed and all perfected, but all we ever made was experimental models."

In fact, one of the early car seats was installed in Knabusch's Chevrolet.

Car seats were not the answer to their financial difficulties, but the entrepreneurs remained open to new business ventures. The La-Z-Boy chairs they manufactured were wholesaled to local retailers. One day, Shoemaker noticed a newspaper advertisement for a La-Z-Boy chair. The chair, which Floral City had sold for $66.75, was retailing for $139.50. Shoemaker showed the ad to Knabusch and remarked that Floral City was "in the wrong business." The profit margins in retailing appeared to be much larger than Floral City's.[17]

At first, Knabusch didn't take the suggestion seriously. He feared that if Floral City retailed La-Z-Boy chairs, the company's relationships with its dealers would be strained. But Floral City had always sold its own chairs and specialty furniture. It seemed natural to display the goods in a showroom. In 1931, Knabusch and Shoemaker partitioned off a small room on the building's top floor so that customers could view furniture samples and place orders.

Soon, Knabusch and Shoemaker were accommodating customers' requests for furniture from other manufacturers. Custom orders increased, and in January 1932, Knabusch traveled to the Grand Rapids Furniture Market to purchase an assortment of furniture for Floral City's display room.[18]

Furniture sales continued to grow, bringing needed cash into the business. In 1932, Floral City Furniture broke even for the first time. The quick success of their retail business convinced Knabusch and Shoemaker to end their manufacturing operations and focus on retailing full-time.

Knabusch later said, "The trouble with making special furniture to order is you make one set-up for your machine and put one piece through, and then you have to make another set-up . . . so it is too costly. You just couldn't make money. I don't care how cheap you would sell it, [customers] would think they were being overcharged."[19]

"Showing" Off

The partners sold their woodworking equipment to a local school and cleaned up the factory's first floor, transforming it into a furniture showroom. They painted draperies around the windows to make the room more attractive for furniture display.[20] While Knabusch concentrated on buying and setting up the furniture store, a new office manager, Herman Gertz, oversaw office duties. Gertz, 22, was a former bookkeeper and teller at Monroe State Savings Bank.[21] He soon began selling furniture in the retail operation and became the store's manager.

Floral City Furniture Store opened in May 1933 with a furniture show featuring Knabusch's latest selections from Grand Rapids. An ad in the *Monroe Evening News* announced the store's grand opening.

Visit our showrooms where you will find a most interesting display of fine furniture! Before any piece is displayed it must pass rigid tests

This logo, designed by Edwin Shoemaker, was used through the 1930s. Because it was difficult to reproduce, it was simplified around 1940.

and critical examination by men of experience who have built fine furniture for years themselves. This assures you of the highest quality for the price at all times. We invite comparison.[22]

Everyone who attended the furniture show received a free flowering shrub, which Knabusch and Shoemaker bought at a local nursery for 5 cents apiece.

A few months later, Floral City bought Rupp & Fleure, a 65-year-old Monroe furniture store that couldn't survive the Depression. Floral City also acquired Rupp & Fleure's inventory and one of its salesmen, Bill Osborne.[23]

Knabusch's marketing wizardry and showmanship helped Floral City Furniture thrive during the Depression. The Furniture Show became an annual event. In 1934, when Floral City began planning its second Furniture Show, Knabusch and Shoemaker found they had too much inventory to display in their showroom. Knabusch drove to Detroit and rented an 80-foot-by-60-foot circus tent. The tent was erected in front of the store and filled with furniture.[24]

"They wondered how in the world a little outfit in the country grew into a tent," Gertz said. "That was something different. Furniture in a tent."[25]

The tent was one of many merchandising brainstorms Knabusch came up with to stimulate sales during the Depression. Realizing that many parents would bring their children to the furniture show, he thought up a unique attraction to hold their attention while their parents shopped: a mouse circus. Knabusch and Shoemaker spent an entire night building a glass-walled stage that housed treadmills and other apparatus that mice could operate by running. They enlisted the help of a neighbor, who caught a dozen mice in his corncrib. Once released into the glass showcase, the mice quickly learned their tricks, said Gertz.

Within a couple of hours, they got to running like mad. They seemed to love it. They'd stretch themselves out and run like mad on the ferris wheel, the teeter-totter, and merry-go-round, which Mr. Shoemaker made. The mouse circus was set up in a smaller tent on the furniture show site. Parents knew where they could find their children after shopping, and they often had

a hard time dragging them away from the show. People would go away from here and tell their friends, their uncles, their brothers.[26]

Floral City Furniture was a neighborly place to shop. It had a reputation for quality, honesty, and integrity. Customer service and convenience were priorities. The store was open daily, including evenings and Sunday afternoons.[27]

As a goodwill gesture, Knabusch gave away fresh fruit (raspberries were a favorite) and vegetables to customers. He loved gardening and rose at

dawn to pick fruit and vegetables from his large garden and orchard before going to work. Much of the harvest was given to customers.

Sometimes, out of necessity, Floral City acquired produce as well. When money was tight during the 1930s, customers sometimes bargained for furniture with wheat, corn, and coal. One farmer paid for a refrigerator with a cow. Floral City cared for a menagerie of animals. Guinea hens served as a burglar alarm.[28]

Despite the difficult economy, Floral City grew during the Depression. Sales increased from $15,372 in 1932 to $35,514 in 1933 and $64,178 in 1934.[29] Knabusch and Shoemaker realized that the store would soon outgrow the two-story building they had constructed in 1927. In 1933, they purchased an outdated school building for $251. Employees worked nights and Sundays tearing it down and transporting the pieces to the Floral City property, where they were stored for two years.

One Sunday morning in October 1935, Knabusch was awakened by noise from contractors resurfacing Telegraph Road. He persuaded the workers to dump the broken concrete on the store property instead of hauling it away. He then summoned Shoemaker and Gertz, and the three men spent the day breaking up the stone for the new store's foundation. Thus construction on the new Floral City Furniture store began. Employees helped complete the new building in 45 days. It opened December 12, in time for Christmas, and was decorated for the season with green burlap "carpet."[30]

The 140-foot-by-80-foot building was more suitable for a retail store than the old, two-story structure. The new building was closer to Telegraph Road and featured large display windows. Parking was ample and convenient. A shipping and receiving room in the back facilitated deliveries.[31] The old building was used for storage, and Floral City rented warehouse space in downtown Monroe until 1937, when it added a warehouse behind the store.[32]

The large showroom provided display space for a wide variety of merchandise. In addition to furniture for every room, the store carried mattresses, large appliances, radios, lamps, and mirrors. One of the best-selling items in the store was the La-Z-Boy® chair.

Customers entering the showroom were immediately drawn to a large goldfish pond designed by Shoemaker. The pond was made of stone and decorated with flowering plants. As the mouse circus had, the fishpond kept

This illustration exemplifies a Floral City Furniture Show. The annual event featured a tent filled with furniture and a mouse circus. Knabusch is pictured on the stairs, and Shoemaker greets a customer at left. In the center is store manager Herman Gertz.

Above: The focal point of the entrance to Floral City Furniture Store was a large fishpond, which held the attention of children while their parents shopped.

Below: Floral City Furniture's annual lamp show featured a giant lamp. When lit, it was visible a mile away.

children entertained while their parents shopped. It served as a focal point for seasonal decorations and merchandising.

Floral City's annual spring furniture show continued to attract large crowds to its tent. In the fall, Floral City staged a lamp show, in which hundreds of lamps were displayed inside the store. With little money for advertising, Knabusch again was challenged to attract customers to the event, and he and Shoemaker constructed the world's largest lamp. The shade measured 20 feet in diameter and was made of multicolored silk panels purchased at Hudson's in Detroit. It hung on an Edison light pole in front of the store. Powered by 1,000 watts of electricity, the lamp could be seen a mile away. A sign in front of the store announced, "Lamp Show, Admission Free."[33]

"The colors showed beautifully, and people would go up and down the street to look at it," Gertz said. "Salesmen would call on us, and they'd take the story all over the United States."[34]

Meanwhile, Knabusch's wife, Henrietta, kept the furniture in the showroom dusted and polished.[35]

Do It Yourself to Do It Right

Floral City continued making fixtures for its La-Z-Boy® chair licensees. The company had

abandoned its exclusive nationwide rights in favor of regional territories. Manufacturers were licensed in Milwaukee, Detroit, San Francisco, Salt Lake City, Seattle, and Denver. Licensees also produced chairs in Canada and Great Britain.[36]

In 1937, Floral City's board of directors, consisting of Shoemaker, Knabusch, Gertz, and two Monroe businessmen, Bernard Hoffmann and Leo Boudinet, began to discuss discontinuing the license agreements. Knabusch and Shoemaker believed the U.S. licensees dedicated more resources to their own products than to the La-Z-Boy chair. The quality of the chairs produced by licensees was not up to Shoemaker and Knabusch's standards. The founders also believed the fixture needed improvement. Competing chairs were less expensive, and the La-Z-Boy fixture prevented variations in chair design.

Shoemaker went to work improving the mechanism, and in May 1939, he and Knabusch applied for a new patent. The improved fixture was easier and less expensive to produce, more durable, and able to accommodate different chair designs. The patent was granted in 1941.

"We changed it drastically at that time," Shoemaker said. "The new design [enabled us] to flare the chair and not cause any problems in operating, as before, we were always handicapped."[37]

Knabusch took the new design to a Detroit concern and asked them to set up a line of chairs and fix the selling prices. "When the line was completed I went back," Knabusch said. "The line was all right but the prices were way too high."[38]

Floral City had stopped manufacturing chairs in 1930 because it couldn't keep up with the demand. Now Knabusch and Shoemaker believed making La-Z-Boy chairs in their own facility was the only way they could maintain quality and keep the prices down. In 1940, the Floral City board voted to build a new manufacturing facility. The company was going to make La-Z-Boy chairs again.[39]

"We didn't want to go into the manufacturing end," Knabusch said. "We had a good retail store business and did not want to take on the additional worries of a manufacturing business. But there was no alternative. If we were going to capitalize on the chair, we would have to make it ourselves."[40]

A Return to Production

A year later, the company split into two corporations. Floral City Furniture continued as a furniture retailer. La-Z-Boy Chair Company was formed to manufacture chairs. Knabusch was president and general manager of both companies, and Shoemaker was vice president. Gertz was secretary-treasurer and assistant general manager of Floral City Furniture and a director of La-Z-Boy Chair. Otto C. Uecker, a former teacher, was secretary-treasurer and assistant general manager of La-Z-Boy Chair and chairman of the board of Floral City Furniture. Dr. Robert Ewing, a doctor specializing in industrial medicine, and Ora Sessions, a railroad executive, were directors of La-Z-Boy Chair and Floral City Furniture, respectively.[41]

La-Z-Boy began production in October 1939. Its dealer network included 400 stores across the country. La-Z-Boy chairs were sold in established department and furniture stores including H. & S. Pogue, Cincinnati; Kaufman Department Stores, Pittsburgh; J. L. Hudson Company, Detroit; Maison Blanche, New Orleans; Gimbel Brothers, New York City; and some Sears and Montgomery Ward stores. La-Z-Boy's wholesale division employed 24 people, including seven salesmen, and maintained a permanent showroom in the Chicago Merchandise Mart Building.[42]

Immediately after returning production to the company, La-Z-Boy purchased five acres of land adjoining its original site and built a new, 27,000-square-foot manufacturing plant.[43] Shoemaker and Knabusch designed the facility, which included office and production space. "We never required an architect," Knabusch explained. "We planned everything ourselves down to each detail, including strength of steel, amount of concrete, and purchased all construction materials ourselves. Actual construction began before blueprints were drawn. Each department was planned according to its own needs and its flow into the next department, and the building sized accordingly. Production balance was the key to the whole thing."[44]

Construction was sometimes hampered by supply shortages due to World War II, already raging in Europe and the Pacific. When the plant was completed in the fall of 1941, it was outfitted with modern windows, ventilation, heating, insulation, and lighting. The factory was divided into specialized areas. One room was dedicated to cutting and sewing and included an electric cutter capable of cutting upholstery materials for 50 chairs at once. In another room, called the picking room, cotton batting was stuffed into upholstered chairs.[45]

Future plans called for a conveyor system, which would move chairs to different stations along a production line, modeled after automotive assembly lines. Such production techniques had never been used in furniture manufacturing before. Knabusch and Shoemaker expected the plant's capacity to eventually reach 500 units a day.[46]

The new factory opened shortly after the October Furniture Show in Chicago. Orders from the show and La-Z-Boy's staff of 14 salesmen throughout the country produced a backlog of

approximately 1,000 chairs. The shop's employees were obliged to work overtime to fill orders by Christmas. Knabusch explained the importance of filling Christmas orders in the employee newsletter.

We have set up an overtime schedule for night work and Saturdays, and [we] are paying the penalty of time and a half. It is only natural that on all such chairs produced, all overtime rates will

Opposite: La-Z-Boy welcomed the public to an open house at its new manufacturing facility in November 1941.

Below: After La-Z-Boy returned to manufacturing, it opened this permanent showroom in the Chicago Merchandise Mart. Each chair had an invitation to "Sit in it, that's all we ask."

cause us to lose money. However, our company is willing to produce these extra chairs at a loss in order to retain the good will and business of the dealers involved. . . . By doing so, we will not only retain the good will of our dealers, but we can also look forward to their patronage next year.[47]

Shoemaker and Knabusch were optimistic about their new production facility. Nine years earlier they had abandoned manufacturing for retailing. Their Floral City Furniture store had gotten them through the Depression, and it continued to thrive. But in order to realize the potential of their La-Z-Boy® chair, they had spent $72,000 on a modern manufacturing facility. On November 25, 1941, when La-Z-Boy Chair Company hosted an open house, Knabusch and Shoemaker believed they were finally ready to reap the fruit of their efforts. But world events were again about to interrupt their business plan. Less than two weeks after the grand opening, Japanese planes attacked the U.S. Pacific Fleet at Pearl Harbor, Hawaii, and on December 8, America entered World War II.

At the January 1942 Annual Shareholders Meeting of the La-Z-Boy Chair Company, Knabusch reported the company would hold off installing the conveyors in the chair factory until management knew how the facility would be used.

"If the time presents itself when we will be able to serve the government in defense work, we will cooperate to the fullest extent," he said. "In times like these, we do not know what we are going to do tomorrow."[48]

By the 1940s, billboards advertising La-Z-Boy® chairs were located throughout the Eastern United States.

CHAPTER THREE

WAR AND GROWING PAINS

1942–1959

*We often wonder how in the name of thunder we met the challenges
that hit us every year.*

—Herman Gertz, store manager

GONE FOR THE DURATIO.

La-Z-Boy

CHAIR FACTORY HAS BEEN TAKEN OVER FOR

WAR WORK

AND MUST VACATE BY AUGUST 10th

The Big Chair with 1000 RECLINING POSITIONS

READING
RELAXING
REPOSING
RETIRING
RECLINING

CHOICE OF MANY FINE COLORS

SPECIAL OFFER

Open Evenings 'til 9 — **FLORAL CITY FURNITURE COMPANY** PHONE 580 — Open Sundays 2 'til 6

THE WAR POSTPONED Edward Knabusch and Edwin Shoemaker's plans to mass-produce La-Z-Boy chairs. The country's political and economic uncertainty was evident at the Chicago Furniture Show in early 1942. Afterward, Knabusch and store manager Herman Gertz reported in *La-Z-News & Floral Views,* the company newsletter, that it was the dullest market they had ever attended.

Most buyers claimed that their warehouses were heavily stocked and very few orders were placed for stock merchandise. In addition to having large inventories on hand, present-day conditions made buyers hesitant to buy very far ahead. It is also true that prices seem to be fairly stabilized in most lines with no immediate indication of drastic raises going into effect.[1]

Nevertheless, La-Z-Boy continued manufacturing chairs in its new factory. Anticipating supply shortages, Knabusch and Shoemaker had experimented with alternative materials and stockpiled supplies. In January 1942, the company had enough materials for one year's production.[2]

During the summer of 1942, the War Production Board investigated the possibility of acquiring the La-Z-Boy plant for the production of aircraft parts for Republic Aircraft. La-Z-Boy made plans to move its production back into its original building, but ultimately Republic Aircraft acquired a larger factory in Toledo.[3]

Joining the War Effort

In August, La-Z-Boy was forced to cease production of the La-Z-Boy chair when Woodall Industries leased the plant for war production. The Monroe business employed about 100 people at the La-Z-Boy plant, where it made seats and seat backs for tanks, torpedo boats, turret guns, and armored cars and produced upholstered components for the captain's quarters in cargo ships.[4]

La-Z-Boy bid on and received contracts for other products, including metal parts for aircraft, tanks, and turret guns and a wood radio operator's desk. The company also completed war work for Monroe Auto Equipment Company, Chrysler Corporation, Cadillac Motor Car Company, Norge Division Borg-Warner Corporation, Hudson Motor Car Company, and Sparks-Withington Company.[5]

An August 1942 ad in the *Monroe Evening News* announced the discontinuation of La-Z-Boy chair production during the war.

La-Z-Boy's new factory proved inadequate to complete all the work, so the company operated out of three Monroe locations. Machine work was done at the Telegraph Road plant; the upholstery department was located in the Beaubien Building; and the Dull Building was leased for storage.[6]

Knabusch sought new contracts while Shoemaker designed and made samples for bids and

Above: Floral City Furniture Store employees gather for a 1944 group shot. Herman Gertz is seated and wearing a suit. Seated to his left are Edward Knabusch and Edwin Shoemaker. Knabusch's dog Boots often found her way into photographs.

Below left: During the war, Edwin Shoemaker helped design seats for tanks, torpedo boats, turret guns, and armored cars.

dies for the work that came in.[7] Gertz recalled Shoemaker's work on tank seats.

"When they had the tank plans all ready to go, they didn't allow enough height for the driver to sit in, and they needed a flatter seat," he said. "So Mr. Shoemaker designed what is equivalent to a metal tractor seat with about a 3.5-inch depression, very flat, and threw on a pad."[8]

When rush jobs came in, everyone helped out. Knabusch sometimes helped Shoemaker make production samples, and Assistant General Manager Otto Uecker spray painted parts.[9]

Victories and Shortages

Knabusch voluntarily took on an additional role during the war. In 1943, the company prepared four acres of land for Victory Gardens. The acreage was divided into 40-foot-by-100-foot lots in which employees planted crops. Knabusch, an avid gardener, helped employees with their gardens before and after work. Participants produced crops that helped them save ration coupons. In addition, the farm animals that the company acquired during the Depression were sometimes slaughtered for food and given away or sold inexpensively to employees. Nine pigs born in 1943 yielded 18 hams, which were given to workers.[10]

War work occupied 85 percent of workers' time in the factory. Floral City's normal inventory of refrigerators, ranges, washing machines, vacuum cleaners, lamps, and floor coverings was severely restricted or unavailable during the war.[11]

Occasionally the plant returned to the furniture business. La-Z-Boy continued to supply fixtures to its Canadian licensee, producing 1,500 in 1945. Dealers continued to send in orders for La-Z-Boy® chairs, and in November 1943, La-Z-Boy received permission to resume chair production using existing inventory, when time was available.

Additional materials for chair production became available in 1944, when La-Z-Boy produced 1,422 chairs. The chairs were distributed to dealers based on the volume of previous purchases.[12]

The company's success in obtaining furniture from suppliers was spotty. At the 1943 Chicago Furniture Show, Gertz found that manufacturers had cut production by 25 percent and established quotas for their customers based on past purchases. Buyers had no assurance of when shipments would be made. Since Floral City bought heavily before the war, it was able to obtain an adequate inventory of items.[13]

Floral City Furniture also adapted to wartime shortages. "They wouldn't allow us to use metal," Herman Gertz said. "You couldn't have upholstered furniture with springs in it. You couldn't even have innerspring mattresses in bedding."[14]

Employees of the La-Z-Boy Chair Company gather around Ed Shoemaker, Edward Knabusch, and Otto Uecker (seated in center row, third, fourth, and fifth from left) in this 1944 photo.

Since metal wasn't available for springs, new mattresses and upholstered furniture were filled with felt or cotton batting. Floral City, however, was resourceful in obtaining springs. It advertised for used upholstered furniture, which it recovered and promoted as such. It was the only furniture store in the area where people could get upholstered furniture with springs. The recycled furnishings were hot sellers.[15]

"All the new upholstered furniture had just plain filling in the seats, but no springs at all," Gertz recalled. "And Floral City Furniture Company very promptly advertised for used upholstered furniture. We reupholstered and stocked hundreds of spring-filled sofas and chairs that no other store had."[16]

One day, salesman Lloyd White was sent out to find more furniture. He found two barns where someone had stored dozens of upholstered chairs and sofas and bought every one of them. Floral City Furniture kept its showroom stocked

Gas rationing during World War II forced Floral City Furniture to curtail deliveries, but the company's inventory of home appliances, lamps, and floor coverings was severely restricted or unavailable during wartime anyway.

and many employees working during those tough times.[17]

On December 15, 1943, fire broke out in Floral City's warehouse. Knabusch and Shoemaker rushed from their homes on hearing the news at about 10 P.M. and helped firefighters tame the blaze by crawling through the building with a hose. About $1,000 in inventory for Christmas delivery was destroyed, as well as the original La-Z-Boy® chair, which had been stored since 1929. Shoemaker returned home at about 4 A.M. with his clothes frozen to his body. The cause of the fire was never determined. Fortunately, insurance covered most of the loss.[18]

Back in the Saddle: A Furniture Frenzy

The end of World War II propelled the country into a manufacturing and buying frenzy. After 16 years of economic hardship and wartime shortages, Americans were anxious to get on with their lives. Record numbers of marriages and births followed the war. During the preceding three years, La-Z-Boy had produced 119,311 seats and backs and 272,935 stampings for the war effort.[19] Now it was ready to help furnish young families' homes.

Initially, shortages of springs, fabric, and steel kept production down to 15 chairs a day and delayed new designs, despite high demand. During the first year after the war, La-Z-Boy produced 4,000 chairs. Dealers continued to send in orders, and the company had a hard time keeping up with demand. Sales reached $100,000 in 1945.[20]

Before the war ended, La-Z-Boy and Floral City had recognized the need for a larger factory and furniture showroom. In 1944, the board approved a plan to purchase land adjacent to the existing factory and build additions worth $65,000. Material and labor shortages prevented construction until after the war, and the longer construction was postponed, the more ambitious the building plans became. The expansion was finished in 1948 and included a new warehouse to replace the one lost in the fire; an addition to the furniture store; and a larger, modern factory to bring all operations on-site.[21]

The furniture store showroom doubled in size. Skylights in the ceiling flooded the room with natural light. The new showroom also featured a larger sales counter, more offices, and added space for carpet displays. A new sales meeting room seated 50 and included complete hookups to demonstrate washing machines, stoves, and other appliances.[22]

Floral City Furniture Store had a reputation for superior service. The store's 25 employees did not earn commissions and were instructed not to pressure customers into buying. A bronze plaque in the store's lobby stated, "Salesmen are instructed not to solicit your order, but to lend their assistance only." Customers felt free to wander through the store without the pressure to buy.

Floral City's spring furniture show and fall lamp show continued to attract large crowds. The 1949 lamp show drew 9,000 visitors in eight days. Traffic and parking managers were posted outside to facilitate parking. The store continued its tradition of creative merchandising. At the 1949 show, a giant lamp tree emerged from the store's famous fishpond. Workers removed a dead tree from the countryside and "planted" it in the center of the pond. Electrical wiring was woven throughout the tree, and lampshades hung from its branches, appearing to grow there.[23]

The redesigned furniture works was a state-of-the-art facility. In order to control quality, the plant was capable of handling all operations, including frame construction, spring assembly, wood carving, and fixture stamping and assembly. The frame construction operation was a major commitment. Prior to and during the war, La-Z-Boy had purchased chair frames from a Louisiana supplier. But in 1946, lumber was scarce, and La-Z-Boy's source was no longer able to supply frames. La-Z-Boy tried other suppliers, including Weis Manufacturing Company in Monroe. But La-Z-Boy chairs required a precise fit of the fixture and the frame, sometimes labeled "the Shoemaker fit" because he was so meticulous.[24] Without this precision, the chair mechanism would not work properly. The owners decided the only way to ensure the quality they demanded was to make the frames themselves.

Into the Woodwork

In 1946, La-Z-Boy established a sawmill and 42 acres of standing timber in Northern Michigan. The sawmill was moved to the La-Z-Boy site. "Despite the fact that this may have been a forced venture, we now feel that it is a most welcome asset to our equipment," Knabusch told employees.[25]

The process also required a dry kiln, a power plant, and a woodworking shop. The timber and woodworking operation was a labor of love for Knabusch, whose interest in and knowledge of woodworking had inspired his entry into the furniture industry in the first place. He personally inspected every woodlot the company bought.

La-Z-Boy hired workers to cut trees and move the heavy logs to a used Navy bomber truck for the trip to the sawmill.[26] The logs were cut into planks and arranged in stacks that exposed all sides to the weather. They air dried for a minimum of three months before entering the dry kiln, which held 50,000 board feet of lumber at temperatures ranging from 110 to 180 degrees Fahrenheit. After drying, the lumber entered the woodshop to be cut into parts for frames, arms, and legs. A new boiler plant burned wood waste, reducing La-Z-Boy's fuel costs.[27]

La-Z-Boy struggled with its woodworking operations in the beginning. Equipment had to be purchased or built, and workers needed training. By 1950, however, Knabusch reported to the board that the quality of frames was up to La-Z-Boy standards and profits were increasing.[28]

In addition to constructing frames, the woodworking shop cut curved pieces of wood for the chairs' arms and legs using La-Z-Boy's patented band saw guide. A separate operation produced wood dowels used in frame assembly.

With the woodworking department, La-Z-Boy could complete all its operations on-site. The metal shop stamped and assembled the La-Z-Boy® fixtures. In the cutting room, electric shears cut through 50 layers of fabric at once. The operator paused to sharpen the knife's blade 10 times for every batch of cloth. Leather required additional care and was cut by hand one piece at a time. Workers sewed together 27 pieces of fabric or leather per chair and eight pieces per ottoman. Women operating button-making machines could produce 100 fabric-covered buttons in 45 minutes.[29]

Chair cushions were made in another area of the shop. Coil spring units were wrapped with cotton batting and inserted into a stuffing machine that drew the cover over a cushion.

The company also acquired wood through something of a community service, said Jim Waltz,

Below: Hardwood logs were cut into planks in La-Z-Boy's sawmill, purchased in 1946.

Inset: La-Z-Boy employed loggers, including Robert Quell, to cut down and prepare timber for the sawmill. The company purchased 42 acres of woods in 1946.

who joined the La-Z-Boy team in 1947. "People would call Mr. Knabusch if they had a tree in their yard they wanted removed. He'd go over there, look at the tree, and if it was what he thought we could use, he would send his logging crew over."[30]

Years later, Waltz would visit Knabusch at his home for quiet chats. On one visit, he found Knabusch among the trees in his back yard.

He drove his Cadillac [back there] with his big bags of birdseed, and he was feeding the birds. He says, "Hey, Jim, come on. I'm just about done. Get in the car." I about split a gut because there we were, weaving back and forth through all these trees in that big car.[31]

The Assembly Line

The assembly line that Shoemaker and Knabusch envisioned in 1939 was finally installed in 1947. All chair components merged at the beginning of the line, which consisted of a series of small workbenches on wheels. Materials for each operation were placed on each bench. A motorized

Supervisors walked along the assembly line, installed in 1947, inspecting each operation.

conveyor moved the benches along tracks in the floor to stations where workers performed individual operations. The line moved through the assembly and packing process. A separate line produced ottomans. With the new production line, workers were trained quickly because each handled only one operation. Supervisors roamed the floor, inspecting the product along the way.[32] Knabusch's daughter, Betty Lou White, recalled the slow pace of the production line.

I was fascinated by the way the workers kept tacks in their mouth and spit them to tack material on the chairs. And I used to run barefoot through the shop!

I spent a lot of time there. . . . I would have peashooter fights with some of the guys. . . . My brother, Charles, and I would pick [vegetables and fruit] from the garden, put them in the wagon, and go through the shop and sell strawberries [and] raspberries.[33]

Production volume was higher than it had been under the old process, in which workers made chairs on individual benches and were required to complete an entire job. Knabusch continued to boast that the modern factory could produce 500 chairs a day, but La-Z-Boy never reached that rate during the 1950s. Generally, workers produced 70 to 120 chairs per day.

Fixture sales increased steadily as La-Z-Boy added foreign licensees. By 1953, Deluxe Upholstering's factory, in Kitchener, Ontario, was devoted entirely to La-Z-Boy® chair production. The plant eventually made its own fixtures, for which it paid a royalty.[34] A Mexican company, Muebleria Internacional, began manufacturing La-Z-Boy

chairs in the mid-1950s.[35] In 1956, I. Lubner, in Johannesburg, South Africa, also began manufacturing La-Z-Boy chairs.[36] An Australian company, Jason Metal Furnishing, was licensed in 1959.[37]

New Designs

In 1948, La-Z-Boy introduced its new, modern, postwar styles. Recliners were not considered high-style items because of their bulk. La-Z-Boy

Upholsterer Earl Blohm spits tacks onto the magnetic end of his hammer before driving them into the chair. Workers stored tacks in their mouths, and when they occasionally swallowed one, they would swallow a small wad of chair stuffing, which wound itself around the tack and rendered it harmless.

occasionally contracted with outside designers to design its chairs but would eventually bring the function back in-house. Outside designers had trouble accommodating the La-Z-Boy mechanism in their designs.[38] La-Z-Boy workers responsible for chair design moonlighted on the Floral City Furniture sales floor to learn customer preferences.[39]

In 1950, La-Z-Boy sales reahed $1 million for the first time. The same year, the company suffered the loss of Vice President and Secretary Otto Uecker, who died suddenly of a heart condition at the age of 46. Uecker had also been La-Z-Boy's sales manager.[40]

With the new factory and lumber operations complete and humming along smoothly, La-Z-Boy was able to concentrate on new products during the 1950s. In 1951, La-Z-Boy introduced the posture chair. The form-fitting chair featured a leg- and footrest that, similar to a dentist's chair, supported the lower body when someone sat or reclined.

In 1952, La-Z-Boy introduced the footrest chair, which eliminated the need for a separate ottoman. The chair's built-in footrest rose to support the feet when the chair reclined, and then it folded down into the front when the chair returned to an upright position. Other furniture manufacturers made chairs with built-in footrests, but only La-Z-Boy chairs reclined. The chair was an immediate success.[41] Within a year, the automatic footrest models comprised two-thirds of La-Z-Boy's production.[42] An extension footrest provided extra length for tall people.

In 1953, La-Z-Boy improved the automatic footrest feature by creating the Otto-Matic Magic Ottoman. It could be raised for leg support when the chair was positioned for sitting or reclining. A hidden button on top of the leg rest could be pushed to release the footrest.

La-Z-Boy introduced two rockers. A platform rocker came out in 1951. In 1955, the company added a built-in footrest to the platform rocker and named it the La-Z-Rocker®. Neither of these models reclined.

La-Z-Boy's next big seller was the Hi-Lo-Matic chair in 1956. When not in use, the chair's back remained in a low position, making it more fashionable than a traditional bulky recliner. Before reclining the chair, someone could raise its back to a comfortable position for any height. By 1957,

Hi-Lo-Matic and Otto-Matic chairs accounted for the majority of La-Z-Boy sales.[43] That same year, La-Z-Boy offered a vibrator option, called 'The Tranquilitor.' The feature could be added to any La-Z-Boy chair for an additional $15.[44]

The Hi-Lo made the recliner more acceptable to those who resisted them earlier, said Edwin Shoemaker's son, Dale. "There was a big resistance to the chairs all through the years—they were rather ungainly looking, supposedly."[45]

The company's final new model introduced during the 1950s was the Relaxaire, a lounge chair with a built-in ottoman. The Relaxaire offered full leg support but did not recline.

In the Public Eye

All of the company's new models were supported with national advertising. La-Z-Boy had been advertising in national magazines since 1947, when it spent $27,000 on its first national advertising campaign. Ads appeared in the *Saturday Evening Post, Better Homes and Gardens, House Beautiful,* and *Holiday,* as well as a number of trade magazines. Knabusch believed that national advertising would encourage consumers to buy La-Z-Boy chairs and build the company's reputation among dealers.[46]

La-Z-Boy employed advertising agencies to plan its advertising until 1952, when Knabusch reported to the board that the agencies weren't providing sufficient guidance. That year La-Z-Boy created a new position, advertising manager, bringing the function in-house for the first time. George Nadeau, a former *Monroe Evening News* writer who had been working as a La-Z-Boy sales representative in the Eastern United States, was named to the new position. Nadeau, 35 and a graduate of the University of Toledo, coordinated advertising and dealer promotions.[47]

In 1953, La-Z-Boy's sales network included 22 salesmen and 3,900 dealers. It maintained permanent displays at all major furniture shows, which were held in Chicago, New York, San Francisco, and High Point, North Carolina, an emerging venue for furniture sales in the South.[48]

La-Z-Boy provided its dealers with sales training, point-of-purchase sales aids, and local advertising assistance. Dealers received cover books, newspaper ad mats, circulars, decals, framed copies of national ads, and radio spot announcements. All dealers also received a one-third-size cutaway model that revealed the chair's quality construction. Electrically operated, one-third-size, fully upholstered chairs were also available for display.[49]

A sales training brochure produced by La-Z-Boy in 1950 offered selling tips to dealers. "Demonstrate, demonstrate, demonstrate! This is the most important rule of all," the brochure instructed. "Sit in the La-Z-Boy yourself and show your prospect its many advantages. Smile pleasantly and look completely relaxed."

After demonstrating the chair's comfort features and reclining ability, the salesmen were instructed to invite customers to try the chair. Salesmen were to offer to hold the customers' hats and coats so they could try the chair just as they would at home. "Don't allow a lady prospect to knock her hat askew when she sits in the chair. It embarrasses her, puts her in a bad frame of mind," the brochure said.[50]

La-Z-Boy hired a new sales manager, Walter Marder, in 1954. Marder came to Monroe from Olean, New York, where he was a furniture sales

executive and president of the National Association of Furniture Manufacturers. He immediately introduced a new sales training program for La-Z-Boy salesmen to present to dealers. He also guided La-Z-Boy toward more efficient advertising buys, which generated more inquiries. At the 1955 annual meeting, La-Z-Boy's board of directors recognized Marder's experience and knowledge of the furniture industry by giving him a seat on the board.[51]

La-Z-Boy's marketing efforts also included some unique publicity events. In June 1957, a La-Z-Boy® chair appeared on television for the first time. *Club 60*, a TV show featuring Dennis James and singer Mike Douglas, originated at the Chicago Furniture Show that summer. The chair was featured in a 5-minute skit as well as a musical number in which Douglas, stretched out in the chair, sang, "I'm going to stay here 'til I die." The show appeared on 72 NBC stations.[52]

The following year, La-Z-Boy chairs were given as prizes on a CBS game show, *Big Payoff*. One chair was given away every week for 13 weeks. The weekday afternoon show appeared on 32 stations.[53]

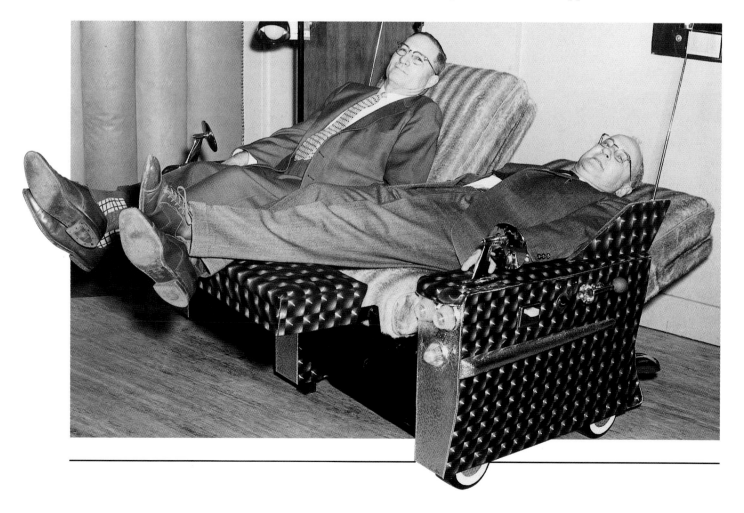

In 1959, Knabusch and Shoemaker created a mink-upholstered loveseat that was auctioned off at the Chicago winter furniture show. The imaginative inventors built the reclining chair out of two Otto-Matic, Hi-Lo recliners mounted on wheels. They added automotive accessories including rearview mirrors, horns, aerials, tail fins, headlights, turn signal lights, exhaust pipes, a radio, and a vibrator. The chair, dubbed the Cadillac-Satellite Chair, drew many people to the La-Z-Boy showroom.[54] It sold for $596.

This stunt spawned the idea for the twin lounger with Hi-Lo-Matic features on each side. It was introduced at the June 1959 furniture show.

Despite the company's new product introductions and marketing efforts, sales during the late 1950s declined. After reaching $2.4 million in 1954, La-Z-Boy sales fell to $1.1 million in 1960. The disappointing dip resulted from a national recession and intense competition in the furniture industry. In 1959, 400 furniture companies made reclining chairs. Some sold for as little as $39.95.[55] These low-cost competitors snagged considerable market share from La-Z-Boy.

The Cost of Business

La-Z-Boy's commitment to quality differentiated its products from competitors'. La-Z-Boy produced the only reclining chair that reclined flat. Its mechanism carried a lifetime warranty, and in 1952, the company reported that it had never had to replace a fixture for having worn out. La-Z-Boy also resisted competing on price. In 1952, the company stated, "La-Z-Boy has never made a chair to fit a specific price range. Prices are determined only after the chair has been produced, tested and, if necessary, improved. No idea of cost comes up until the chair is completed with all ingredients necessary for quality, comfort, and

long life. Designers and engineers tackle new ideas in an effort to accomplish perfection—not with the attitude they must make something cheap."[56] Nonetheless, La-Z-Boy eventually bowed to competitive pressure and introduced a $99.50 model during the mid-1950s.[57]

Quality construction wasn't the only reason La-Z-Boy's costs were higher than its competitors'. The company's labor costs were also higher. Most furniture makers were locating in the Southern United States, where labor costs were lower than in Michigan. La-Z-Boy's location near Detroit also made it difficult to keep costs down. Nearby automotive plants were unionized, and their workers were among the highest-paid manufacturing workers in the country. La-Z-Boy and other manufacturers in the region were pressured to compete for workers.

In 1954, La-Z-Boy factory workers voted for union representation.[58] Two years later, the workers went on strike, demanding higher wages. During the seven-week work stoppage, La-Z-Boy estimated it lost 4,200 chairs, contributing to the year's poor sales.[59]

Another strike occurred in 1959. After working without a contract for four months, La-Z-Boy workers struck, and negotiations dragged on for months. La-Z-Boy and its workers finally settled on November 25. The agreement included increased wages, a seventh paid holiday, and a provision for a union shop.[60]

The four-month strike was a wake-up call for the La-Z-Boy board of directors, composed of Knabusch; Shoemaker; Gertz; Marder, who was treasurer; Dr. Robert Ewing; and Moritz Brueckner, a former salesperson for Shaw and Slavsky, a Detroit manufacturer and distributor of pricing and merchandising equipment. Brueckner was hired as a sales manager and was named vice president in 1960.[61]

Since La-Z-Boy had only one production facility, the labor strike had completely halted the company's output for four months. At year-end, La-Z-Boy recorded its first financial loss. Knabusch believed the company should protect itself against future losses by opening a new factory in the South. The board agreed, and thus began a search for the site of La-Z-Boy's second manufacturing plant.

In a publicity stunt at the 1959 Chicago Furniture Show, La-Z-Boy auctioned the Cadillac-Satellite, a one-of-a-kind mink loveseat. The dual recliner on wheels was accessorized with horns, rearview mirrors, headlights, taillights, and a radio. Edward Knabusch sits in the passenger seat, beside a fully reclined Edwin Shoemaker.

La-Z-Boy employees outside the new, 60,000-square-foot plant in Newton, Mississippi, in April 1961

CHAPTER FOUR

ROCKING THE WORLD OF RELAXATION

1960–1969

We don't get lost in the community. We're a part of it.

—Richard Micka, vice president of administration,
on La-Z-Boy manufacturing facilities

SHORTLY AFTER THE CONCLUSION of La-Z-Boy's second labor strike in three years, Ed Knabusch left on a driving tour of 10 Southern states. The strike had convinced Knabusch that La-Z-Boy Chair Company should have a second manufacturing plant. Locating it in the nonunion South would keep labor costs down and help the company compete with other furniture makers.[1]

Knabusch looked for a location that had easy access to raw materials. A small, comfortable town, like Monroe, was also a priority. La-Z-Boy was one of Monroe's largest employers and contributed generously to the community. Knabusch wanted the company's new plant to be located in a similar environment.

Knabusch returned to Monroe with no firm decision on the new location, but two months later, four visitors from Newton, Mississippi, arrived on his doorstep. Knabusch summoned Shoemaker for a meeting with the gentlemen.

"It was a nasty afternoon," Shoemaker recalled. "It was snowing a bit, and they came out with no rubbers on, no overcoat, no topcoat, or anything. I don't even think they had hats."[2]

The Newton city officials had flown to Michigan to convince Knabusch and Shoemaker to locate La-Z-Boy's new plant in their town. Newton was a city of 4,000 located about 60 miles east of the Mississippi state capital, Jackson.

Newton was predominantly rural, and nearby were plentiful supplies of timber, cotton, and other raw materials used in La-Z-Boy® chairs. The town's industries had shut down, and city officials were anxious to attract a new employer.

"We had a lead on a site in Newton, Mississippi, and when [the Newton officials] found that out, they parked on our doorstep, and we couldn't get away from them," Shoemaker said.[3]

The Newton officials made a generous offer. They proposed a seven-acre site formerly occupied by Mississippi Oil Mills, which processed cottonseed oil. Newton offered the city-owned land to La-Z-Boy tax-free for 20 years for an annual rental fee of $18,000.[4]

La-Z-Boy accepted the proposal, and on May 6, 1960, Knabusch, Shoemaker, William "Mac" McLeod, and Dewey Turner loaded a truck with 1,300 pounds of metal chair fixtures and other components, tools, office supplies, and baggage. They drove for two days, traveling 919 miles to Newton, Mississippi, where they saw the setting of their new plant for the first time.

The Reclina-Rocker®, the first reclining rocking chair, was introduced in 1961 and instantly became a best-seller.

Above left: William "Mac" McLeod, a natural mechanic, was named manager of the Newton, Mississippi, plant in 1960.

Above right: Dewey Turner became office manager of the Newton plant in 1963. *(Photos courtesy of Harry Revell Fine Photography.)*

Heading South

"They always picked smaller rural towns, like Monroe," said Vice President of Administration Richard Micka, who joined the company in 1968. "We're near big cities, but we're still in an agricultural setting, and the people are all pretty close knit. They have strong value systems, and everybody knows everybody."[5]

The weeds on the seven-acre site were as high as the foursome's pickup truck. Two warehouses, previously occupied by the cottonseed-oil processor, were a shambles. Knabusch and Shoemaker stayed for 10 days, helping to clear a pecan grove, hire electricians, carpenters, and plumbers, and unload and set up equipment. They tore down one warehouse and cleared land surrounding the second building. They attempted to build the new plant around the second warehouse but eventually had to remove it as well.[6]

From their first day on the site, the men were deluged with Newton residents seeking jobs. The first two men hired were J. J. "Pete" Roach and Glen Strickland, who worked with McLeod and Turner over the next six months to set up the plant. In November 1960, the 60,000-square-foot plant opened and began producing La-Z-Rocker® swivel chairs.[7]

The Newton plant was a wholly owned subsidiary of La-Z-Boy Chair Company and was called La-Z-Boy Inc. (The name was later changed to La-Z-Boy South.) The plant was almost an exact duplicate of the Monroe facility. When it was dedicated on May 30, 1961, 1,200 people attended an open house—an incredible turnout from a community of only 4,000 people.[8]

McLeod, who had begun working at La-Z-Boy in 1940 as a janitor, was named the Newton plant manager. He had observed upholsterers in Monroe and often stayed late in the plant to learn the craft. Within a year, he was an upholstery foreman. He became general foreman in 1943 and plant superintendent in 1946. McLeod shared many qualities with Shoemaker and Knabusch. He was a natural mechanic who wasn't afraid to get his hands dirty.[9] Taking McLeod's place as Monroe plant manager was Lorne Stevens, who had come to La-Z-Boy in 1949 and had moved up from upholstery foreman and senior line foreman in the upholstery department.[10]

Dewey Turner was Newton's first office manager. He had begun working in La-Z-Boy's wood room in 1946 and soon learned other jobs in the assembly and shipping departments. He

Below left: Lorne Stevens filled McLeod's position as Monroe plant manager in 1960.

Below right: J. J. "Pete" Roach was one of the first employees hired at the Newton plant. *(Photos courtesy of Harry Revell Fine Photography.)*

became an upholsterer in 1948 and began studying accounting the same year. After serving in the Korean War, Turner worked in La-Z-Boy's purchasing and production departments. He had a reputation as a hard worker.[11]

La-Z-Boy's 1963 Board of Directors: standing, from left, Dr. Robert Ewing; Herman Gertz, secretary; Moritz Brueckner, vice president for sales; and Wilmer Knake, treasurer; and seated, Edward Knabusch, left, and Edwin Shoemaker.

The First Reclining Rocker

Amid the optimism, La-Z-Boy stockholders heard bad financial news. At the 1961 La-Z-Boy annual meeting, Treasurer Walter Marder reported that the company was operating at a loss for the second year. For the first time in the company's history, it failed to pay a dividend.[12]

At the same meeting, stockholders saw a demonstration of a new La-Z-Boy® chair that had received incredible attention at the January furniture show. The chair combined the popular features of the platform rocker and the reclining chair: It rocked and had a built-in footrest, and it also reclined. Dubbed the "Reclina-Rocker®," the chair utilized an entirely new, patented mechanism. No other furniture maker offered a reclining rocker.

Dale Shoemaker recalled the day his father told him about his idea for a chair that reclined and rocked. "'Somebody's got rocks in their head,' I thought. But it took off like gangbusters."[13]

La-Z-Boy produced its first Reclina-Rocker in December 1960 and then made more to take to the January furniture show, where buyers swamped the company with orders. The Reclina-Rocker was immediately La-Z-Boy's most popular product and one of the fastest-selling furniture items in the industry. By 1962, it accounted for 82 percent of La-Z-Boy's sales.[14]

The Reclina-Rocker® reversed La-Z-Boy's sales slump. The company produced more than twice as many chairs in 1962 as in 1961. Sales more than doubled, rising to $3.3 million. In 1963, sales nearly doubled again, reaching more than $6 million. The Monroe workforce jumped from 70 to 148, and a second shift was added. Newton employment leaped from 18 to 75. The company was soon producing 400 chairs a day.

By 1963, the popularity of the Reclina-Rocker made the company's earlier chairs obsolete, and La-Z-Boy discontinued its old-style recliners. The Reclina-Rocker mechanism could be adapted to a wide variety of styles. Early American furnishings were popular during the 1960s, and in 1963, La-Z-Boy introduced the Americana 600 series of Reclina-Rockers. The series was

inspired by a lounge chair Thomas Jefferson invented.

The Reclina-Rocker was also popular around the world. La-Z-Boy licensees in Mexico, Canada, Australia, and South Africa produced Reclina-Rockers. Furniture makers in both England and Switzerland began making La-Z-Boy® chairs in 1964 to supply the European market.[15]

In 1963, while en route to negotiate a licensing agreement in Japan, La-Z-Boy Treasurer Walter Marder died in a plane crash. Marder, 62 when he died, had brought a wealth of furniture-industry experience and knowledge to the company when he arrived in 1954. He had served on the board of directors and had worked as sales manager, treasurer, and assistant to the president. W. C. Knake joined the board as treasurer following Marder's death.[16]

Supplying the Demand

The company expanded its Monroe shop and office and added a third dry kiln in 1963. The Monroe plant then measured 100,000 square feet. The Newton plant, in operation for only two years, was enlarged to 94,000 square feet.[17]

But the plant expansions weren't enough to meet the demand for La-Z-Boy chairs. That same year, La-Z-Boy purchased a building in Monroe owned by Weis Manufacturing Company, where Ed Knabusch had worked from 1919 to 1925. The 180,000-square-foot Weis facility was transformed into La-Z-Boy's third manufacturing plant. Wood and metal parts and fabric covers were made at the Telegraph Road plant, which by then housed the company's research and development departments, and shuttled to the new shop for assembly.[18]

Plant expansion continued nonstop through the 1960s, but La-Z-Boy still had trouble keeping up with consumer demand for Reclina-Rockers. By 1965, sales totaled $14.8 million. The following year, sales jumped an astounding 41 percent to $20.8 million.

In 1966, La-Z-Boy opened its fourth plant, in Redlands, California. Redlands was a town of 34,000 people 65 miles east of Los Angeles in an area whose

Above: La-Z-Boy Treasurer Walter Marder died in a plane crash on his way to Japan in 1963.

Below: After an assembly plant opened in Monroe in 1963, the Telegraph Road building became La-Z-Boy's headquarters for research and development.

Edward Knabusch's son, Charles (far left), moved to Redlands, California, to become office manager at the new plant. Courtney Leckler (center) managed the upholstery department at La-Z-Boy West, the name given the Redlands plant. D. A. Kennedy (near left) was named vice president of La-Z-Boy East.

orange groves were falling to developers. Known as La-Z-Boy West, the plant supplied dealers in the Western United States, reducing shipping costs to the region. Mac McLeod served as the Redlands plant's manager. His ability to establish the Newton plant and manage its phenomenal growth was considered a "production miracle." Pete Roach replaced McLeod as Newton plant manager.[19]

Other Redlands appointees included 26-year-old Charles T. Knabusch, Edward Knabusch's son, as office manager. He was a graduate of Cleary Business College and had worked in the La-Z-Boy accounting department since 1961.[20] Courtney Leckler headed the Redlands plant's upholstery department. Leckler was a 20-year La-Z-Boy employee from the Monroe plant's upholstery department.[21]

"It's tough to get a plant started," Leckler recalled. "We were very quality conscious right from the beginning. It was hard to get the right people. But once we got going, we always made a profit, and we were proud of the chairs we made. Everybody went out of their way to do a good job."[22]

Redlands was a bedroom community with little business at the time, typical of the towns Knabusch and Shoemaker chose. "Mr. Knabusch and Mr. Shoemaker both were from a small town, and when they expanded and built factories in other places, they chose small towns, I think, because of the closeness of the people," said Kathi Stiefel, who came to the La-Z-Boy office in 1966. "They always thought [of] their workers as part of the family."[23]

California real estate was more expensive than at La-Z-Boy's other locations. Furthermore,

hardwood wasn't readily available, and the threat of earthquakes limited the use of some machinery. So the 75,000-square-foot Redlands plant was established as an assembly plant only, while La-Z-Boy searched for another facility to supply Redlands with parts.[24]

The search was short: In July 1966, La-Z-Boy purchased a furniture plant in Florence, South Carolina, owned by Furniture Industries. The 135,000-square-foot plant produced bedroom furniture and employed 100 people. The plant was located on 31 acres that had been Florence's first industrial site. In 1910, it had been the location of a lumbering operation that went bankrupt in 1920. Subsequently the property was sold to a manufacturer of wood parts for automobile bodies. When the auto industry switched to steel car bodies, this venture also went bankrupt. In 1937, J. H. Stelling and H. H. Shelor founded Furniture Industries, which reorganized in 1957 after Stelling's death. Shelor was named president; J. H. E. Stelling Jr., vice president; and D. A. Kennedy, secretary. La-Z-Boy purchased the company from those three men,[25] and Kennedy remained as vice president of La-Z-Boy East. La-Z-Boy retained Furniture Industries' 100 employees and converted the plant to produce wood parts for the Redlands plant, which began producing Reclina-Rockers a few months later.[26]

Unlike the Newton plant, which was financed through a bank loan, all La-Z-Boy's expansion during the mid-1960s was financed entirely through profits. In 1965, Knabusch told stockholders, "We don't have a single penny of debt. No mortgage, no debts whatsoever. All our growth has been financed out of profits."[27]

Efficiency Experts

In 1967, after 17 months of preparation, La-Z-Boy installed an NCR data processing system in its general offices in Monroe. The system streamlined and centralized a number of operations and enabled the staff to produce a daily report on the status of every chair on order by every dealer. An average day's orders of approximately 1,800 chairs could be reviewed in 15 minutes. The daily report included dealer's name, order number, La-Z-Boy's acknowledgment number, style number, fabric number, order date, expected shipping date, and the plant producing the chair. This new system saved countless hours

and eliminated duplicate information at different locations.

The system also helped track inventories at La-Z-Boy warehouses and plants and produced custom reports on production projections, scheduling, parts purchases, and orders by style.[28]

Things also became more efficient in the accounting office, said retired Secretary-Treasurer Gene Hardy, who performed La-Z-Boy's first audit in 1967.

When Fritz [Jackson, CFO] and I first came, La-Z-Boy was running a problem with cash. They always had to borrow in the fall of the year, when their big Christmas season was coming up.

The problem was in their accounting system. We found about a million dollars sitting in desk drawers in the accounting office. That was an amazing discovery. We couldn't believe it. They would never deposit a check in the bank until they could figure out who gave the check to them and what invoice they were paying.[29]

The hivelike Monroe plant could not produce enough chairs to meet demand during the 1960s, necessitating more La-Z-Boy plants. Sales skyrocketed after the introduction of the Reclina-Rocker®, keeping Monroe workers busy.

The founders were so busy engineering and introducing new products that making money was almost an afterthought, Hardy said.[30]

Celebrity Spokesman

La-Z-Boy's national advertising also took a new turn in the mid-1960s. Since 1947, La-Z-Boy had been advertising in national magazines such as *House Beautiful, McCall's, Reader's Digest, Ladies' Home Journal,* and *Better Homes and Gardens.* Ads had also appeared in newspapers and on radio and television. The ads spotlighted relaxation and comfort and generally featured a man or woman beaming in a La-Z-Boy. The chair's lifetime warranty was also a selling point. By 1966, La-Z-Boy's advertising budget exceeded $500,000.[31]

Then in 1967, La-Z-Boy changed its magazine, newspaper, and trade magazine ads to feature a celebrity spokesman: singer and actor Bing Crosby. The magazine ads pictured Bing and his wife, Kathryn, relaxing in La-Z-Boy® chairs in their home. Bing says, "Man, this is really relaxing . . . an evening at home with Kathryn in our La-Z-Boy chairs."

A Changing Company

Directing La-Z-Boy's advertising during the 1960s were Moritz Brueckner and Gary Schroeder. Brueckner had served as sales manager since 1958, and in April 1968, he was named executive vice president. He assisted Knabusch in company administration and was the administrative chief in Knabusch's absence.[32]

Knabusch continued as chairman and president of the company, but, at age 68, he was ready to groom future La-Z-Boy management. Shoemaker, who served as executive vice president of engineering and product development, was not involved in the company's administration beyond his department. Brueckner represented La-Z-Boy's first expansion of top management beyond the two founders.

Succeeding Brueckner as sales manager was Gary Schroeder, who was named vice president of sales. He had been with La-Z-Boy since 1964 as director of new product planning and marketing.

Bing and Kathryn Crosby appeared in La-Z-Boy ads during the 1960s.

A graduate of Susquehanna University, Schroeder had been vice president and director of a furniture distribution outlet in Peru, Indiana, and a furniture buyer for a Pittsburgh, Pennsylvania, company.[33]

Schroeder added other celebrity spokespersons to La-Z-Boy advertising. Betsy Palmer and Bess Myerson recorded radio commercials for NBC and CBS radio, respectively.[34] In fall 1969, La-Z-Boy sponsored 60-second *Tonight Show* commercials in which announcer Ed McMahon demonstrated a La-Z-Boy® recliner.[35]

Another advertising campaign ran concurrently with the celebrity ads. Spurred by the consumer

La-Z-Boy salesmen attended a sales training session in Monroe in 1965.

movement in the United States, which encouraged businesses to provide complete information about their products, La-Z-Boy began running ads in 1967 that contained detailed information about the construction of La-Z-Boy® chairs.[36] Revealing how its chairs were made was nothing new for La-Z-Boy. The company always emphasized its chairs' quality construction and, since the first chair was exhibited in 1929, had provided a lifetime warranty on its chairs' mechanisms.

Style Council

Under the guidance of Shoemaker, La-Z-Boy engineers and designers constantly improved the chairs' comfort, style, and durability. Shoemaker oversaw chair design, selection of materials, layout of plants, tooling and dies, and production methods. He worked closely with David White, director of styling and design. White was the son of Floral

City Furniture salesman Lloyd White and was a graduate of Kendall School of Design, in Grand Rapids, Michigan. He began working at La-Z-Boy in 1961 and had become the company's chief chair designer. In fact, La-Z-Boy chairs were promoted in the furniture industry as "David White designs."

La-Z-Boy's smooth gliding mechanism, adjustable tension control, comfort selector footrest, and other refinements were all products of La-Z-Boy's Engineering Department.

In 1966, the company introduced the Continental La-Z-Loungers, a reclining lounge chair with an "off the floor" look. At the same time, La-Z-Boy introduced a new, three-position footrest mechanism on all its recliners. It was called the Comfort Selector, and it gave users a choice of three footrest positions on the Reclina-Rocker®, whether or not the chair was reclined.[37]

La-Z-Boy still had two Reclina-Rocker product lines. Its charter line sold at furniture stores and accounted for most of La-Z-Boy's sales. In 1968, this group had 29 styles and 5,000 dealers. The company's Americana Collection featured 16 styles and was sold in 150 department stores. Both lines featured 250 colors and patterns.[38]

In 1968, La-Z-Boy engineers collaborated to develop a revolutionary new shipping carton called Mini-Pak. The carton reduced freight costs, saved warehouse space, and resulted in less freight damage than the carton it replaced. It measured only 31,972 cubic inches and stood only 30 inches tall, whereas its chunky predecessor took up nearly 50,000 cubic inches and needed 10 more inches of headroom.

Furniture vans hauling La-Z-Boy chairs could hold 52 chairs packaged in the old, L-shaped cartons, which were stacked with the back of one chair resting on the seat of another. By contrast, 78 of the new Mini-Pak cartons could fit in a furniture van. Because of the new cartons' more compact size and efficient handling, La-Z-Boy received a special shipping rate that was one-sixth less than the previous cost.

The Mini-Pak was not just a packaging change. To fit into smaller cartons, La-Z-Boy chairs were shipped with their backs removed. The dealer or customer could assemble them without tools.[39] "The detachable chair back was really an innovation for the company," Richard Micka said. "It was a landmark patent and a defining moment for La-Z-Boy. It increased sales dramatically."[40]

Mini-Paks could be carried by one person whereas the former carton required two handlers. Also, Mini-Paks came with a convenient tear strip, eliminating damaged upholstery that could result from slicing open a carton with a knife.

Because dealers could store more chairs in the same amount of space, they could carry larger inventories of La-Z-Boy chairs packaged in Mini-Paks. Dealers could also reduce delivery costs by encouraging take-home sales since Mini-Paks fit in most standard car trunks.[41]

La-Z-Boy's Comfort Selector feature provided for three footrest positions while someone sat or reclined. The footrest was controlled by a handle on the chair's side.

Shifting Gears

By the end of the 1960s, La-Z-Boy was again experimenting with new products. In 1969, the company introduced the Sofette, a space-saving reclining loveseat. The Sofette had two independently operating reclining seats and was marketed to people who lacked room for both a sofa and a recliner. The chair was introduced in 1969 and went into production during 1970.[42]

The Sofette was a product consumers had requested, said furniture store owner Charles Dewey.

Through the years, we've had scores and scores of requests for a reclining sofa by La-Z-Boy. We even had a backlog of names of people who wanted such a unique sofa. When we found out last summer that the Sofette was available, we acquired more names on our list. When our first shipment of four Sofettes arrived, we put one on the floor. In a matter of minutes, it was sold. . . . We have every reason to believe that the Sofette will be the hottest furniture item in America in 1970.[43]

The introduction of the Sofette produced an immediate backlog of orders. With all plants on double and triple shifts, expansion again was necessary. In 1969 all plants were enlarged, and La-Z-Boy broke ground for its sixth plant, in Neosho, Missouri.

Floral City Furniture was also growing. Sales in 1969 were $1.9 million. That year, Floral City broke ground for its first expansion since 1946. The Knabusches moved their home, just north of the

furniture store, to a new location to make room for a larger showroom.

At 78,000 square feet, the expanded Floral City building was one of the largest furniture stores in the Midwest. Its showroom spread over 39,500 square feet, an increase of 16,500 square feet. It included rooms for carpet, Drexel furniture, Early American furniture, and La-Z-Boy® chairs. Floral City was La-Z-Boy's largest one-store account, selling about 2,000 La-Z-Boy chairs per year.[44]

Floral City Manager Herman Gertz was named president of the corporation in 1969. Knabusch was chairman of the board, and Shoemaker was Floral City's secretary/treasurer. Other board members included Norman T. Smith, vice president of purchasing, and Lloyd White, vice president of sales.[45]

Alice Vagt had been bookkeeper for Floral City since 1941. She recalled the generosity of Ed Knabusch.

He had a boat, and he'd say, "You all get ready. Tonight, we'll have a party on the boat." This would happen all summer long. He would get the food ready himself. It wasn't Mrs. Knabusch that would do it. She was not all that well. He'd clean the vege-

Floral City Furniture sold more La-Z-Boy chairs than any other outlet during the 1960s.

tables and everything himself and invite everybody who worked [at Floral City Furniture]. And if you couldn't be on the boat today, why, maybe he'd throw a second party tomorrow so the rest could come. He was just the kindest person I think I ever knew.[46]

Knabusch often cooked for his employees, said Gene Hardy. "Mr. Knabusch really valued the shareholders and people who had supported the company when it was struggling, so for the annual meeting he would barbecue beef. He would invite the shareholders for the meeting and serve them roast beef sandwiches and things like that. It was a tradition as we started accumulating more shareholders."[47]

When the meal was eliminated, attendance at annual meetings dropped from an average of 125 to about 37, Hardy said. "They were coming for the roast beef sandwiches."[48]

No Decline for Recliners

By the end of the decade, recliners were the fastest-growing segment of the furniture industry, and La-Z-Boy was the leading recliner manufacturer. As Americans became more affluent and enjoyed more leisure time, recliners became a standard furnishing in family rooms or living rooms. Hotels and vacation condominium builders added recliners in front of televisions. La-Z-Boy entered the contract market when it teamed up with a mobile home manufacturer that included a recliner with every mobile home sale.[49]

In many ways, La-Z-Boy was an exception in the industry. It was the country's 11th-largest furniture maker. Its sales had grown from $1.1 million in 1960 to $42.7 million in 1969. It employed 1,823 people in five plants.[50]

Most large manufacturers were located in the South, and the furniture market had followed suit; its center had moved from Chicago to High Point, North Carolina. But La-Z-Boy plants were regionally located: in the North, South, East, West, and, soon, Midwest.

The industry's upholstery makers faced additional challenges. Upholstered furniture had higher labor costs than case goods and was largely custom-made. Consequently, this segment earned the lowest profits in the industry.[51]

Furniture industry advertising was often left to retailers, and *Fortune* reported little brand-name identification. But La-Z-Boy had long been an advertising leader as well. It had advertised its brand for better than 20 years in magazines and newspapers and on billboards, television, and radio. The name La-Z-Boy was becoming synonymous with recliners, and the company was careful to protect its trademarks and patents.

La-Z-Boy's products were being recognized locally and internationally. In a 1964 Michigan Week contest, the Reclina-Rocker® was named Product of the Year in Monroe and throughout its region.[52] In 1969, La-Z-Boy received the American Furniture Mart's Pacemaker Award for 40 years of achievement in the home furnishings industry. *Furniture World* and *Furniture South* magazines gave La-Z-Boy their Design Award for outstanding design in its class, judged by a national group of leading retail furniture executives.

La-Z-Boy was also honored in Europe. In 1969, La-Z-Boy's Italian licensee, Sergio Pizzetti of Industria Della Poltrona Pizzetti of Rome, received the Mercurio D'Oro, described as the Oscar of European trade. It recognized La-Z-Boy for productivity and economic collaboration policy and particularly for the manufacturing and distribution in Italy of Reclina-Rockers. The award was well publicized in Europe.[53]

As the decade came to a close, La-Z-Boy looked forward to the opening of its sixth plant. The plant would help meet the demand for Reclina-Rockers and accommodate the company's plans for growth in a new area—contract sales. Vice President of Sales Gary Schroeder was planning a big push in the contract field. Schroeder told the *Monroe Evening News* in 1969 that La-Z-Boy planned to "go into the contract business next year on a big scale."[54]

Mr. Howell of *Gilligan's Island* and the voice of Mr. Magoo, actor Jim Backus was also the voice of La-Z-Boy during the 1970s.

CHAPTER FIVE

FIFTY YEARS OF RECLINING

1970–1979

A solid foundation for the next 50 years has been laid. We are staffed, equipped, and ready to meet the challenges of the years ahead.

—Edward Knabusch, 1979

JUDITH CARR'S ENTRY INTO THE company was an unusual one. While working in a restaurant at a local Holiday Inn, Carr served Mr. and Mrs. Shoemaker and two of La-Z-Boy's licensee guests from Australia. When one of the licensees asked Carr what Monroe was famous for, she replied, "George Custer and La-Z-Boy Chair Company."

The licensee asked, "How would you like to meet the inventor of the first La-Z-Boy® chair? This is Mr. Ed Shoemaker."

Carr, 33 at the time, jokingly asked, "Mr. Shoemaker, can I work for you when I grow up? I just think the world of La-Z-Boy."

Shoemaker's wife poked him in the ribs with her elbow and said, "Eddie, that's the kind of person you need at La-Z-Boy, somebody enthusiastic."[1]

Three weeks later, Carr got a call from the head of La-Z-Boy's Personnel Department about an opening in the Customer Service Department.

"I ended up getting a job as a clerk typist for less than I was making at the restaurant," Carr said. "But I didn't care because I had my foot in the door."[2]

A Family Business

The La-Z-Boy family is strengthened by its open-door policy. "It has always been a company where you could walk in and talk to our top management, which is a really special thing," Carr said. "There's always been a good rapport between our upper management and the rest of our employees. A lot of our upper management people will wander around the office and visit with people and are available if you want to talk to them."[3]

That tradition began long ago with Ed Knabusch, said his daughter, Betty Lou White. "Nobody called him Mr. Knabusch. He wanted to be called Ed."[4]

Knabusch and Shoemaker imprinted the company with a family feel early on with picnics in the Knabusches' backyard and along Lake Erie, swimming pool parties, and an annual Christmas party.

"Today, we have an annual summer picnic for employees, and we have a Christmas luncheon in the auditorium," Carr said. "Even though now we're a couple-billion-dollar-a-year company, we still have a lot of tradition being carried on, which is fabulous for morale."[5]

La-Z-Boy commissioned a series of family-life paintings for its magazine advertising during the 1970s.

Employees are so closely knit that La-Z-Boy retirees eat lunch together on a regular basis. "Once people become affiliated with La-Z-Boy, they are forever a part of the family," Carr said. "Our scrapbooks are full of obituaries, weddings, and other events. You [don't] have to be somebody famous to get in La-Z-Boy's scrapbook. All you have to be is affiliated with the company. That's about as nice a legacy as anybody could ask for."[6]

Passing the Baton

La-Z-Boy had experienced a decade of strong growth before the economy slowed in 1970. The company's sales increased 3 percent in 1970 to $44 million.[7] The years of 20 percent to 40 percent growth were over, but La-Z-Boy remained optimistic about future sales. The furniture market was expected to nearly double during the first half of the 1970s, with sales climbing from $5.5 billion to $10 billion.[8]

The company began the decade with organizational and personnel changes and a new product line. Knabusch's attempt to groom Moritz Brueckner as his successor ended abruptly when Brueckner left the company in December 1969. A few months later Knabusch named his son, Charles, to the position of vice president and assistant to the president. Three years later, Edward Knabusch stepped down as president of the company, remaining as chairman of the board, and Charles Knabusch, 33, was named president. David White was executive vice president, and Gary Schroeder was executive vice president of sales and marketing. The three young executives joined Ed Knabusch, Eddie Shoemaker, W. C. Knake, Herman Gertz, John A. Cammenga, Robert Ewing, and S. J. Newton on the board.[9]

The La-Z-Boy Chair Company board of directors in 1971 included (standing, from left) Herman Gertz, Gary Schroeder, Charles Knabusch, Edward Knabusch, Edwin Shoemaker, S. J. Newton, Robert Ewing, and (in front, from left) W. C. Knake and John Cammenga.

In 1972, La-Z-Boy became a publicly traded company. Through underwriter Merrill Lynch, Pierce, Fenner & Smith, La-Z-Boy offered 320,128 shares and raised money to finance new plant construction.

"The idea is, if the public owns the stock, they'll look at your product and they'll buy your product," said Fritz Jackson, who worked as chief financial officer at La-Z-Boy until he retired in 2001.[10] The offering tripled the number of La-Z-Boy shareholders to 3,000. La-Z-Boy stock was quoted over the counter using the ticker symbol LAZB.[11]

La-Z-Boy continued to grow internationally. In 1970, it signed a licensing agreement with Kosuga and Company, Limited, of Tokyo, Japan. The company produced La-Z-Boy® chairs for sale in Burma, Hong Kong, India, Japan, Korea, Malaysia, Indonesia, Okinawa, Pakistan, Taiwan, and Thailand.[12]

Attracting Partners

La-Z-Boy entered into a joint venture with Jason Industries, its Australian licensee, in 1972. This alliance was La-Z-Boy's first ownership in a foreign operation.

The new company was named La-Z-Boy International Pty. La-Z-Boy had worked with Jason Industries since 1959. It manufactured furniture and building materials. Jason sold La-Z-Boy chairs in Australia, Burma, Ceylon (now Sri Lanka), Fiji, India, Kuwait, the Loyalty Islands, Malaysia, Mauritius, New Caledonia, New Guinea, New Hebrides (now Vanuatu), New Zealand, the Solomon Islands, Thailand, and Tonga.[13]

La-Z-Boy's licensees in West Germany and Italy covered the European market. South African licensee Associated Furniture Companies manufactured chairs and owned a chain of 26 retail stores in African countries.[14]

Diversity of Products

Until 1970, La-Z-Boy's products had been marketed to the home furnishings customer. But La-Z-Boy broke into an entirely new market that year when it began producing swivel and reclining desk chairs for the contract and institutional markets.[15] La-Z-Boy had long known the potential of the contract market, which included offices, hospitals,

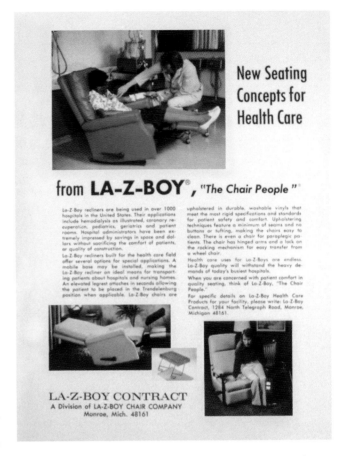

Above: La-Z-Boy advertised its Contract Division products in health care magazines. The durable chairs became increasingly common in hospitals and nursing homes in the 1970s.

Below: La-Z-Boy chairs made patients' visitors comfortable and doubled as beds for overnight guests.

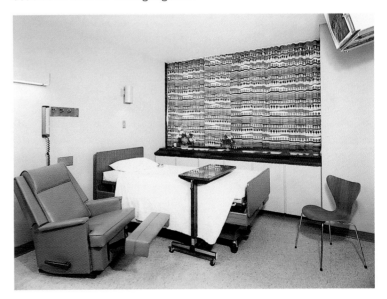

nursing homes, motels, and mobile homes. As early as 1953, La-Z-Boy had advertised its chairs as a way for stressed businessmen to relax. But at the time, La-Z-Boy did not have the production capacity to make both residential and contract furniture.

In 1970, though, La-Z-Boy established a separate sales force to sell to the lucrative contract market. Twelve salesmen, under the direction of Contract Sales Manager Bernie Bell, serviced accounts at 2,300 dealers. "The biggest potential," Gary Schroeder said at the time, was in the office contract market.

There is an estimated $50 billion being invested in total office furnishings during the '70s, and most of the home furnishings manufacturers are not ser-

vicing the office field. We feel we have something better, more comfortable, and more appropriate for office contract than exists commercially today.[16]

La-Z-Boy Contract offered executive chairs with or without leg rests and reclining action. It also produced coordinating chairs for reception areas, meeting rooms, desks, and executive offices.

At the same time, La-Z-Boy® chairs were becoming more common in hospitals and nursing homes, which hailed the chairs' solid construction and durability. La-Z-Boy® recliners were used in pediatric, geriatric, coronary recuperation, and hemodialysis units. Patients in these units felt more at ease in chairs than in bed because lying on their backs was associated with illness. The chairs doubled as portable beds for patients' overnight guests. For patients who had trouble operating the recliner's footrest lever, La-Z-Boy offered its Lectra-Lounger electric recliner, whose back and footrest motion were controlled by the push of a button.[17]

New products in the consumer line included the La-Z-Glider®—a plastic plate attached to the

La-Z-Boy's office products included a reclining executive chair.

chair's rocker base increased mobility. The Leg Rest Comfort Extension was an option that provided extra reclining length for tall people.[18]

In 1973, La-Z-Boy introduced two new low-silhouette chairs. Interior designers had long complained that recliners were too big and bulky, but the size had been necessary to accommodate the reclining mechanism. La-Z-Boy told buyers, "Each year, La-Z-Boy gets bigger and bigger . . . this year, we got smaller and smaller." The ads referred to La-Z-Boy's Hi-Lo recliner—a La-Z-Lounger with a low back. When the occupant reclined the chair, a hidden headrest popped up from the chair's back."[19]

La-Z-Boy's second new product was a swivel rocker called the La-Z-Rocker®. When the occupant leaned back in the chair, the back gave slightly. La-Z-Boy called the La-Z-Rocker "The chair that breaks its back for you."[20]

In 1974, La-Z-Boy introduced a mobile base that provided mobility to patients using La-Z-Boy Reclina-Rocker® recliners in the health care market. The wheeled base allowed the chairs to be moved easily and to rotate 360 degrees when the leg rest was disengaged.[21]

La-Z-Boy production capacity increased when the Neosho, Missouri, plant opened in 1970. The 180,000-square-foot plant produced Sofettes. Heading La-Z-Boy Midwest was Verl Manor, a veteran of the Monroe plant's wood room who had most recently served as director of production planning and methods engineering. Manor had worked for La-Z-Boy since 1947.[22]

Neosho was located in southwestern Missouri in the foothills of the Ozark Mountains. The city had been hit hard by the closing of a military base and was seeking new industry. Mac McLeod, by then semi-retired, had supervised construction of the Neosho plant.

Workers Strike a Blow

Neosho workers rejected union representation, and in 1971, La-Z-Boy's Monroe workers were the only ones in the company represented by a union. Since the long labor strike of 1959, La-Z-Boy and its union employees had enjoyed a cordial relationship. Contracts had been settled long before deadlines. But the United Furniture

Mac McLeod looks over some of the 83,000 cubic yards of rock that had to be removed from the site of the Dayton, Tennessee, plant.

Workers of America, which represented Monroe workers, and La-Z-Boy clashed in 1971 when the union rejected La-Z-Boy's contract offers.

Union members were receiving a higher combination of wages and fringe benefits than workers at any other reclining chair manufacturer. In fact, the union had used La-Z-Boy's contract and high wages as an example for other furniture manufacturers to follow. It had even used the high wages and fringe benefits as a propaganda tool to win an election at La-Z-Boy's Florence, South Carolina, plant.[23]

Florence workers voted for union representation, and when negotiations for its first contract were postponed until a Monroe contract was signed, workers at both plants walked out. Although production at the Monroe plants stopped, the Florence plant remained open. The strikes dragged on for two months, with violence reported at both locations. Union negotiators blocked Monroe workers' efforts to conduct a secret vote on contract proposals.[24] Linking the two contracts remained a major point of contention.

On September 29, the La-Z-Boy board of directors discussed the union's rejection of its offers. The board studied the economic situations at all La-Z-Boy plants. It discovered that the cost of producing chairs in Monroe was higher than at any other plant. The board advised the union that if its offer were rejected, the Monroe plant

At a ground-breaking ceremony in 1972, Edward Knabusch pulled the lever on his La-Z-Boy® chair, setting off a dynamite charge on the site of the Dayton, Tennessee, plant.

would be shut down permanently and operations transferred to other facilities.[25]

A week later, both sides made concessions, and the Monroe strike ended October 5. Florence workers agreed on a contract and returned to work on October 25.

Gaining Momentum

La-Z-Boy opened two more plants in 1973. La-Z-Boy Tennessee opened in Dayton, Tennessee, a town of 5,000, in December. Before construction began, La-Z-Boy learned that 83,000 cubic yards of rock had to be removed from the site. Four months later, Knabusch led an unusual ground-breaking ceremony. While seated in a La-Z-Boy chair, he pulled the chair's footrest lever, setting off a charge of dynamite that exploded in the distance. Construction of the 314,000-square-foot plant took much longer than expected, due to bad weather.[26]

When the plant began producing Reclina-Rockers®, in December 1973, it was the largest of

La-Z-Boy's manufacturing plants. John Cammenga was named vice president of La-Z-Boy Tennessee. Cammenga, formerly vice president of manufacturing, had been with La-Z-Boy since 1966 and on the board of directors since 1969.[27] James Marunick was named plant manager. He had been chief industrial engineer in Monroe.[28]

The introduction of La-Z-Boy's swivel rocker in 1973 necessitated additional production capacity. La-Z-Boy couldn't afford the time to build a plant, so in January it purchased an old Pet Milk plant in Siloam Springs, Arkansas, about 60 miles south of the Neosho plant. The 75,000-square-foot facility had been built in 1943. It was converted quickly, and production began in June.[29] After a large addition, the plant totaled 121,274 square feet.[30]

Cutting Costs and Consumption

Like La-Z-Boy's earlier plants, the new plants were self-sufficient. With the exception of the Redlands, California, plant, all facilities were responsible for kiln drying lumber, cutting frame parts, stamping mechanisms, sewing covers, and assembling the product. A new operation at all plants was polyurethane fabrication. Producing the materials to stuff the chairs' upholstered parts resulted in substantial cost savings for the company.[31]

Chair frames became another area in which increased costs led to new materials. One day's production at the Telegraph Road plant alone used 20,000 board feet of wood, equivalent to 35 trees at least 60 feet high and with a diameter of 30 inches.[32] Wood was scarce during the 1970s, and its cost was climbing. La-Z-Boy experimented with a few plastic parts during the early 1970s and gradually began using plastic for frame parts. La-Z-Boy engineers found that plastic lent more versatility to carved designs and assured uniformity and strength.[33]

The 1973 embargo halting oil exports to the United States from Middle Eastern oil-producing countries spurred another recession and motivated businesses to trim energy consumption and conserve materials. La-Z-Boy found ways to grind up wood chips and sawdust not burned for fuel, combine them with a bonding agent, and mold them into unexposed chair parts. Similarly, poly scraps were recycled into usable padding.[34]

Instead of scarce and expensive natural gas and fuel oil, La-Z-Boy plants burned their unrecyclable wood waste in nonpolluting boilers to cut costs and maintain production during cold winters.[35]

La-Z-Boy added other environmentally friendly processes during the 1970s. A state-of-the-art paint system for metal parts slashed paint usage by 75 percent and cut spray booth maintenance costs by 90 percent. An electrostatic wood finishing process reduced the amount of sealer and lacquer used by 60 percent and kept the air cleaner.[36]

Fabric Centers

Cover material was La-Z-Boy's most expensive inventory item, and in 1974, the company took steps to reduce its fabric costs. Prior to 1974, cover material was shipped from mills to each La-Z-Boy plant. Shipments were hand-posted and entered into a computerized inventory. The method was often inaccurate, and the company kept much more fabric in its inventory than it needed. With seven plants and more than 1,000 fabric styles and colors, La-Z-Boy needed a way to handle fabric more efficiently and economically.[37]

The solution was the computerized Fabric Processing Center, opened in 1974 in Florence, South Carolina. The five-story building, the only facility of its kind in the world, housed all upholstery fabrics for the entire company. It could hold 20,520 rolls of fabric, or more than 1 million yards, enough to upholster 150,000 La-Z-Boy chairs. Its computerized inventory system kept track of the exact yardage of every pattern of fabric at all times.[38]

The building was outfitted with computer-operated automatic stackers and control units. Fabric from the mills arrived at the center, where it was inventoried and transported by the stackers to its storage areas. The stackers were crane assemblies that traveled over steel rails at 500 feet per minute. Responding to signals from an NCR Century 251 computer at La-Z-Boy corporate headquarters, the stackers automatically picked and loaded fabric to be shipped to La-Z-Boy plants. The Fabric Center could handle 1,400 fabric transactions in an eight-hour shift.[39]

Less than two years after the Fabric Center opened, La-Z-Boy had reduced its fabric inventory from 2.2 million yards to 1.4 million yards, saving the company $1.3 million. The $2 million plant paid for itself in two years.[40] It doubled in size in 1980.

Farewell to Floral City Furniture

In 1974, Floral City Furniture Store closed permanently and sold its land and building to La-Z-Boy Chair Company. The retail store had operated since 1931 and had grown to 78,000 square feet. In 1973, the store's sales totaled $2.5 million.[41] Although sales had been increasing, the store's profits were declining, leading to the decision to close the business.[42]

It was a sad day for employees, recalled Lloyd White, who started with Floral City Furniture in 1940. "I had tears in my eyes that day." Although Floral City closed its doors, the friendships sparked there would remain. Past employees are rounded up each year for an annual breakfast. "It's sort of a Floral City Furniture reunion," White said.[43]

Alice Vagt recalled a farewell dinner for the women in the office. "Mr. Shoemaker and Mr. Knabusch came," she said. "Few people ever quit Floral City. Everyone stuck around. I often say that if they had stayed open, I would probably still be working there if they let me. It was fun to work there. It was a happy place to be."[44]

Vagt recalled the generosity and integrity her bosses shared.

They are the best I've ever had. Wealth did not show with either of them. It didn't change their personalities, and they gave so much that nobody found out about it until [much later]. They didn't want it to be known all over—they just gave. A lot of people could have patterned after them.[45]

Motion Furniture

With increasing competition during the 1970s, recliner manufacturers continually introduced new styles and improvements to win the battle for customer dollars. Many furniture makers streamlined recliners, attempting to transform their bulky lines and "beer and baloney" image, according to *Furniture/Today*. In 1975, La-Z-Boy introduced the Wall-Recliner®, a reclining chair that could be positioned one inch from a wall and reclined

without hitting the wall. Subsequently, La-Z-Boy embellished the idea and gained sales with its Wall-Recliner Sofette and Wall Reclina-Rocker®. La-Z-Boy was the first to develop a wall-proximity recliner that rocked. The chair included all the features of La-Z-Boy's Reclina-Rocker®, including

La-Z-Boy® chair covers were produced in the Sewing Department at the Neosho plant. From left are Laura Loving, Wanda Duncan, Lora Harding, Billie Renfro, and Edith Call.

the three-position footrest. La-Z-Boy also introduced La-Z-Mates®—a matching Reclina-Rocker and La-Z-Rocker®.

Motion or action furniture, as it was called, was a fast-growing segment of the furniture industry. It was estimated that recliner sales would grow 12 percent a year through the decade. La-Z-Boy was the largest motion chair manufacturer, with a 26 percent share of the market in 1976.[46] Another fast-growing segment of the furniture industry was sleep sofas. Their sales were expected to increase 10 percent annually. David White told the *Monroe Evening News* in 1977 that by 1980, 50 percent of sofas purchased by consumers would be sleeper units.[47]

La-Z-Boy saw an opportunity in these figures. In 1978, the company introduced its first nonchair product: a sleep sofa called the La-Z-Sleeper®. It had a counterbalanced opening mechanism that operated easily and quietly; an exclusive, sinuous wire mattress support deck; an innerspring mattress; and an adjustable headrest for reading and TV viewing. Like La-Z-Boy chairs, La-Z-Sleeper mechanisms had a lifetime warranty.[48]

Brand Awareness

La-Z-Boy continued to advertise its brand heavily during the 1970s. Beginning in 1970, Jim Backus and his alter ego, Mr. Magoo, recorded radio and television spots for La-Z-Boy.

In the mid-1970s, La-Z-Boy added sports personalities as spokespersons. New York Jets quarterback Joe Namath was the most visible one. He appeared on television and radio, often during sports events. He was also featured in magazine advertisements. Other La-Z-Boy spokespersons included football coaches Don Shula, Rick Forzano, and Bo Schembechler.[49]

La-Z-Boy's advertising investment paid off. A national poll on brand-name awareness confirmed that La-Z-Boy had become the most recognized name in the furniture industry.[50]

In 1975, La-Z-Boy capitalized on its brand-name recognition when it authorized furniture stores to use the La-Z-Boy name in recliner specialty stores. Recliner specialty shops were not a novel idea, but using a manufacturer's name in a retail logo was believed to be an innovation, according to *Home Furnishings Daily.*[51]

"There was a feeling that the brand was strong enough to carry its own retail entity," said John Case, who started his sales and marketing career with La-Z-Boy in 1979. "The challenge was to open up a La-Z-Boy store with an independent owner—and that might be three miles down from a general furniture store that was carrying La-Z-Boy."[52]

Showcase Shoppes

The independently owned stores were called La-Z-Boy Showcase Shoppes. About 10 shops opened in 1975. A year later, there were more than 150 La-Z-Boy Showcase Shoppes across the country. A typical Showcase Shoppe was 4,000 square feet and displayed 250 La-Z-Boy chairs. Shoppe owners were encouraged to display La-Z-Sleeper® sleep sofas in coordinating fabrics.[53]

When the stores first opened, they generated "scores of rumors, half-truths, and total misconceptions on the part of many in the industry," *Retailing Home Furnishings* reported. "Several manufacturers . . . called them thinly disguised franchises trying to pass themselves off as totally independent furniture stores. Others considered the concept to be little more than a built-in annuity for the Michigan recliner giant. . . . Many retailers feared price fixing and/or severe price discounting."[54]

La-Z-Boy officials denied the accusations and pointed out that there were few restrictions on Showcase Shoppes. They were required to buy a certain amount of La-Z-Boy merchandise and could not carry competing recliners. They could, however, sell noncompeting furniture and accessories.[55]

When the industry speculated that Showcase Shoppes could hurt sales in La-Z-Boy's existing network of 8,000 dealers, Gary Schroeder insisted the Shoppes would raise consumer awareness of La-Z-Boy® recliners. "This is supplemental in our present marketing. We will only put them in areas where it will help our current market penetration and not hurt our present accounts," Schroeder told *Retailing Home Furnishings.* He also pointed out that most Showcase Shoppes were owned by current dealers.[56]

La-Z-Boy lost a lot of distribution at first—as the company opened chair stores, it lost independent dealers. But the sales from those chair stores were significant. La-Z-Boy finally stemmed the tide of defections and proved to its dealers that the product was sold to them at the same price it was sold to Showcase Shoppe owners. La-Z-Boy's credibility and the power of the brand carried the retail stores to success.[57]

Paul Opfermann had been employed by La-Z-Boy for three years when he left the corporate office and started his own Showcase Shoppe in 1975.

I was 23 or 24 and had no intentions of getting into the retail business. But I was encouraged by my brother-in-law [Executive Vice President David White] to pursue the opportunity. I had no money. He and Betty Lou [David's wife and Ed Knabusch's daughter] loaned me the money to start the business with a line of credit from Monroe Bank and Trust, which was very closely associated with La-Z-Boy

Opposite: Early La-Z-Boy Showcase Shoppes' 4,000-square-foot stores displayed chairs in long rows.

corporate. With that help we started our first store, in Warren, Michigan.[58]

In 1978, La-Z-Boy stopped authorizing Showcase Shoppes, saying that at 208 shops, "It had fulfilled its original intention of using these shops to help it penetrate major marketing areas."[59] The Showcase Shoppes had helped La-Z-Boy penetrate urban areas, where its sales typically were weak. In New York, for instance, La-Z-Boy had been unable to sell its chairs in department stores because it was unable to give the stores exclusivity in the market. The Showcase Shoppes helped La-Z-Boy add dealers in areas such as New York.[60]

The driving force behind the opening of the Showcase Shoppes was Gary Schroeder, whom many credited with La-Z-Boy's hitting the $100 million sales mark in 1976. Schroeder was described as tough, bombastic, combative, outspoken, and shrewd. He was well known and admired by many in the industry. He was a former president of the National Association of Furniture Manufacturers.

Chairman of the Board Ed Knabusch relaxes for a photo with board members (from left) John Cammenga, Charles Knabusch, David White, and Gary Schroeder.

Some claimed that Schroeder created the sales machine—and to some degree the marketing machine—that drove the business up so dramatically.[61] But while many credited him with making La-Z-Boy the furniture industry force that it was, others criticized him as authoritarian. *Retailing Home Furnishings* reported that detractors saw him as "willing to sacrifice profits in pursuit of sales and as lacking in regard for retail accounts."[62]

Ed Knabusch asked for Schroeder's resignation in January 1977.

Last Days of Monroe Assembly

La-Z-Boy's new products and increased retail outlets spurred sales during the late 1970s, but profits did not increase. In 1978, Ed Knabusch and the La-Z-Boy board of directors made the difficult decision to close the Monroe Assembly Plant permanently on January 1, 1979. The plant had been unprofitable for four or five years. Its labor costs had always been higher than other plants', and its three-story structure was not as efficient as the company's newer plants. About 300 workers lost their jobs.[63] Closing the plant was a difficult move for Knabusch, who had always supported the local community and through the years had often walked through the Monroe plant, meeting workers. Knabusch also had sentimental feelings for the plant because he had worked in the building during the 1920s, when it was owned by Weis Manufacturing.

La-Z-Boy retained some manufacturing operations at its Telegraph Road facility, and some workers transferred there. In addition to corporate offices, the Telegraph Road building then housed product development, woodworking, tool and die, and customer repair.

"That was one of the most difficult times for the company," Judith Carr recalled.

Our founders agonized over that decision, but it came at a time when the economic climate in Michigan and other parts of the Midwest was very poor. Those were the years the steel industries were going down, the automobile industries were going down. The tax base was very difficult for business in this part of the country. You could go

to another state and get a much better deal on doing business.

It was a combination of things. Labor relations were very strained at that time, and we were producing in a very antiquated building. It had narrow passageways, and it was hard to transport goods from one part of the plant to the other. And to build another facility just wouldn't have been good business at the time.[64]

After unsuccessful attempts to sell the outdated factory, La-Z-Boy gave the building to the city of Monroe, which converted it into senior citizen housing. It was the first project in Michigan in which an industrial facility was renovated for residential use.[65]

It was not the first time a city benefited from the company's philanthropy. "If you'll look at every

A worker cuts fabric at La-Z-Boy's eighth plant, in Tremonton, Utah. Built to serve the booming Western market, the 212,000-square-foot plant housed production and assembly operations.

area they put a plant in, the first thing they do is authorize a certain amount of money to go to some of the local charities or hospitals or something like that," said retired sales representative Bill Gallagher. "They are certainly and always have been outstanding corporate [citizens]."[66]

Acquiring Deluxe

In 1979, La-Z-Boy acquired its Canadian licensee, Deluxe Upholstering, located in Waterloo,

Ontario. In 1929, Deluxe had become La-Z-Boy's first foreign licensee, and the two companies had worked together successfully for 50 years. La-Z-Boy purchased the 125,000-square-foot Canadian facility from The Molson Companies. Deluxe became a wholly owned subsidiary named La-Z-Boy Canada. David W. Eby, president of Deluxe since 1968, was named president of La-Z-Boy Canada. The subsidiary had 110 employees and produced 160 chairs a day for sale in Canada. Its 1978 sales totaled $5.5 million.[67]

The Canadian plant was La-Z-Boy's seventh manufacturing facility. An eighth plant opened in 1979 in Tremonton, Utah. Built to serve the growing market in the West, it housed all production and assembly operations in 212,000 square feet. Charles Nocella, formerly vice president of La-Z-Boy Arkansas, served as vice president of the new plant, known as La-Z-Boy Utah.[68] Wally Swiderski, plant superintendent of the closed Monroe Assembly Plant, replaced Nocella as vice president of La-Z-Boy Arkansas.[69]

La-Z-Boy Midwest Vice President Verl Manor died suddenly in November 1979. The popular Manor was only 56 when he suffered a fatal heart attack. Manor had been a La-Z-Boy employee for 32 years. He had established the Neosho plant and led the operation since 1969. At the time of his death, Neosho was La-Z-Boy's largest plant.[70]

Recliner's Anniversary

As La-Z-Boy Chair Company celebrated the 50th anniversary of the reclining chair in 1979, it announced record sales of $146 million. But net income had declined for the second year in a row.

With the introduction of wall proximity models, reclining chairs had gained popularity. Manufacturers had modernized chair styles to boost sales in urban areas and move chairs from the recreation or family room into living rooms. The company had climbed to the top of the action furniture market (it made more than double the sales of its nearest challenger), but competitors were anxious to gain a bigger piece of the pie, and they sometimes beat La-Z-Boy to the market with contemporary styles and popular features.[71]

La-Z-Boy Midwest Vice President Verl Manor looks over the Neosho plant's wood burner. The energy-efficient unit recycled wood waste into heat. Manor died suddenly in 1979.

La-Z-Boy upgraded its Showcase Shoppes and provided the owners with in-store signage, sales training, and other merchandising assistance. This display was used in a photo shoot.

CHAPTER SIX

BRAND CONSCIOUS

1980 – 1989

Pat Norton's experience at Ethan Allen, in terms of what is needed to make a proprietary store system reach its potential, was invaluable to our development. His vision led to the creation of what is now our La-Z-Boy Furniture Galleries network, which is a key element of our business success.

—Kurt Darrow, President, La-Z-Boy Residential

LA-Z-BOY BELIEVED IT WAS IN A good position to compete in the 1980s. Only 20 percent of households had recliners, so sales potential was high.[1] La-Z-Boy's share of the motion chair industry had slipped somewhat, but the company still held the largest share of the market—a respectable 21 percent.[2] Strong brand identification was a valuable asset in the brand-conscious 1980s, and La-Z-Boy happened to be the furniture industry's most recognized brand.

Despite an uncertain economy, La-Z-Boy sales grew in 1980, reaching a record $158.2 million. La-Z-Boy reintroduced its close-to-the-wall recliner, the Reclina-Way®, in 1979. Wall-proximity chairs had been big sellers for many furniture makers, but sales of La-Z-Boy's previous model had been disappointing. The new Reclina-Way accounted for 30 percent of La-Z-Boy sales in 1980. The same mechanism was used in the Reclina-Way Sofette, introduced in 1980.[3] In 1981, La-Z-Boy introduced two other popular features. Swivel-Stop was a feature added to La-Z-Boy® swivel rockers that locked the chair in a fixed position when not in use. The mechanism served as a safety feature, keeping the chair stable while the user sat down or got up. It also kept the chair facing in the desired direction while unoccupied.[4]

The Swivel-Stop was the first innovation engineer Larry LaPointe worked on after he came to La-Z-Boy in 1980. The director of mechanical engineering and test laboratories recalled working with Knabusch and Shoemaker. "I always had a good feeling about those two guys," LaPointe said. "They made you feel right."[5]

La-Z-Boy's most unusual product was the Back Jack, a multipurpose leisure seat introduced in 1980. La-Z-Boy purchased all patent and trademark rights to the seat from Concept Engineering, of Lincoln, Nebraska. The Back Jack had a foam cushion, and its washable canvas duck cover stretched over a tubular frame. It could be used as a floor seat or, flipped over, as a backrest, with the cushion forming a head pillow. The seat could be customized with a screen-printed logo; it sold for between $20 and $25. It served a purpose similar to a beanbag chair's but was less expensive and more portable.

Back Jacks were made at La-Z-Boy's Siloam Springs, Arkansas, plant. In addition to La-Z-Boy's conventional distribution channels, Back Jacks were sold at home centers, sporting goods stores, and national chain stores, as well as in mail-order

---

"Jake Jr." was a 6-foot, 190-pound wooden model used to test La-Z-Boy® chairs. He was the creation of La-Z-Boy woodworker Clarence "Jake" Kohler.

Above and left: Back Jack leisure seating was introduced in 1980. La-Z-Boy's most unusual product, the patented portable seats and backrests sold for about $20.

catalogs.[6] La-Z-Boy hired two marketing executives to support the product's marketing and distribution, but ultimately Ed Knabusch didn't like the Back Jack, and it was discontinued after about two years.

In 1981, La-Z-Boy had 11,000 dealers, including 210 Showcase Shoppes. Dealers ranged in size from small stores in rural areas to the company's largest account, Montgomery Ward, with 400 stores. La-Z-Boy treated all of its dealers the same, Knabusch explained to *Retailing Home Furnishings:* "We still treat the smaller dealer the same as a big account. There is no favored treatment, no discount structure, for larger stores."[7]

But many small stores were going out of business during the economic downturn of the early 1980s, and La-Z-Boy recognized that it needed to revamp its dealer network. Traditional La-Z-Boy dealers, who accounted for a major percentage of net sales during 1981, continued to be suspicious of La-Z-Boy Showcase Shoppes. Showcase Shoppes had many advantages for La-Z-Boy. The use of the La-Z-Boy name in the name of dealers' stores enhanced consumers' awareness and perception of La-Z-Boy products. In addition, their

quicker turnover led to higher sales volumes. But La-Z-Boy still struggled with the Showcase concept and often had to placate its other dealers who felt that the Showcase Shoppes were unfairly competing with them.[8]

Norton Joins the Team

In 1981, La-Z-Boy hired Patrick Norton as senior vice president of sales and marketing. Much of his responsibility was managing La-Z-Boy's network of Showcase Shoppes. Norton, 58, was a well-known furniture industry executive who was serving as senior vice president and board member at Ethan Allen (a division of Interco), the country's largest furniture manufacturer. In his 19 years at Ethan Allen, he had worked at all levels of the company's sales and marketing departments and had helped develop the company's admired Gallery program. Ethan Allen had 300 independent showcase stores. Prior to his tenure at Ethan Allen, Norton, a World War II army air force veteran of 33 combat missions, had worked in the retail furniture field in his native St. Louis, Missouri, since he was 17.[9]

"I looked around the industry and realized that La-Z-Boy was in trouble," Norton recalled. "I offered my services because I felt that I knew how to fix what was wrong."[10]

Edward Knabusch was not quite ready intellectually to open the company up to an outsider. "The founders found it very hard to admit that there was anything wrong," Norton said.[11]

"Pat Norton was kind of a tough sell for the owners," said Rocque Lipford, an attorney who joined the board of directors in 1979. "David White was the catalyst behind bringing him in, and Charles [Knabusch] agreed with him. They felt the company needed this new blood."[12]

La-Z-Boy would not be the firm it is today without Norton, said John Quinn, a sales representative who came to the company in 1970.

It was around 1980 that we were beginning to have some pretty serious problems. We got very complacent, and our management lacked a lot of direction. Pat Norton was clever enough to research

Above: Patrick Norton (standing) worked with the sales and marketing team to improve La-Z-Boy Showcase Shoppes during the early 1980s.

Right and below: To achieve a uniform look, La-Z-Boy Showcase Shoppes were remodeled and upgraded during the 1980s from the style at right to the facade below.

Shortly after he was named La-Z-Boy senior vice president of sales and marketing in 1981, Pat Norton (center) attended his first stockholders meeting. He is shown here with Ray Cullum, vice president of sales (right), and Fritz Jackson, treasurer.

the industry and realize that La-Z-Boy had some tremendous potential but also was starting to have some problems.

This was probably the key decision in the history of La-Z-Boy. Had we not done it, chances are we would eventually have either been sold or merged.[13]

The industry watched with interest as Norton moved from Ethan Allen to La-Z-Boy. Norton told *Furniture/Today* that his first and highest priority at La-Z-Boy was "developing a really efficient distribution system. We want to service fully a two-pronged distribution system. We are committed to the Showcase Shoppes as we are committed to conventional furniture and department stores. But it's now our job to guarantee that both can function profitably."[14]

Norton was committed to a strategy he had successfully implemented at Ethan Allen, in which the company's products were marketed through galleries in furniture and department stores and in single-product-line stores. In both outlets, retailers displayed groupings of products from a single manufacturer. "Manufacturers are discovering that the impact of their principal effort is diluted when their products are scattered throughout retail showroom floors."[15]

Norton immediately began upgrading and revising La-Z-Boy's distribution, which was sparse in major East Coast, West Coast, and Southern metropolitan markets. La-Z-Boy had always been strong in the Midwest; its competitors envied its 40 percent share in some Midwestern states. But many of the company's dealers were poor performers, and Norton discontinued them.

"He wanted us to sell the *right* dealers instead of *a lot* of dealers," Quinn said.[16] By 1987 La-Z-Boy had pared its accounts by 40 percent, keeping 4,500 dealers.[17]

Quinn recalled a pivotal sales meeting soon after Norton's entry.

He said we had to become more professional . . . had to learn how to do advertising, presentation, and sales training—all the things that helped the dealer move the product. He believed in selling through, not just to, and he told us it would take a lot of work and a tremendous commitment. He also told us that day that there would probably be a number of people who wouldn't make it. As it turned out, he was right. But he was exceedingly patient throughout the process. Those who didn't make it weren't willing to pay the price, or they weren't willing to do things a different way.[18]

Upgrading the company's existing chain of Showcase Shoppes was another priority. Norton developed a unified exterior for the stores. Inside, he created a recommended architecture and floor plan that included 12 to 14 environmental settings in which coordinated groupings of La-Z-Boy® recliners, sleep sofas, and swivel rockers were displayed. This was a significant departure from the original Showcase Shoppes' practice of lining up recliners in rows.[19] The stores' average size increased about 10 percent a year.

La-Z-Boy planned for the average Shoppe to grow to 8,500 to 9,000 square feet.[20]

La-Z-Boy expanded its Showcase department to support the stores with advertising, sales training, site selection, product display, and merchandising. La-Z-Boy also helped owners select styles and fabrics suitable for their markets.[21]

John Case explained what Norton's entrance meant to the company.

At that time, the stores were not very disciplined or consistent at all. [Pat] came in with his experience at Ethan Allen, and the real disciplined store era began. He cleaned them up and created that consistency.[22]

A New Image

Upgrading the environment in which La-Z-Boy® chairs were displayed helped Norton achieve another of his goals: updating the recliner's image. Norton believed the recliner had become a commodity and that it deserved better. "What we really want to do is reposition the La-Z-Boy chair as the chair that a consumer feels she must have," he told *Furniture/Today.*[23]

Norton looked at the company's product line and saw changes were needed. Two weeks after his arrival, he lined up the 40-some chairs before the 10 top sales representatives.

"He had the chairs numbered by volume [sold] and the year they were introduced," Quinn recalled. "Turned out that probably 15 percent of our line was doing maybe 90 percent of our volume, which was way out of balance."[24]

La-Z-Boy sleep sofas were displayed in Showcase Shoppes. They were promoted for their style and comfort.

In fact, the five best-selling chairs were all at least 10 years old.

"We had also lost sight of comfort," Quinn added. "He made us sit in those 45 chairs for a day. Then we virtually redid the line."[25]

New styles and products helped stimulate sales. Between 1981 and 1983, 70 percent of La-Z-Boy's products were new. Styles and fabrics in all product categories complemented each other and represented a broad range of prices. In 1983, for the first time in its history, La-Z-Boy introduced stationary loveseats and sofas.[26] The Signature II® sleep sofa was introduced in 1984 with a half-million-dollar advertising campaign. Signature II replaced La-Z-Boy's previous line of sleep sofas.

Signature II emphasized fashion, and its ads delivered the message that you don't have to sacrifice style when you buy a sleep sofa.

In 1984, La-Z-Boy introduced a line of motion furniture called Motion-Modulars®. Modular sofas emerged in the 1970s and by the mid-1980s had become the fastest-growing segment of the upholstered furniture industry. La-Z-Boy's motion products included love seats, sofas, chairs, and corner groups that could be mixed and matched to fit any design need. The seating units could be ordered as recliners, sofa beds, or stationary furniture.[27] Many of the Motion-Modulars were fashioned in the popular Eurostyle, which featured plump saddlebag arms, double-pillowed seat backs, and shirred front rails.

As Norton predicted, new styles and a new environment in which to sell them helped improve the perception of the reclining chair. Price points rose from around $359 to $400 or $420. Multiple product sales increased.[28] In 1985, La-Z-Boy's sales totaled $282.7 million.[29] By 1986, its share of the motion chair market had increased to 25 percent. Sales rose not only in Showcase Shoppes but also in the motion chair industry as a whole.[30]

La-Z-Boy's new styles and products were supported with extensive national advertising. In 1982, a new pair of spokespersons began representing La-Z-Boy Chair Company. Actor and former Detroit Lions player Alex Karras and his wife, actor Susan Clark, began appearing in La-Z-Boy advertising. Karras and Clark were chosen because research revealed that husbands and wives decide jointly to purchase a recliner, but the woman makes the final decision. Karras and Clark were thought to have universal appeal to both genders. Shortly after they first appeared in La-Z-Boy ads, the couple began

The La-Z-Boy Spring Sale.
Feet Up, Prices Down

In celebration of spring, your authorized La-Z-Boy dealer has a great new selection of genuine La-Z-Boy recliners on hand. All ready for you to stretch out in, look over and size up. And all marked with low sale prices that will sweep you right off your feet.

Like spring, however, both the recliners and the sale will be gone before you know it. So see your La-Z-Boy dealer right away. While his stock is up and his prices are down.

La-Z-Boy

See these and other great La-Z-Boy chairs on sale now at these participating dealers:

Inverness   Brentwood   Avenger

Right: Charles Knabusch was named chairman of the board of La-Z-Boy Chair Company in 1985.

Below: La-Z-Boy co-founder Edward Knabusch relinquished his position as chairman of the board in 1985. He died in 1988.

Opposite: Former Detroit Lions player Alex Karras was La-Z-Boy's spokesperson from 1982 to 1988. He often appeared with his wife, actor Susan Clark.

starring in a popular weekly prime-time comedy, *Webster.* Their appearance in the top-20 show enhanced their value as spokespersons.[31]

During the 1980s, the company boosted its ad budget and scheduled four two-week periods of high-impact advertising annually. In 1983, La-Z-Boy placed TV spots on prime-time shows for the first time. Magazine advertising increased to include women's and home magazines as well as *People, TV Guide, Reader's Digest, Parade,* and *New York Times Magazine.* La-Z-Boy's television commercials touted the company's recliners, but beginning in 1985, La-Z-Boy began diversifying its magazine ads to support sleep sofas, stationary sofas, Motion-Modulars, and swivel rockers as well.[32] This strategy put less emphasis on brand-name awareness, which stood at an enviable 86 percent in 1985, and began to spread the message that La-Z-Boy made more than just recliners.[33] When dealers tied in with the ads, consumers responded with increasing sales.

End of an Era

In 1982, Herman Gertz, who had worked for La-Z-Boy Chair Company and Floral City Furniture since 1931, retired from his position as director and secretary of the company. Gertz had been president of Floral City Furniture and had been on the La-Z-Boy board since its founding in 1941.

Following his retirement from the corporation, Gertz continued his job as administrator of the La-Z-Boy Chair Foundation, a charitable organization associated with the company.[34]

The company passed another milestone when Ed Knabusch relinquished his position as chairman of the board in 1985, the year he turned 85 himself. He continued to hold a seat on the board and serve as a company advisor. Charles Knabusch, 45, was named chairman of the board.[35]

Eddie Shoemaker, a healthy 78, was named vice chairman of the board. He lived part-time in Arizona but maintained an office at La-Z-Boy headquarters.

Other senior executives were closing in on retirement. Three long-time employees would retire in 1989. Lorne Stevens, vice president of manufacturing, ended 40 years of service to the company. Dewey Turner, vice president and general manager of the Newton, Mississippi, manufacturing facility, retired after 42 years. And Ronald Waterfield, vice president of fabric, retired after 25 years with La-Z-Boy.[36]

The departures threatened to shake the company's sense of tradition. Charles Knabusch recognized the need to perpetuate La-Z-Boy's history, and in 1985, he authorized the establishment of a La-Z-Boy Museum and Archives in the Monroe headquarters. The museum told the story of the company's founding and displayed photos, memorable chairs, manufacturing equipment, and awards. The archives preserved historic photographs, publications, documents, and memorabilia. Judith Carr was named museum director and archivist.

Technology and Testing

During the 1980s, manufacturing firms embraced new technology that sped up product

IF THESE WALLS COULD TALK

YOU CAN'T HELP BUT FEEL CONNECTED to history when you stand in the La-Z-Boy Museum, surrounded by chairs, machinery, and tools from the company's early years. Among them are the drafting table used by Edwin Shoemaker and novelty furniture that Edward Knabusch made in his garage workshop. But beyond the artifacts, you notice the building itself, especially the brick walls. Uneven mortar is visible between the bricks, laid in 1927, when Knabusch and Shoemaker, broke and full of dreams, built their company's first factory in the middle of a cornfield. This is where the two made the wood-slat chair and, later, the first upholstered reclining chair, which they named the La-Z-Boy®. This is where Otto Uecker and Herman Gertz helped the founders guide the young enterprise; where Dewey Turner, Lorne Stevens, and Mac McLeod learned lessons about furniture manufacturing they would take to plants across the country; where Knabusch's beloved dog Toodles happily wandered the shop floor.

The building was transformed into a retail furniture showroom in 1931 and returned to manufacturing in 1941. Soon after, it was leased to Woodall Industries for war work. After the war, the original brick building became a storage facility for the Floral City Furniture store, and La-Z-Boy Chair Company moved to a new building next door. When Floral City Furniture closed in 1974, the store and the La-Z-Boy office building were connected to create a larger headquarters for the growing La-Z-Boy Chair Company. Through countless renovations and additions, the three-story brick structure in the northeast corner of the building remained. With no heat or air conditioning, the drafty appendage that rises one story above the rest of the building served only as a storage facility and a sentimental reminder of the past—until 1984, when Charles Knabusch had an idea.

Knabusch's father and Edwin Shoemaker were aging, and they held memories that would be lost forever if not preserved. Knabusch envisioned a museum that would chronicle the history of this American success story. He and Vice President of Administration Richard Micka put out a call for volunteers to develop a company museum and archives that would be housed on the second floor of the original brick building. They asked employees to contribute old products, photographs, and other memorabilia to the collection. Donations trickled in from employees as well as retirees, Monroe residents, sales reps, and La-Z-Boy plants.

Judith Carr, a buyer in the company's purchasing department and a local history buff, volunteered to help. She spent lunch hours and work breaks cataloging and organizing the donations in the drafty brick building. She accumulated furniture, tools, machinery, photographs, old advertisements, fabric sample books, dealer sales aids, and documents. The Shoemaker and Knabusch families contributed items related to the founders' childhoods, including some of the furniture the boys made before forming their partnership.

La-Z-Boy's maintenance staff cleaned up the building's second floor and outfitted it for displays. Carr and Fabric Department employee Becky Brasher organized the exhibits in time for a grand opening during the 1985 stockholders

meeting. The museum was a resounding success for the company and the community.

Carr continued to organize the collection as additional artifacts came in. Shoemaker spent many hours reviewing documents and identifying items donated to the museum. By 1988, the displays had outgrown the building's second floor, and the museum expanded to the first floor, where workstations were set up to show how the early La-Z-Boy chairs were made by hand. During the early 1990s, the museum was renovated and air-conditioned.

When Carr announced her retirement in 1995, Knabusch asked her to work part-time as museum director. Since then, the museum has been open two days a week for tours. Visitors include furniture industry people, dealers, historians, La-Z-Boy retirees and employees, senior citizens groups, and schoolchildren. The museum has also gained the attention of the media and has been featured on *The Today Show, CBS Sunday Morning, History's Lost & Found, CNN News, Modern Marvels,* and National Public Radio's *Morning Edition.* It has also been written up in the *Chicago Sun Times, Detroit Free Press, New York Times, Wall Street Journal,* and *USA Today.*

Among the items on display are the original wood-slat chair; 40 recliners, dating from the 1930s to the 1970s; a Gossiper telephone stand; the crystal radio Shoemaker was working on when he first visited his cousin's workshop; a World War II tank seat; cutaway chairs and miniature chair models used in displays; and machinery from the original factory.

But the greatest artifact of all is the structure itself. The company and the rest of the building have expanded around it, and mega-retailers like Wal-Mart, Staples, and McDonald's now line once rural Telegraph Road. But the 1927 structure remains. It houses the company's historical artifacts and reminds employees and the community of the foundation on which La-Z-Boy Incorporated was built—brick by brick.[1]

Above: Judith Carr, museum director, and Richard Micka, vice president of administration, prepare for the opening of the La-Z-Boy Museum in 1985. The museum contains photos and artifacts that tell the company's history.

Opposite: The original Floral City Furniture building, built by the founders, still stands today and houses the museum. The cousins dug the basement and sewers, mixed the cement, laid the foundation, and built the walls themselves in 1927.

New technology, installed under the direction of Vice President of Engineering Marvin J. Baumann, helped streamline manufacturing.

development and streamlined manufacturing. In 1981, under the direction of Marvin J. Baumann, vice president of engineering, La-Z-Boy began using an Electric Discharge Machine, a computer-controlled metal-cutting device, to produce dies. The machine read engineers' layouts and translated them into actual dies quickly and accurately.[37] When it was paired with a computer-aided design (CAD) system, La-Z-Boy was able to move from engineering concepts to finished product faster than ever before. The CAD system allowed engineers to view a product blueprint and a three-dimensional perspective of the product or part on computer screens at the same time. When the size or shape of a part was altered, engineers could immediately see how the change affected the product's finished appearance or operation and could generate a new blueprint immediately.[38]

The company also acquired a Camsco Pattern Machine. It made patterns for wood, fabric, or metal directly from engineers' drawings. The machine helped La-Z-Boy use materials more efficiently and reduce waste. It also aided quality control by improving parts standardization.[39] Both of these machines reduced the time needed to produce dies and parts from several weeks to a few hours.

Larry LaPointe recalled the boom in technology. "Even with the good tools we have here, I still sometimes go back to those old methods because they really are good methods to use," he said. "I'm probably the only one left in corporate headquarters who still has a drawing board."[40]

LaPointe was put to work on a testing laboratory that opened in 1985 at the Monroe Research and Development facility.[41] The lab housed equipment used to test frames, mechanism, springs,

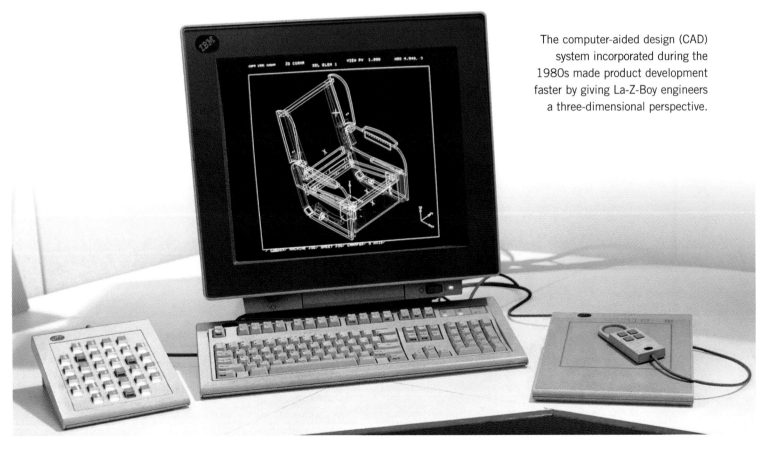

The computer-aided design (CAD) system incorporated during the 1980s made product development faster by giving La-Z-Boy engineers a three-dimensional perspective.

Carved from rock maple, "Jake" was used to test support and durability of residential and contract chairs. The new science of ergonomics required the consideration of human factors in furniture design.

padding, fabrics, glues, and reinforcements and simulated wear likely to be encountered in homes or businesses, LaPointe said.

Up until that point they just used a lot of good common sense, but they really didn't have a procedure for every product to go through, and I was asked to come up with a formal testing program. Now we start people out in the test plant because it's a good way to learn about the product—you see firsthand what's going to work and what's not. It's like a chain, and a product is only as good as its weakest link. So what we do in the lab is find those weak links.[42]

La-Z-Boy's was the first lab to be accredited to 17025, formerly the International Standards Organization (ISO) 25. The certification recognizes companies that meet and maintain accepted industry guidelines. Other manufacturers have visited the lab before designing their own, LaPointe said.

The lab was the home of "Jake Jr.," a 6-foot, 190-pound wooden model of a man used in many testing procedures. Jake was the creation of Clarence "Jake" Kohler, a La-Z-Boy woodworker, who carved it out of rock maple. The model was used to test residential and contract chairs for support and durability. The new science of ergonomics required furniture makers to consider human factors in furniture design. Since American workers were spending more time at computer workstations, seating manufacturers had to develop seating that was not only attractive but functional and healthy as well. Jake was used to test chairs' comfort and lower body, lumbar, and upper body support.[43]

But Jake was not the only body testing chairs, Carr said.

One year they hired a young student to be a chair tester, and he would actually study while he was rocking. He'd flip the footrest open and put it down and flip it open and put it down and rock and read. I don't know how he'd do it. I'd get dizzy. That hit the papers nationwide—a guy making money sitting in a chair. It was a great story.[44]

La-Z-Boy's use of technology also extended to the production process. An automatic lumber stacker uniformly stacked wood for drying. Overhead conveyors moved components throughout the plants. Conveyors in the sewing department moved precut fabric to work stations where operators guided it through semiautomatic sewing machines. The automation helped plants use space more efficiently and speed up production.[45]

The addition of automated equipment at all plants was part of a large expansion and modernization program during the second half of the decade. Several plants were enlarged beginning in 1985.

La-Z-Boy purchased and enlarged a second plant in Waterloo, Ontario. The 200,000-square-foot plant tripled the company's manufacturing space in Canada. A 120,000-square-foot addition to the Tremonton, Utah, plant boosted La-Z-Boy's West Coast production. Increased sales of the company's Signature II® sleep sofas necessitated a 74,000-square-foot expansion of the Siloam Springs,

Arkansas, plant.[46] The Florence, South Carolina, Dayton, Tennessee, and Newton, Mississippi, plants also expanded.

Contract Furniture Division

Growth in La-Z-Boy's contract sales led to the acquisition of a casegoods plant in Leland, Mississippi. In 1983, La-Z-Boy contracted with an office casegoods manufacturer to produce a line of desks, credenzas, conference tables, and cabinets. Two years later, La-Z-Boy bought a factory and began producing the furnishings itself. The plant was modernized immediately after La-Z-Boy acquired it.

Lorne Stevens, vice president of manufacturing, explained why La-Z-Boy began making office casegoods: "We had been making contract seating for a good number of years. In marketing our product, we felt it would be best to have a package program that would address the total industry."[47]

Using its engineering expertise, La-Z-Boy upgraded the quality of the casegoods products, adding central locking systems, improved slide mechanisms on drawers, and more durable finishes.[48]

The Contract Division became a separate sales and marketing entity in 1984.[49] Although office furniture was the largest segment of the contract market, La-Z-Boy continued to manufacture products for health care and hospitality. Its reclining chairs and Signature II® sleep sofas were selling well to hotels and motels.[50] La-Z-Boy acquired RoseJohnson Inc. in 1986 to provide a more complete selection of office furnishings to customers.

When La-Z-Boy first entered the contract market, it sold its furniture through office furniture retailers. Since 65 percent of office furniture was purchased by architects, interior designers, and contract dealers, who outfitted whole floors or

La-Z-Boy President Charles Knabusch and Monroe Office Manager Don Blohm look over a display of La-Z-Boy Contract products. In 1983, La-Z-Boy began producing office casegoods such as desks, conference tables, and credenzas.

ROSEJOHNSON

IN 1986, LA-Z-BOY EXPANDED ITS OFFICE furnishings line with the acquisition of RoseJohnson Inc., in Grand Rapids, Michigan. RoseJohnson had an established presence in the market and specialized in wall panels and components for open office layouts. It also supplied guest room furniture for hotels and motels.[1] At the time of the acquisition, RoseJohnson's annual sales totaled approximately $20 million.[2]

RoseJohnson was formed when Rose Manufacturing Company, a specialist in acoustical screens and partitions, merged with Johnson Furniture Company, a wood furniture maker, in May 1983. Johnson Furniture Company had been founded in 1903. It produced fine residential furniture exclusively until 1963, when it expanded to include contract cabinet lines. Between 1968 and 1976, Johnson was owned by Holiday Inn. In 1976, James G. VanOosten and Albert Smith purchased the company and continued to supply Holiday Inn. In 1981, the company began producing its first proprietary contract line of hotel and motel furniture.[3]

Rose Manufacturing Company began in 1917 as Rose Carving and produced legs for local furniture manufacturers. The company was incorporated in 1935 and began producing frames for upholstered sofas, chairs, and footstools. It began making office chair frames during the 1950s, and in 1969 it produced its first acoustical screens for Holiday Inn on a contract basis.[4]

La-Z-Boy operated RoseJohnson as a wholly owned subsidiary. Robert Lindblom was chairman of the RoseJohnson board, and James VanOosten was president.[5]

RoseJohnson's signature product line, Progressions+ office systems, received the 1986 ROSCO Commendation Award for product design from the Resources Counsel Inc.[6] La-Z-Boy's Contract Division designed office chairs to coordinate with the RoseJohnson products. During this time, with workers' jobs requiring more and more time seated at computers, ergonomic seating became increasingly important. In 1984, La-Z-Boy introduced the Adagio Collection of office seating scientifically engineered for computer workstations.[7]

La-Z-Boy's Adagio line of office chairs was ergonomically designed for comfort and back support.

---

entire buildings, La-Z-Boy also established relationships with these customers, participated in more trade shows, and opened and remodeled showrooms in major professional market centers.[51]

On Acquisitions

While the acquisitions in La-Z-Boy's Contract Division were positioning the company as a complete supplier of office furnishings, the same strategy was at work in La-Z-Boy's Residential Division. La-Z-Boy recognized that to become a complete supplier of home furnishings, it had to produce more than chairs and sofas. In the mid- to late 1980s, La-Z-Boy acquired furniture companies that produced products and styles new to La-Z-Boy. These included Burris Industries, Hammary Furniture, and Kincaid Furniture Company.

All of La-Z-Boy's acquisitions were operated as wholly owned subsidiaries of La-Z-Boy Chair Company. La-Z-Boy recognized that the companies had solid reputations in the furniture industry, with established identities, products, and customer bases. Some operations were integrated with La-Z-Boy's to improve efficiency. These included research, computer-assisted product design, tooling and factory engineering, centralized purchasing, transportation, and administrative support.[52]

Fritz Jackson spoke of the company's acquisition strategy.

We had a couple of rules: We never wanted to acquire anybody who didn't want to be acquired by us, and we always tried to acquire those who had the same philosophy as to how to treat people and how to grow. You've got to grow. If you don't grow, you die.[53]

Devil in the Details

La-Z-Boy designers and engineers added and improved features on La-Z-Boy® chairs, sofas, and sleepers during the latter half of the 1980s. In 1986, La-Z-Boy introduced its Uni-Flex Comfort System on Signature II® sleep sofas. The new mechanism made opening the sofa easier and eliminated snagged sheets. The company also added 3 inches to the length of the bed's fold-out platform and mattress without increasing the depth of the sofa's seat. Signature II beds measured 74 inches as a result.[54]

Two chairs with electric controls came out in 1986 and 1987. La-Z-Boy introduced its Lectra-Lounger power recliner in 1986. It was operated by fingertip switches instead of a hand lever, and individual switches operated the seat back and footrest, allowing for infinite positions. La-Z-Boy had introduced a power recliner in 1970, but there had been little consumer interest. The company believed that a growing market of upwardly mobile baby boomers and older consumers would purchase the new models.[55]

In 1987, La-Z-Boy introduced a power lift chair with reclining capability. The Lectra-Lift chair featured electronic controls that lifted and lowered the seat to help people stand and sit.[56] LaPointe boasted about this product.

BURRIS INDUSTRIES

IN JULY 1985, LA-Z-BOY ACQUIRED BURRIS Industries, a Lincolnton, North Carolina, manufacturer of motion chairs and upholstered furniture. Burris was founded in 1936 as a cedar-chest maker. It later added low-priced upholstered furniture, and in 1962, it began making reclining chairs, its strongest seller. This good fortune led to the manufacture of coordinated family room groupings of upholstered sofas, love seats, stationary chairs, and recliners.

During the mid-1960s, Burris became a pioneer in the use of molded polyurethane for chair and sofa frames.[1] During the year before La-Z-Boy acquired the company, Burris's sales totaled approximately $10.6 million. After acquiring Burris, La-Z-Boy streamlined the subsidiary's product lines so that its efforts concentrated on the high end of the motion chair market.[2] Burris sold its products in finer department stores and furniture stores.[3]

Donald Twitty, former corporate manager of industrial engineering at La-Z-Boy, was named vice president of Burris Industries Inc. Marty Goodwin, a former Burris sales representative, was appointed vice president of sales.[4]

La-Z-Boy acquired Burris Industries in 1985. Burris is the maker of high-end upholstered motion chairs.

HAMMARY FURNITURE

HAMMARY FURNITURE JOINED THE La-Z-Boy family in 1986. Hammary produced quality living room furniture, including tables, entertainment centers, brass-and-glass tables and étagères, and upholstered furniture. Hammary was noted for its elegant touches, such as carved panels, inlaid and burled surfaces, and brass accents, and was sold in department and furniture stores. It also had a very successful in-store gallery program.[1]

Hammary had been founded in 1943 in Lenoir, North Carolina, by Hamilton and Mary Bruce. It made canvas-covered lawn chairs until 1947, when it began producing occasional tables. Upholstery was added in 1960, and the company became known as "The Living Room Source." In 1968, U.S. Industries acquired Hammary, and the company expanded rapidly. By 1982, it had six plants. After being acquired by Hanson Industries in 1984, it was consolidated into three plants, which La-Z-Boy acquired.[2]

Hammary continued making its upholstered furniture, tables, and cabinets and began producing a line of occasional tables called La-Z-Boy CompaTables® for the La-Z-Boy Residential Division. CompaTables complemented La-Z-Boy® upholstered furniture and were displayed and sold in La-Z-Boy Showcase Shoppes.[3]

Hammary's La-Z-Boy CompaTables were displayed in Showcase Shoppes with La-Z-Boy chairs, sofas, and sleep sofas.

HAMMARY®

I think we have the best lift chair out there as far as comfort and longevity. It required an extensive amount of engineering to really get it right so that it would hold up for our customers. Recliner chairs aren't a necessity for people. They're more of a luxury for people, whereas a lift chair is a necessity for people who need it. People who use lift chairs quite often live in [them]. So we take a lot of pride in that product.[57]

In 1988, La-Z-Boy replaced the mechanism in the Reclina-Way® wall recliner, making it even easier to operate. In 1989, the Twincliner sofa was introduced. The sofa's end units featured pop-up footrests.[58]

Getting into Galleries

La-Z-Boy continued to refine its Showcase Shoppes. Since redefining the concept in the early 1980s, La-Z-Boy had enlarged and restyled the stores and opened new Shoppes. All Showcase Shoppes met strict La-Z-Boy standards for size, location, layout, signage, interior displays, sales training, and customer service. By 1989, approximately 300 Showcase Shoppes were selling La-

KINCAID FURNITURE COMPANY

ITS FINAL ACQUISITION OF THE 1980S brought La-Z-Boy into new areas of the home. Kincaid Furniture Company, of Hudson, North Carolina, produced solid wood dining room and bedroom furniture in a wide range of styles. The company had been founded by J. Wade Kincaid in 1946. Kincaid originally made cedar chests and wardrobes, and over the years its product line expanded to include bedroom and dining room furniture for middle- and upper-middle-income families. Wade Kincaid was chairman of the board of Kincaid, and his son, Steve, was president.[1]

Steve Kincaid explained the company's early specialty. "Back in the '40s up [in] the Northeast and Mid-Atlantic states, the property tax was based upon the number of rooms you had in your home. A walk-in closet was a room. [Our] initial product was a cedar wardrobe and cedar chest. A lot of people would buy these stand-alone wardrobes for their clothing to eliminate extra rooms and save substantially on taxes in the '50s."[2]

Wade Kincaid, left, founded Kincaid Furniture Company in 1946. His son, Steve, serves as president.

Kincaid said La-Z-Boy was the company's "white knight" in a hostile takeover attempt by Ladd and Nortek. "The one thing that attracted us to La-Z-Boy as a possible parent company was the integrity they have and the way they are viewed by their customers, their vendors, and employees," Steve Kincaid said. "When La-Z-Boy acquired Kincaid, it was a big step for us. But it was also a big step for La-Z-Boy because they really got into furnishing the whole home."[3]

Z-Boy® upholstered furniture and CompaTables® by Hammary.[59] To complete the vignettes in Showcase Shoppes, La-Z-Boy contracted with a lamp supplier in 1987 to produce lamps that complemented the room settings. The lamp line was known as La-Z-Boy CorreLites.[60]

A description of La-Z-Boy Showcase Shoppes appeared in the 1987 La-Z-Boy annual report:

The concept behind La-Z-Boy Showcase Shoppes is to display La-Z-Boy® furniture in professionally arranged, well-accessorized room vignettes. In this way, shoppers can see how their selections can complement a room at home, how new moods can be created by coordinating colors and fabrics, and how modular, motion, or sleeper units can introduce extra comfort and functionality. Customers are assisted by salespeople whose experience in home

CorreLite lamps were produced for La-Z-Boy to complement room displays in La-Z-Boy Showcase Shoppes.

decorating can be genuinely helpful in making decisions. Service departments are equipped to ensure continuing after-the-sale customer satisfaction.[61]

"We wanted the stores to have the aura of a national chain even though the stores are independently owned," added Kurt Darrow, who started as an assistant national accounts manager in 1979.

We have really attempted to broaden our appeal to the consumer and be a full upholstery resource without giving up our strength in chairs. When you think of a recliner, the first thing you think of is La-Z-Boy. We like that recognition, and we don't want to lose that.[62]

La-Z-Boy extended the display concept to include independent furniture stores in medium-size markets. Many of these stores opened La-Z-Boy Galleries, floor space dedicated to vignettes of La-Z-Boy furniture.

La-Z-Boy In-Store Galleries accommodated eight or more room vignettes. Galleries averaged 3,800

THE BELOVED MR. K.

EDWARD KNABUSCH BARRELED through adversity without blinking an eye. What he lacked in education, the tenacious farm boy with an eighth grade education made up in creativity and optimism. During his early years in business, he constantly came up with ideas to market the La-Z-Boy® chair. Board member Herman Gertz recalled Knabusch carrying paper and a short pencil with him at all times. He jotted down ideas as they came to him, day or night.[1]

In 1980, Knabusch gave the Weis building to the city of Monroe for $1.

Co-founder Edwin Shoemaker recalled that board member Oliver Golden tried to make Knabusch more fiscally accountable. During the Depression, when the company was just getting on its feet, Golden wanted to know how much money Floral City made every day. Knabusch couldn't be bothered with daily reports. He was too busy bartering furniture and appliances for produce, chickens, or a cow—surely earning loyal customers for life. "[Golden] always criticized Ed quite a bit because Ed was too optimistic for him," Shoemaker said.[2]

"Mr. Knabusch just didn't believe in the concept of failure," La-Z-Boy Museum Director Judith Carr said. "It never occurred to him. He figured if you worked hard and you kept plugging, you were going to be OK, and it worked. It really worked. He always had a way to keep things going."[3]

Knabusch represented Floral City Furniture, and later La-Z-Boy Chair Company, to bankers, suppliers, and dealers. He spoke for the company in the furniture industry and in the general press. He marketed the La-Z-Boy chair around the world, establishing dealers across the United States and licensees in Australia, South Africa, Mexico, and Europe.

But no matter how far he traveled or how successful he became, Knabusch never forgot his Midwestern values and Christian ethics. He loved people and was as comfortable with business and community leaders as he was with

workers in La-Z-Boy plants. His daughter, Betty Lou White, recalled that for many years, the family lived next door to La-Z-Boy headquarters. When he walked to work in the morning, he'd go out the back door and walk into the machine shop to say hello to the employees and pass out apples he picked from the orchard next to the shop.[4]

Knabusch never gave up his walks through the plants and offices. He loved to chat with employees, who affectionately called him "Mr. K."

Knabusch also enjoyed gardening and wildlife. One of his favorite pastimes was walking in the woods. He supported conservation efforts and transformed 560 acres of land he owned in northern Michigan into a game preserve.[5]

Knabusch contributed time and money to many religious and civic causes. He was president of the former Monroe Lutheran Hospital Association for 16 years and director of the Monroe Lutheran Home for 18 years. He served as president of Grace Lutheran Church and helped supervise the church's construction. He also donated to the Monroe YMCA, the Monroe Historical Society, the Joslin Diabetes Foundation, Monroe churches, and many other organizations.

He received countless civic and industry awards, including the Monroe County Bar Association's Liberty Bell Award, the First Realtor Award, the Monroe Exchange Club's Certificate of Appreciation, the Sertoma Service Award, and induction into the American Furniture Hall of Fame.[6]

Knabusch's values, which were shared by co-founder Edwin Shoemaker, still echo in the halls and the boardroom of La-Z-Boy Incorporated. The company continues to give generously to the community and maintain the ethical business standards established by its founders.

Knabusch was survived by his wife of 60 years, Henrietta; his son, Charles; his daughter, Betty Lou White; seven grandchildren; and nieces and nephews.

Knabusch proudly shows off his first LAZBOY vanity license plate in 1974.

square feet, but some dealers allocated as much as 6,500 square feet. In 1987, about 37 La-Z-Boy Galleries were in operation. By 1989, there were 94. Some furniture stores that participated in the Gallery program reported sales gains of up to 40 percent.[63]

La-Z-Boy supported its dealers with local and national advertising, promotional tools, and a comprehensive sales training program called "Retail Sales Power." The furniture industry regarded the program as the standard for retail sales training.[64]

The La-Z-Boy name was responsible for much of the success. Other furniture manufacturers had attempted to put up stores with their name on the door with little success, John Case said. "A lot of them failed because they haven't invested in [their] brand—it's not a recognized name by the consumer. That's the real key."[65]

A Death in the La-Z-Boy Family

In 1988, La-Z-Boy lost one of its founders when Edward Knabusch died at the age of 88. Knabusch had led La-Z-Boy for 61 years, transforming the company from a two-man operation into the country's largest manufacturer of upholstered furniture. But Knabusch was not only a giant of the furniture industry; he was also a noted humanitarian, conservationist, and benefactor.

Many former and current employees remembered "Mr. K." as a man who walked through the La-Z-Boy plant talking to workers and passing out apples and other produce from his home garden. But hand-in-hand with his genuine country charm went a self-taught business acumen that made La-Z-Boy a household name.

Shortly after his death, Knabusch became one of the first industry pioneers inducted into the American Furniture Hall of Fame. Knabusch was recognized with this and other industry and civic awards not only for his entrepreneurial spirit but also for La-Z-Boy's reputation in the industry and the business world at large. La-Z-Boy reflected the Midwestern values and Christian ethics of its founders. It was known as an ethical corporation that gave back to the communities in which it did business. Knabusch and Shoemaker both personally donated time and money to civic causes and authorized La-Z-Boy to make corporate contributions in the cities that were home to its plants.[66]

MISS AMERICA'S THRONE

SINCE HER CHILDHOOD, THE SIGN greeted everyone who entered her hometown: "Welcome to Monroe, the home of General George Custer, La-Z-Boy® chairs, and Monroe shock absorbers."

"It was just a wonderful thing to have the La-Z-Boy Chair Company here in my own hometown," said Kaye Lani Wilson, who was crowned Miss America in 1988. "My Dad was a staunch supporter of anything local, so we had La-Z-Boy chairs in every room."

Her connection to the furniture giant would grow deeper as she got older. She began competing in pageants locally in 1981 to pay for nursing school. She graduated in 1985.

"The pageants pushed me out into the public eye, and so I began working closely with a lot of nonprofit groups, helping people raise funds. And every single fundraiser I have been involved with, La-Z-Boy Chair Company was on the top of the list donating a chair or money. They have been so supportive. I don't know what this community would do without La-Z-Boy."

Wilson's dream of opening a hospice in Monroe began in 1982. As always, La-Z-Boy was there to lend support. "I questioned my ability when people looked at me and said, 'There is no way you can do this.'"

But a talk with Edward Knabusch gave her hope. "He said, 'You can do this.' If anyone would be able to tell me it can happen, that a dream can grow, it would be him. Just to know that La-Z-Boy Chair Company supported me and people like Mr. Knabusch supported my work really meant a great deal and really kept me focused."

The company provided more than $10,000 seed money and furniture for the office. The hospice opened in the fall of 1988. "It takes some communities 10 years to get funding approval and certification. It's a very long process," Wilson said. "With their help, it took 45 days!"

The company's consistent support for charitable causes probably stems from the founders' original goal, Wilson added. "I think it is kind of ironic because they were trying to provide comfort in people's homes. And they have managed to continue that thought and that mission by doing even more. It's not just the company, but La-Z-Boy is made up of some great individuals who know the importance of supporting their community."[1]

Kaye Lani Wilson, Miss America 1988, has worked closely with La-Z-Boy in her charitable efforts.

The company continued to demonstrate its commitment to the community and the environment after Knabusch's death. In July 1989, Charles Knabusch announced that La-Z-Boy would no longer use furniture foam containing chlorofluorocarbons (CFCs), a chemical blamed for the erosion of the earth's ozone layer.

CFCs were widely used as blowing agents to form the bubbles in polyurethane foams. When they escaped into the upper atmosphere, however, CFCs were believed to damage the ozone layer that filters the sun's rays. La-Z-Boy used 80 million to 90 million board feet of foam annually. (A board foot is equal to a 12-inch-square piece of foam 1 inch thick.) La-Z-Boy's decision to discontinue the use of CFCs was purely voluntary, and the company urged other furniture manufacturers and suppliers to follow its lead.[67]

These business decisions did not go unnoticed. In 1989, La-Z-Boy was recognized in a *Lear's* article about social investing—investing in companies that have a record of charitable contributions, protect the environment, and make socially responsible decisions. In the article, The Calvert Group, a

Bethesda, Maryland, investment advisor, listed La-Z-Boy as a good corporate citizen and recommended its stock.[68] In 1991 and 1992, *Fortune* magazine would rank La-Z-Boy first among residential furniture manufacturers and in the top 40 percent of 306 companies determined to be "America's Most Admired Corporations." The ranking was based on a poll of more than 8,000 executives, directors, and financial analysts who evaluated companies' quality of management, products, and services; human resources policies; environmental responsibility; and wise use of corporate assets.[69]

A Position of Comfort

Between 1980 and 1989, La-Z-Boy sales had grown from $158 million to $553 million. La-Z-Boy and its five subsidiaries had 8,000 employees. La-Z-Boy stock was listed on the New York Stock Exchange in 1987 and on the Pacific Stock Exchange in 1989 with the symbol LZB.[70]

As La-Z-Boy entered the 1990s, it was positioning itself to sell a broad range of home and contract furnishings. Its product line and distribution system had advanced far beyond what they had been in 1980, and La-Z-Boy continued to refine its products and its dealer network. In 1989, La-Z-Boy unveiled a plan for a new generation of furniture stores called La-Z-Boy Furniture Galleries.

Store owner Ed "Big Ed" Breunig Jr. recalled the switch to galleries. "We all agreed to change the name of the stores from Showcase Shoppes to Furniture Galleries," he said. "Part of the reason was the word 'shop' connotes something small. We all spent a lot of money to change all our signing and redo our stores to bring them up to speed."[71]

The money was well spent, and La-Z-Boy always supported the dealers, Breunig Jr. said. "Over the years, La-Z-Boy would put together steering committees, and we would help them understand what some of our needs were on the floor. They were very helpful in spending the money to do the research to find out how different products would work in the stores. They've been a great partner in progress."[72]

The stores would be larger than Showcase Shoppes and would feature the full La-Z-Boy® product line. The concept was tested when a prototype La-Z-Boy Furniture Galleries store opened in Las Vegas in 1989.[73] La-Z-Boy was taking furniture retailing to a new level of professionalism and service. "That's when the company really took off," Norton recalled.[74]

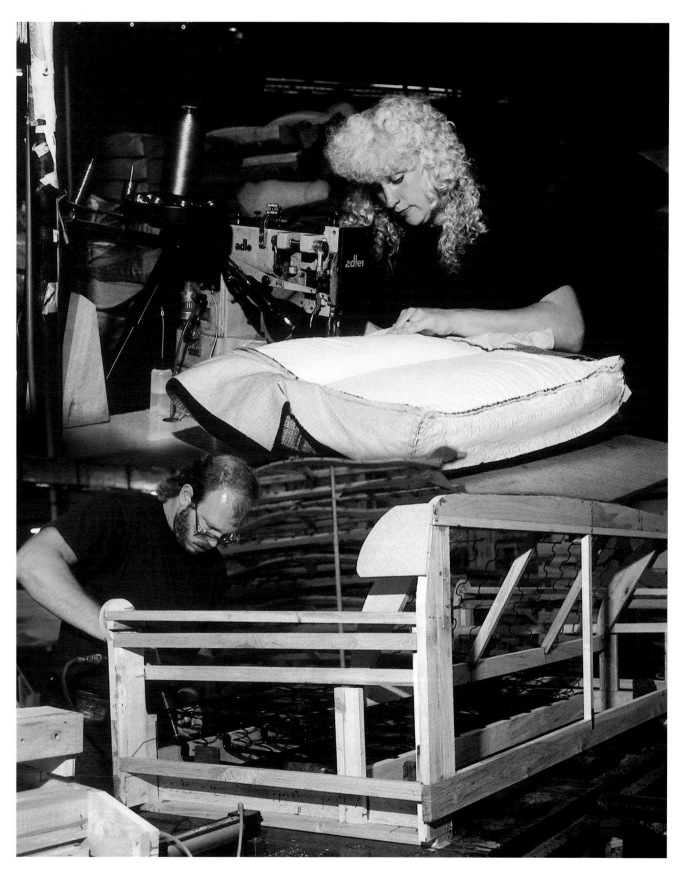

La-Z-Boy employees at work in the Dayton, Tennessee, furniture plant, where an upholstery division was added in the early 1990s

CHAPTER SEVEN

THE MAKING OF A HOME

1990–1995

*I never had difficulty making a moral decision because I knew if I
made the right one, the firm was behind me.*

—John Quinn, retired La-Z-Boy sales representative

IN ITS 1990 ANNUAL REPORT, La-Z-Boy Chair Company told stockholders, "La-Z-Boy isn't just a chair company anymore. We've become a full-line manufacturer, able to furnish virtually every room in America's homes in comfort, quality, and style."[1]

In 10 years, La-Z-Boy had transformed itself from a manufacturer of recliners to the country's third-largest residential furniture maker. The transformation had breathed new life into the company, and by 1991, La-Z-Boy was the largest producer of brand-name sleep sofas and the nation's largest independent manufacturer of upholstered furniture.[2] Its Burris, Kincaid, and Hammary acquisitions gave La-Z-Boy the means to supply living room, dining room, and bedroom furniture as well. It was also becoming a larger player in the contract market.

Between 1985 and 1990, La-Z-Boy's annual sales had more than doubled to $592 million. Its manufacturing capacity had increased 120 percent. Furniture industry growth had slowed in 1989 and 1990, but La-Z-Boy's sales had grown faster than the rest of the industry's. In 1990, La-Z-Boy was included in the *Fortune* 500 list for the first time.[3] La-Z-Boy had the products, the people, and the plants to be a full-line furniture manufacturer.

Blueprint for the '90s

As it entered a new decade, the company outlined a "Blueprint for the '90s" to clarify its new position in the industry.

La-Z-Boy had long been the most recognized name in furniture, but it had always been associated with recliners. Now La-Z-Boy's challenge was to position itself in consumers' minds as a full-line furniture manufacturer. La-Z-Boy wanted American families to think of La-Z-Boy when they shopped for furniture for any room in their homes.

"The challenge for us was to expand it and not walk away from our heritage and equity with the recliner," said John Case. "So what we've done over the years is we've run parallel campaigns—promote and advertise recliners under the La-Z-Boy name, then have separate campaigns in magazines showing the other [furniture] categories."[4]

Ed "E-3" Breunig III, a La-Z-Boy store owner, said customers who visit his family's Furniture Galleries store all say the same thing. "We call it the 'Gee factor.' People walk through the door, see five

La-Z-Boy Furniture Galleries began to replace Showcase Shoppes in the early 1990s.

La-Z-Boy Furniture Galleries had a standardized exterior that included several windows to admit natural light.

or six fashionably accessorized vignettes, and they go, 'Geez, I didn't know La-Z-Boy made all this.'"[5]

Therein lies the company's goal, said John Case.

We've said publicly to our dealers that our long-term goal is . . . that no one ever walks in and says that, because they'll know we make all that. We've had significant growth in the non-reclining-chair categories. That has been our growth opportunity.[6]

The blueprint also called for improving the quality of distribution, gaining financial strength, expanding production capacity, and improving production efficiency.[7] La-Z-Boy had recently modernized many of its plants. It opened new upholstered furniture plants in Dayton, Tennessee, and Tremonton, Utah. Kincaid, Hammary, and La-Z-Boy Contract plants were also modernized and expanded.[8]

All La-Z-Boy facilities were linked by an electronic communications system, which allowed divisions at different locations to work together.

For instance, the design and engineering department in Monroe could provide design services to other divisions and control automated equipment at distant manufacturing sites. The system also helped coordinate the flow of business data throughout the company.[9]

Furniture Galleries

A major part of La-Z-Boy's repositioning strategy was its new line of stores. Pat Norton had been refining La-Z-Boy's proprietary stores since 1981. After upgrading the Showcase Shoppes, he instituted research on consumer buying patterns, which revealed that "consumers don't really love shopping for furniture, and when they do, their needs of product quality and fair price are closely linked with buying from a store that keeps them from making a mistake."[10] Norton used this research to develop the next generation of furniture stores—La-Z-Boy Furniture Galleries. *Upholstery Design & Manufacturing* magazine described the Galleries as "idea centers that show retail consumers how to make their homes more beautiful and comfortable."[11]

The first of La-Z-Boy's Furniture Galleries opened in Las Vegas in 1989. It served as a merchandising laboratory, where La-Z-Boy could test product mix and presentation, sales production, price, and store size. The Las Vegas store measured 17,500 square feet, about twice the size of a typical La-Z-Boy Showcase Shoppe. Unlike Showcase Shoppes, which emphasized motion furniture, Furniture Galleries featured a complete line of La-Z-Boy® upholstered and wood furniture, including Burris upholstery, Hammary occasional tables, and Kincaid entertainment centers, all of which boasted the La-Z-Boy trade name.[12]

The stores were divided into four separate galleries. The Family Room Gallery featured sleep sofas and loveseats, reclining sofas, and Motion-Modular®

groupings. The Living Room Gallery featured La-Z-Boy® stationary sofas, loveseats, chairs, and tables. A Leather Gallery displayed leather-upholstered furniture. A Chair Gallery offered a selection of La-Z-Boy® recliners and rockers. Room settings were accessorized with lamps, area rugs, wall art, and accessories chosen by La-Z-Boy.

Over the next two years, 42 La-Z-Boy Furniture Galleries opened across the country. La-Z-Boy tweaked the concept, and in 1992, it unveiled what would be a prototype La-Z-Boy Furniture Galleries store in Las Vegas, Nevada. The freestanding store measured 13,600 square feet—smaller than the

Furniture Galleries merchandise was displayed in quadrants— living rooms, family rooms, recliners, and leather.

1989 Las Vegas store. It had an open, airy floor plan that allowed customers to look across the selling floor and see a variety of fabrics and textures on display. The store had a standard exterior and large windows on three sides, admitting natural light.[13]

La-Z-Boy planned to replace its Showcase Shoppes with 300 to 350 Furniture Galleries during the decade.[14] Showcase Shoppe owners who may have been reluctant to make the transition to the larger stores were persuaded when they learned that Furniture Galleries' revenues were substantially higher than Showcase Shoppes' on a dollars-per-square-foot basis.[15]

La-Z-Boy maintained strong relationships with its dealers. "Very few people totally understand the inner soul of this company," Norton said, explaining that La-Z-Boy regarded its dealers very highly. "I don't believe there's a more retailer-oriented company in this industry than La-Z-Boy. The independent dealer is terribly important to us. We could not survive without him." Norton pointed out that La-Z-Boy's strategy wasn't to increase

Custom furniture orders increased in La-Z-Boy Furniture Galleries, where fabrics were displayed in Design Centers.

square footage but to increase sales. La-Z-Boy provided its dealers with the tools they needed to grow their businesses.[16] In 1992, La-Z-Boy Furniture Galleries, Showcase Shoppes, and in-store Galleries accounted for only 42 percent of sales.[17]

Connections

In 1992, La-Z-Boy linked its independently owned Furniture Galleries with its corporate headquarters through a computer system used for electronic order writing and inventory management. The Sequel System from GE Retail Systems allowed the stores to order directly from La-Z-Boy via electronic data interchange. The system gave La-Z-Boy headquarters the ability to see what its retailers were selling, not just what they were buying from La-Z-Boy. It allowed retailers to track their orders from production to delivery. A GE Retail Systems spokesperson told *Furniture/Today* that La-Z-Boy's system would be "the most comprehensive and widespread electronic order network in the furniture industry."[18]

La-Z-Boy Furniture Galleries also accommodated custom orders, which had increased 10 times between 1981 and 1989.[19] In 1993, La-Z-Boy introduced a video catalog to facilitate custom orders. Studies had shown that 70 percent of custom-order customers walked out of the store without buying, often because they couldn't visualize what the finished product would look like. The La-Z-Boy Screen Test[®] video catalog allowed customers to see how various fabrics would look on a piece of furniture they were considering.[20]

La-Z-Boy's extensive consumer research helped it shape its Galleries formula and the company's product mix. Popular products introduced during the early 1990s included Reclina-Way[®] reclining sofas, whose end units functioned as close-to-the-wall recliners, and a chaise recliner that eliminated the gap between the recliner's seat and footrest when reclined, providing added leg comfort.

Cost-Conscious Consumers

Another merchandising goal was to broaden the price range of La-Z-Boy[®] products. Most La-Z-Boy[®] furniture was priced in the midrange. To attract high-end customers, La-Z-Boy offered Burris recliners, which were labeled La-Z-Boy Classics[®] in 1991.[21] By 1993, La-Z-Boy phased out the Burris name altogether.[22]

In 1991, La-Z-Boy went after budget-minded customers with a $299 recliner called the La-Z-Rest[®] rocker recliner. La-Z-Boy was reluctant to market low-priced products because it feared it could not provide at $299 the excellent quality its products were known for. But dealers demanded the lower price point to remain competitive.

The Reclina-Way sofa was introduced in 1990. The sofa's end units functioned as wall recliners.

To develop the $299 recliner, La-Z-Boy's engineering, design, and manufacturing departments eliminated some of the "bells and whistles" normally found on a La-Z-Boy® chair. La-Z-Rest® didn't offer the three-way ottoman or adjustable seat tension and was available in a limited selection of fabrics and colors. The chair had fewer parts and utilized a frame constructed of hardwood and plywood, which proved to be stronger than La-Z-Boy's all-hardwood frame. The La-Z-Rest chair carried the lifetime La-Z-Boy warranty.[23]

Engineers also developed a more efficient assembly process for the La-Z-Rest: Components of the chair were produced "off-line" and came together in the assembly operation.[24] A year after its introduction, the La-Z-Rest label was abandoned, and the lower-priced chair was renamed La-Z-Boy Reclina-Rest®.

In 1992, La-Z-Boy introduced the American Home Collection® stationary sofas. The line was built on newly engineered frames that allowed designers to create trendy new styles.[25] Like La-Z-Boy Classics®, the American Home Collection was aimed at high-end customers. When the American Home Collection was introduced, La-Z-Boy became a serious player in the stationary market, according to *Furniture/Today*.[26]

La-Z-Boy dealers asked for another product during the early 1990s. Functional features were very popular options on motion upholstery. Consumers loved modular seating units equipped with practical features like storage drawers and drop-down tables, as well as gimmicks like hidden telephones and stereo speakers. Dealers believed function added value to furniture and appreciated the products' higher profits. La-Z-Boy accommodated

The American Home Collection of stationary upholstery helped establish La-Z-Boy as a manufacturer of stylish furniture for living rooms and family rooms.

the dealer requests when it began offering storage drawers, snack trays, and massage on its motion chairs and sofas in 1993. The company's La-Z-Touch® line of massage recliners was particularly well received. The line of four chaise reclining chairs featured six motors in the back, seat, and footrest.

"We were not eager to get into this category," Norton said. "But, in order to be fair to our dealers, we needed to do it. It was an issue of keeping them competitive."[27]

In 1994, La-Z-Boy Contract introduced an executive chair with massage. The Pulse IV® massage option was operated by a remote-control unit. La-Z-Boy was the first in the industry to offer a massage chair for the office.[28]

La-Z-Boy's subsidiaries updated their product lines as well. Hammary and Kincaid made some lines that carried the La-Z-Boy name and were sold in La-Z-Boy Furniture Galleries. They also continued to make their own signature lines, which were sold by independent furniture stores.

Former Sealy Furniture Company President Fred Preddy was named president of Hammary in 1990.[29] Under Preddy's direction, Hammary revamped its upholstery lineup, lowering the products' price points to harmonize with the company's midrange occasional tables. Hammary, which had been producing some of its occasional tables overseas, shifted production back to the United States. Despite a trend in the furniture industry toward overseas production, La-Z-Boy and its U.S. subsidiaries produced all products domestically, where they believed quality was superior.[30]

In 1991, Hammary introduced a new line of modular entertainment centers called Video-Centers. The centers catered to the growing home theater trend, in which people stored large-screen televisions, VCRs, stereo equipment, and speakers in modular units, along with video and audio tapes and CDs.[31] Hammary's revised upholstery, entertainment center, and table lines coordinated so dealers could display and sell complete living room or family room furnishings.

Changes were also taking place at Kincaid. In 1990, Jerry Kiser, who had served for 23 years in a variety of management posts at Broyhill Furniture, was named to the new position of senior vice president of operations.[32] Kincaid wanted to become the country's largest manufacturer of solid wood furni-

ture. In 1991, it introduced several new lines of solid wood heirloom furniture.

Hall of Fame

In 1992, Edwin Shoemaker joined Edward Knabusch in being inducted into the American Furniture Hall of Fame, one of the highest honors the industry can bestow. Shoemaker was recognized for his inventiveness and engineering genius. The induction ceremony program noted that "Shoemaker was among the first to project the physical properties of recliners as a science. If there were such a thing as the 'Father of Motion Furniture,' he would be a candidate for that title."[33]

Three years later, Patrick Norton was inducted into the Hall, making La-Z-Boy the only furniture company with three Hall of Fame inductees. In Norton's 14 years with La-Z-Boy, sales had increased more than sixfold, from $155 million to nearly $1 billion. "Pat's keen insight and his remarkable ability to motivate people have contributed greatly to the success of the company and the industry as a whole," Charles Knabusch said.[34]

Home Furnishings Council

Norton's contributions to the industry included service on the board of the American Furniture Manufacturers Association and on the liaison committee with the National Home Furnishings Association. Norton was instrumental in forming the National Home Furnishings Council (HFC), an association of furniture manufacturers, retailers, and suppliers united to increase furniture sales.[35] The group hoped to gain a larger portion of discretionary dollars consumers spent on home entertainment and computers.[36]

The HFC sponsored an interior design cable television show called *Haven* and invested in additional advertising and public relations. HFC ads were meant to "arouse Americans to the importance of a warm and comfortable home environment," according to an ad agency spokesperson.[37] HFC advertising strove to boost furniture sales in general.

La-Z-Boy had a strategy for building long-term relationships with customers who would remain loyal to the La-Z-Boy brand. In fall 1994, La-Z-Boy surprised its 1,400 dealers by announcing that it would discontinue La-Z-Boy's long-standing co-op ad funding. The funds went instead into a $20 million national advertising and customer referral program that began in 1995.

Case explained that the campaign was meant to establish relationships between dealers and consumers.

We're looking at this not so much as a selling proposition but rather as a relationship establisher. A relationship may never pay off. Then again, if a consumer who saw the commercial happened to be at the later stages of the shopping process, they may come in right away and buy several thousand dollars worth of furniture. Or the relationship may pay off in a few months or next year and the next year.[38]

Business Galleries

The La-Z-Boy Contract Division developed a wider range of products during the early 1990s. It also improved its distribution by developing in-store Business Furniture Galleries, beginning in 1991. The galleries displayed La-Z-Boy® desks, cabinets, seating, and accessories in modular settings.[39] By 1995, La-Z-Boy had 34 Business Galleries in dealerships across the country.[40]

In 1994, the RoseJohnson Division merged with the La-Z-Boy Contract Division, and the RoseJohnson name was discontinued.[41]

La-Z-Boy Contract introduced ReVisions modular office components in 1993. This line included desks, credenzas, file cabinets, hutches, and wardrobes designed for small and midsize business and home offices. The easy-to-assemble components were made from 125 manufactured parts and could be configured in thousands of ways.

Engineering, design, sales, and manufacturing representatives worked together to develop the ReVisions line in an unusually short time. Gary Vanderwood, director of design and merchandising, said the company moved three times faster than expected in reaching full capacity with the ReVisions line. A CAD line between Monroe headquarters and the manufacturing plant in Grand Rapids, Michigan, facilitated the project. A PC-based inventory system gave the project a "running start,"

Vanderwood said. New, computerized equipment streamlined the production process.[42]

The ReVisions line was a step toward La-Z-Boy's design team concept launched in 1995. Teams of designers, engineers, cost analysts, and technical staff worked together to design new products. The company's goal was to compress the design curve until new product ideas could be completed and shipped to customers within 90 days of introduction.[43]

Another step in improving the production process came when La-Z-Boy launched a Total Quality Management program in 1995. The program included process controls; computer tracking; step-by-step result measurement; specific, individual quality targets; and reduced handling.[44]

Streamlining production required constant updating of plants and installation of automated, computer-controlled equipment. Although furniture required hand assembly, many processes in La-Z-Boy plants were automated. In 1995, La-Z-Boy built a new plant in Siloam Springs, Arkansas. The 400,000-square-foot plant doubled the size

Kincaid introduced several new lines of solid wood heirloom furniture in 1991 with the goal of becoming the country's largest manufacturer of solid wood pieces.

of the plant it replaced and tripled its efficiency, according to Norton.[45] The original Siloam Springs plant had been built in 1943.

A Symbiotic Relationship

In 1995, La-Z-Boy acquired upholstered-furniture maker England Inc. Charles Knabusch said the acquisition "gives us the ability to have an entry-level price point that we would have a hard time filling."[46]

England benefited from the merger as well. Rodney England, president of England Inc., said La-Z-Boy allowed the England family to keep a sense of pride in owning and running a family business.

They've been very open minded about our business model, very understanding that the things

we do sometimes do not conform to what they see as their business model at La-Z-Boy.

They've been a great partner to England to give us the freedom to do what our model calls for and what works for us.[47]

England Inc. had 2,500 dealers, mainly smaller stores, which La-Z-Boy considered a strong point because of the challenges of dealing equitably with both independent dealers and its proprietary stores.[48] England had a "huge, strong, independent

ReVisions modular office furniture was introduced in 1993. The line included 125 parts that could be configured in thousands of ways to form desks, credenzas, file cabinets, hutches, and wardrobes designed for business and home offices.

dealer base," Norton said. "They've made their living on mom-and-pop stores scattered all over this country. We're trying very hard to solidify our base with those folks."[49]

"You know, there are not too many relationships where you feel as at home and at ease as we do [with La-Z-Boy]," Rodney England added.

They're very genuine people. One time we presented a very aggressive five-year business plan. It called for about $7 million or $8 million in capital expenditures, and it opened new plants in different states to expand our customer base and our manufacturing capabilities. Pat Norton looked at me and said, "Rod, are you sure

ENGLAND INC.

L A-Z-BOY ACQUIRED ENGLAND/CORSAIR, a privately owned manufacturer of budget-priced upholstery, in 1995. England/Corsair was founded as England Upholstery Manufacturing Company in 1964. The company was owned by brothers Eugene and Dwight England and their father, Charles, a silent partner. Eugene left the manufacturing company for the retail furniture store in 1969, and Dwight operated the business with new partners Wayne and Kenneth England. Charles continued as a silent partner until his death in 1980.

Dwight expanded the business in the 1980s, beginning with a division to produce contemporary furniture. The division took the name Corsair, which had been the name of a chair company founded by the England family during the 1960s. When the England and Corsair divisions united in the late 1980s, England/Corsair emerged as the trademark for all England upholstery products.

England built new plants and expanded sales throughout the United States and Canada. In 1983, the company introduced the Quadrant Delivery Program, a revolutionary idea in the furniture industry. Quadrant delivery was a commitment to deliveries every four weeks and truckload deliveries in two weeks. It had a major impact on the furniture industry.

In 1992, England changed its name to England/Corsair. When La-Z-Boy bought the company, it operated six plants and employed 1,500 people. The company was known for its low-priced chairs, sofas, love seats, and motion

upholstery and gave La-Z-Boy the ability to have an entry-level price point.

Like Hammary and Kincaid, England/Corsair operated as a separate entity. Rodney England served as president. Dwight England, who had been involved in the merger discussions, died shortly before the agreement was finalized.[1]

A vignette displaying budget-priced upholstered furniture manufactured by England/Corsair, which La-Z-Boy acquired in 1995

that this plan is not a little bit too aggressive? Are you sure you can pull all this off?" I said, "Pat, there's only one thing that worries me." Of course he thought he'd hit the homerun button, that there was some part of that plan that I had some reservations about. I said, "The only thing I'm worried about is how mad you're going to be when we pass La-Z-Boy up." He cracked up laughing.[50]

The acquisition pushed La-Z-Boy sales closer to the $1 billion mark,[51] but Norton downplayed the milestone. "We are not just buying companies because we want to increase our volume. We're buying companies that we think will all come together and help us serve the retailer."[52]

No Limits

La-Z-Boy's growth was not confined to North America. La-Z-Boy had been exporting furniture for 25 years, and in 1995, it was exporting to more than 30 countries. Licensing agreements in England, Germany, Italy, South Africa, Japan, New Zealand, and Mexico contributed $26 million in La-Z-Boy sales during 1993.[53]

La-Z-Boy expected the Pacific Rim market to grow considerably during the rest of the 1990s. In 1993, La-Z-Boy introduced the Asian chair in Japan. It was a scaled-down recliner for the Asian market, whose people were often shorter and whose living rooms were typically smaller. La-Z-Boy was careful when naming the chair for the Asian market, where references to laziness were insulting. In Japan, the translation came close to "man sleeps."

In Taiwan, it was called "happy chair." In Korea, it translated to "person or boy relaxes."[54]

The same chair was named Small Comforts® and marketed in the United States as a chair for short people. The smaller chair did not sell well in Asia or or North America and was discontinued.

In fiscal 1995–1996, La-Z-Boy sales totaled $947 million. A large part of the company's "Blueprint for the '90s" had come to fruition. La-Z-Boy's 1995 advertising campaign was attracting consumers' attention and broadening the company's brand name. The Total Quality Management system was compressing delivery schedules. The company's product lines had been broadened so that La-Z-Boy could meet the needs of furniture buyers in a variety of price ranges. Its 130 Furniture Galleries were the second-largest network of Gallery stores in the country.[55]

But the company experienced a great loss as well that year, when retiree Herman Gertz, former president of Floral City Furniture and La-Z-Boy board member, died. Gertz had been an integral part of the company's early history and, following his retirement from the corporation, had served as administrator of the La-Z-Boy Chair Foundation. Gertz was also a civic leader and philanthropist. He co-founded the Herman and Irene Gertz Foundation, which supported various local causes. He was a champion of Monroe County tourism and a supporter of the Monroe Chamber of Commerce.[56]

Herman Gertz, one of the first Floral City Furniture employees, died in 1995. His connection to La-Z-Boy spanned seven decades.

In 1999, La-Z-Boy introduced this commemorative reproduction of its original reclining chair. It sold for $399.

CHAPTER EIGHT

HOLDING ON TO HISTORY

1996–1999

We are certainly proud of our tradition, of our founding fathers and families. That's a strong foundation that we have built from, and those traditional values are consistent with the way we conduct business today.

—Gerald Kiser, president and CEO, 2002

IF THERE WERE ANY question that La-Z-Boy had moved beyond its roots as a chair maker, it vaporized in 1996, when the company changed its name from La-Z-Boy Chair Company to La-Z-Boy Incorporated. At the company's annual stockholders meeting, Secretary-Treasurer Gene Hardy declared, "Chairs are now no more than 40 percent of our business," and stockholders voted to change the name to reflect the company's diversity.[1]

The same year, La-Z-Boy articulated a new vision. After remaking itself into a supplier of furniture for every room in the home, La-Z-Boy declared that it wanted to be "regarded globally as the premier provider of home, office, and institutional furniture in all market segments in which we directly compete."[2] La-Z-Boy strove to be number one not just in the home but in offices, hotels, and hospitals. And it wanted to capture this position throughout the world.

"To make this mission a reality, we're fundamentally changing our infrastructure," Charles Knabusch told stockholders in the 1996 annual report. Some of the changes Knabusch referred to had been in the works for years. The company's design team concept, which began with a few product lines, was now operating company-wide, including at the plant level. Sales and marketing provided consumer preference input to teams of cost analysts, designers, frame engineers, and

LA-Z-BOY
INCORPORATED

manufacturing technology specialists. Together, these professionals created quality products, developed efficient production methods, and brought products to market sooner. La-Z-Boy's Quality, Value & Improvement Program also helped increase productivity.[3]

Simultaneously, La-Z-Boy continued to put the latest technological innovations to work to improve its operations and manufacturing. During 1996 and 1997, La-Z-Boy began using an electronics-based system in its Residential Division. Bar codes and electronic scanners tracked dealer orders from the moment they were received until the product was shipped. The system lowered labor costs; reduced raw material, work-in-process, and finished goods inventories; improved truck loading efficiency; and provided instant updates to La-Z-Boy's management information system.[4]

International growth also received careful attention. La-Z-Boy designed product, manufacturing, and distribution systems that were appropriate for different regions and countries.

The La-Z-Boy Chair Company name was changed to La-Z-Boy Incorporated in 1996 to reflect the company's growth since its days as a chair maker.

New opportunities opened in Canada when the North American Free Trade Agreement (NAFTA) eliminated tariffs on U.S.-Canadian trade in 1994. While La-Z-Boy Canada had been making La-Z-Boy® recliners since 1929, Canadian customers had never been exposed to the full line of La-Z-Boy® products before NAFTA took effect. In 1996, La-Z-Boy Furniture Galleries opened in Calgary, Edmonton, and Winnipeg, and 54 Canadian retailers opened La-Z-Boy in-store galleries.[5]

Also in 1996, La-Z-Boy opened a La-Z-Boy Furniture Galleries store in Madrid, Spain. It was the first gallery outside North America.[6]

La-Z-Boy's dealer network expanded at home as well in 1996 when Sears HomeLife stores began

selling La-Z-Boy products. HomeLife began in 1993 as 20 freestanding furniture stores and furniture departments inside Sears stores and by 1996 had grown to approximately 140 stores.[7] La-Z-Boy debuted in 46 of them on the West Coast and spread across the country during the next two years.[8] "This is a great move for Sears and a great move for us," Pat Norton said. He believed La-Z-Boy would be reaching new customers in Sears stores, which had a loyal customer base.[9]

La-Z-Boy was named 1997 HomeLife Furniture Quality Source of the Year for providing the highest-quality merchandise in the furniture category. Sears also granted La-Z-Boy a Partners in Progress award as one of the company's top suppliers. La-Z-Boy competed with more than 10,000 companies for the citation.[10] Unfortunately, HomeLife did not produce the profits Sears had hoped for, and in 1998, Sears sold the chain to Citicorp Venture Capital.[11]

Meanwhile, La-Z-Boy's largest dealer, Montgomery Ward, was also having financial difficulties. Ward filed for Chapter 11 bankruptcy in 1997, saddling La-Z-Boy with about $3.1 million in bad debt expense. Ward had 400 stores in 43 states and accounted for almost 5 percent of La-Z-Boy sales. Montgomery Ward remained in business and put a financial recovery plan in place.[12]

New Introductions

La-Z-Boy wheeled out several new products between 1996 and 1999. The Reclina-Glider® Swivel Recliner attracted attention with its gliding movement. Complements from La-Z-Boy® occasional chairs were designed to go with larger La-Z-Boy® upholstered furniture. La-Z-Boy's Signature Selects® collection was a low-priced line of upholstered seating produced for La-Z-Boy by England/Corsair.[13] La-Z-Boy's Chair and a Half was an extra-wide occasional chair that hid a twin-size bed.

In 1996, La-Z-Boy and its subsidiaries began introducing licensed products. Hammary and Kincaid teamed up to produce a new line of furniture titled Ducks Unlimited. The collection was licensed by the 750,000-member Ducks Unlimited, a conservation group dedicated to preserving waterfowl and wetlands. A portion of sales supported the group's conservation efforts. The furniture was designed for people who loved the outdoors and included an eclectic mix of wood, upholstery, leather, glass, metal, and painted finishes. Hardware and fabrics were inspired by

Left: Sears HomeLife began selling La-Z-Boy products in 1996.

Below: The Chair and a Half could become a twin-size bed.

Opposite: The Ducks Unlimited collection was marketed to people who loved the outdoors. A portion of the collection's profits supported wetlands preservation.

nature, and many featured proprietary Ducks Unlimited artwork.[14] Hammary's 200-piece collection included living room seating, home entertainment units, occasional tables, and home office furniture. Kincaid introduced 100 bedroom, dining room, and occasional pieces for the collection. The products were cross-marketed with other licensees' products.[15]

End of an Era

The 1990s were a transitional time for La-Z-Boy management. Many of La-Z-Boy's vice presidents—men who had been with the company for 30 or more years—retired. Among them were Courtney Leckler, vice president La-Z-Boy West; Marvin Baumann, vice president product planning and development; Charles Nocella, vice president manufacturing; Louis Roussey, vice president human resources; and Ted Engel, vice president La-Z-Boy Dayton.[16]

Meanwhile, Charles Knabusch had been warned by doctors of a heart problem. He realized the importance of grooming the next generation of management. In 1996, when he was 56, Knabusch appointed Gerald Kiser vice president of operations, replacing Nocella. Kiser had been vice president of operations at Kincaid since 1990. He had successfully dealt with quality, productivity, and profitability problems and had turned Kincaid into a profitable company.[17]

The following year, Kiser was named to the newly created position of executive vice president and chief operating officer. Kiser was in place as the company's next president, but nobody anticipated how soon or how tragically he would move into the position. In October 1997, while playing golf during the International Home Furnishings Market, in High Point, North Carolina, Charles Knabusch suffered a fatal heart attack. He was only 57.

Knabusch had been president of La-Z-Boy since 1973, when La-Z-Boy had 2,500 employees, five plants, and annual sales of $52.7 million. He had become chairman and chief executive officer in 1985. Knabusch had maintained a vision for the company. In the mid-1970s, he had predicted that La-Z-Boy would reach $1 billion in sales,[18] and the company hit that milestone shortly before he died. At the time of his death, La-Z-Boy had grown to 12,000 employees and 31 plants.

Knabusch shared many of his father's traits. He was known as an ethical businessman and a good leader. He was friendly with employees, often eating lunch with workers in the cafeteria and playing bridge with them on breaks. He was an outdoorsman and a family man and former president of the American Furniture Manufacturers Association. Knabusch was active in the Monroe Family YMCA and the Boy Scouts and had recently been appointed by Michigan Governor John Engler to the Natural Resources Trust Fund Board. He also sat on the Monroe Bank and Trust board of directors and was a trustee of Mercy Memorial Hospital.[19]

But Knabusch's leadership style contrasted with his father's. He had a more relaxed, unassuming way. He didn't seek publicity and always gave credit to others. "He was not a one-man show," Gene Hardy said. "He surrounded himself with capable people, solicited ideas from them, and gave them a free hand in executing their own plans."[20]

Kurt Darrow described Knabusch as "a guy who allowed you to make your own decisions and make your own mistakes and learn from them."[21]

Pat Norton said that Knabusch was "very supportive. He was very interested in the growth of the company and interested in the growth of the dealers' business."[22]

Knabusch remained humble throughout La-Z-Boy's growth years, fabric supplier Rob Culp said. "He remained the same guy. He worked very hard to stay behind the scenes and gave the credit to everyone else. He was smart enough to empower his employees." Bernhardt President Alex Bernhardt said, "I knew him as a man of integrity and as a totally forthright man. He was ethical, honest, straightforward, and a good negotiator."[23]

Knabusch was survived by his wife, June, three sons, one daughter, seven grandchildren, one great-grandchild, and a sister.[24]

Because Knabusch surrounded himself with a talented management team and had initiated a succession plan, the company remained on course following his death. Kiser, 50, was named president and chief operating officer. Norton, 75, was named chairman of the board and retained responsibility for the company's sales and marketing. Frederick "Fritz" Jackson, 69, was promoted from vice president to executive vice president of finance. The CEO position remained vacant, and the three men composed the Executive Committee. "The three of us are working together in harmony to ensure a successful transition and the continued growth of the company," Norton told *Furniture/ Today.* "I have the highest regard for Jerry. He's an excellent operations man and an excellent choice for president."[25]

The sudden death of La-Z-Boy President and Chairman of the board Charles Knabusch in October 1997 dealt a shocking blow to the company.

Another Blow

But the management change represented more than a change of president. For the first time in its history, La-Z-Boy was not being led by a founder, a family member, or even a Monroe native. And just a few months later, the company was dealt another blow when co-founder Edwin Shoemaker died at the age of 90.

Shoemaker was remembered as a gentle soul, a generous benefactor, and the engineering genius behind his more outgoing cousin, Edward Knabusch. Although he didn't seek attention, it was Shoemaker's invention of the first reclining chair in 1928 and the Reclina-Rocker® in 1960 that made La-Z-Boy a household name. "He devoted his entire life to his work and has been the heart and soul of La-Z-Boy. He was a gentleman in the truest sense," Norton said.[26]

Board Member Rocque Lipford was particularly amazed with one aspect of Shoemaker. "He never really came to grips with all his wealth. It never changed the man an iota. In fact, he was still the kind of guy who, if you could buy something for six cents cheaper over there, he would go and do that. I've never seen anything quite like it."[27]

Courtney Leckler added, "We often wondered if he ever knew how many millions he had."[28]

Shoemaker spent winters in Sun City, Arizona. During the rest of the year, he lived in Monroe and spent time at the company he co-founded. He maintained the titles of executive vice president of engineering and vice chairman of the board until his death. "He still would look at innovations and challenge them at times," Case said. "He had an engineer's mind, and it never rested."[29]

Jim Waltz attended the same Lutheran church as Shoemaker. The two not only worked together at La-Z-Boy but also collaborated to dig a basement under their church, Waltz said.

Now this doesn't sound like much, but our church is big, and he [organized] having that basement dug out completely and putting in cement block for support—putting a floor in there and stairs and everything—and he engineered the whole thing.

A young Edwin Shoemaker stands with the belt-driven machinery used in his cousin's makeshift workshop in a garage. Shoemaker died in March 1998.

You wouldn't believe the stuff that man could do. He was the head honcho, directing all the men working on the church. We had engineers come in to take a look at it all, but Mr. Shoemaker was on the same level if not higher.[30]

When Shoemaker asked Waltz to help him replace some bricks in the church building one evening, Waltz didn't know what was in store for him.

"It was getting after dark, and I was thinking, 'What in the world is he going to do?'" Waltz mixed cement and carried it up the ladder to Shoemaker. The only light available was a light in the churchyard. "I couldn't believe that he could work under those conditions, but we did it," Waltz recalled.[31]

Shoemaker also took an active role in establishing the La-Z-Boy Museum and Archives. He spent days in the archives going over company records and memorabilia with Museum Director Judith Carr.

Shoemaker died in Sun City while napping in his La-Z-Boy® recliner, and Jay Leno acknowledged him that night on *The Tonight Show*, Lipford said. "He said 'The man who made the couch potato possible died today in his La-Z-Boy.' I thought how much Mr. Shoemaker would have laughed at that. He would have taken great pleasure in knowing that somebody like Jay Leno would acknowledge him on TV."[32]

Dale Shoemaker found his father looking peaceful in his chair when he came to the house to take him to dinner. "He had gone to church that morning and told friends he had never felt better in his life," Dale said. "Felt like he did when he was in his 40s."[33]

John Weaver, retired trust officer and retired La-Z-Boy board member since 1971, said, "If I have any choice, I hope I lean back in my La-Z-Boy for a nap just like he did."[34]

A MECHANICAL GENIUS

ONE DAY DURING THE EARLY 1980S, an elderly gentleman visited a La-Z-Boy Showcase Shoppe in Phoenix, Arizona. He introduced himself as Eddie and browsed the showroom. Just another snowbird from the North, the store's manager thought. But he soon discovered that Eddie was Edwin Shoemaker, co-founder of La-Z-Boy and the inventor of the La-Z-Boy recliner.

Shoemaker and his wife, Ruth, spent winters in nearby Sun City, and one of Eddie's favorite pastimes was visiting the Showcase Shoppe. He strolled into the back room to see "what the fellas are having to fix today," recalled La-Z-Boy sales representative Steve Matlock.[1] Shoemaker would watch the workers and occasionally help them adjust and repair the chairs that he invented.

From the time he was 8 years old and made his sister a doll cradle from ice cream and popsicle sticks, Shoemaker loved to tinker. "I've always observed how things were made. If it was something that could come apart, I'd take it apart and put it back together again," he told the *Monroe Evening News*.[2]

Shoemaker was the quiet half of the team that founded Floral City Furniture Company. While his more outgoing cousin, Ed Knabusch, managed the sales and marketing end of the business, Shoemaker worked at his drafting board, inventing the products that made La-Z-Boy the best-known name in the furniture industry. He was responsible for more than 30 La-Z-Boy patents. In addition to creating the products, Shoemaker also made much of the machinery and laid out the early plants. His genius made him a multimillionaire. But in Sun City, the humble, quiet gentleman was not too good to get his hands dirty in the store's back room.

When Shoemaker returned to Michigan during the warmer months, he enjoyed visiting La-Z-Boy headquarters, where he maintained an office. He would stop by the engineering department, where new products were developed and tested. Director of Product Safety and senior mechanical engineer Larry LaPointe recalled, "He had such a great mind. I very much respected his opinion on things. He could look at a design and tell right away if it was going to be any good or not. He didn't have much formal education, but in my estimation, he was a genius."[3]

Shoemaker remained healthy and keen witted throughout his life. He strongly supported the La-Z-Boy Museum and spent many hours reviewing the company's records and identifying many of the materials donated to the archives. In 1991, Marvin Baumann, La-Z-Boy vice president of product planning and development, said,

"One thing I always saw about Eddie Shoemaker was the bond he had with his wife, Ruth," added Lipford. "They were inextricably intertwined. They were indeed interesting to watch. I think we all learned something from them."[35]

Kathi Stiefel, who came to La-Z-Boy in 1966, recalled her favorite story about Shoemaker.

He was just a real sweetheart and liked to visit with the employees. He would go throughout the building. I was working late one night, and he came walking through. Apparently [he] didn't see me and turned the lights out on me. He was very conservative. He was a little shook up when he heard me yell. So I always think about him when someone leaves their lights on. He would turn them off.[36]

In the Face of Change

The loss of Shoemaker so soon after Charles Knabusch's death rocked La-Z-Boy. It reinforced a challenge faced by the executive committee—moving from a family decision-making process to corporate decision making without losing the culture

---

"I once said I'd like to know everything that man forgot. But I changed my mind because I realized he's never forgotten anything."

La-Z-Boy Museum Director and retired employee Judith Carr said working closely with Shoemaker to set up the museum was a privilege. "I knew when I was sitting here with him I was spending some really special time with a really special person. And he considered himself just one of the employees. We went to a retirement party one night . . . and he stood up and said a few words to congratulate the person who was retiring, and he said, 'We sure work for a nice company, don't we?' You

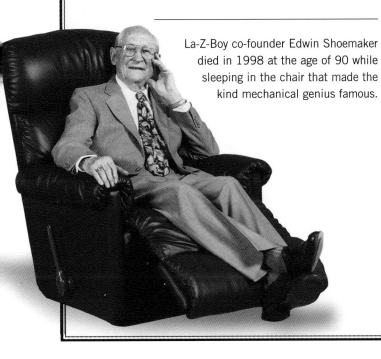

La-Z-Boy co-founder Edwin Shoemaker died in 1998 at the age of 90 while sleeping in the chair that made the kind mechanical genius famous.

know, the man was a millionaire, inventor, co-founder of the company, but as far as he was concerned, he was just one of the people who worked here."[4]

Shoemaker was a generous benefactor to Trinity Lutheran Church, the Monroe Lutheran Home, and the Monroe County Historical Society. He financed an extensive renovation of the Lutheran Home's chapel in honor of his wife, Ruth. The chapel was crafted with English oak paneling, stained-glass windows, a granite floor, and a 2,306-pipe organ built in England.[5]

In addition to being inducted into the American Furniture Hall of Fame, he was named to the Business Hall of Fame of the Southeastern Michigan Chapter of Junior Achievement and received the Governor's Award and the local Minuteman Award. And he was recognized when his name came up as the answer to the question, "Who invented the La-Z-Boy?" on the game show *Jeopardy* and in the fifth edition of the game Trivial Pursuit®.

He was a member of the International Lutheran Layman's League, Valparaiso University President's Club, American Red Cross, Salvation Army, and Monroe YMCA.[6]

Shoemaker remained active until his death at the age of 90. In March 1998 in Sun City, he returned home after having lunch with friends, sat down to rest in his La-Z-Boy recliner, and died in his sleep. He was survived by sons Dale and Robert, daughter Mary Kaye Johnston, six grandchildren, and seven great-grandchildren. His wife, Ruth, died previously.[7]

established by the company's founders. Norton shared his insights into the corporate culture.

The romance of this company dates back to Shoemaker and Knabusch. I am very fortunate. I spent 20 years with a company [Ethan Allen] where a couple of brothers-in-law started the business and built it, and they were as different as day and night, and neither of them would have been worth a damn without the other. I came over here to another company that was exactly the same thing. Neither one of these guys would have been successful by himself, but together they were unbeatable. In certain ways, they had a totally different outlook, and in other ways, they were identical. You don't often see that. That's what took this company

from $1 million in 1961 to where it is today. It's not only what these guys did but the foundation that they laid.

I know one of the things that worries the hell out of me is the worry of losing the thing that really made the company great, and that's the principles that these two guys laid down.[37]

Hardy recognized the challenges that confronted the new team.

I like some of the decisions they've been making—to recognize early any losses or you have to close plants. It certainly affects people. In the old days, we probably didn't make those decisions as fast as we should have because of the care for the employees and the care for the

CARETAKER OF THE LEGACY

THERE WEREN'T MANY JOBS AVAILable in 1939, when Pat Norton graduated from high school. The country was still suffering the effects of the Depression. Norton began working in the furniture department of a high-end department store in his native St. Louis, Missouri. "That's where I could get a job, pure and simple," he told *Furniture/Today*.[1]

It was the beginning of a furniture industry career that has lasted more than 60 years. Norton worked at the department store for a year before joining the U.S. Army Air Force and flying 33 combat missions in the South Pacific during World War II. After being discharged in 1945, he returned to St. Louis and the furniture industry. He managed retail furniture stores, and eventually was a partner in four, until 1962, when he joined Ethan Allen as a salesman. Within four years he was vice president of sales. Norton's retailing expertise helped him build Ethan Allen's proprietary retail network into the largest furniture gallery network in the country.[2]

After 20 years at Ethan Allen, Norton, 59, joined La-Z-Boy, where he thought he would spend his last six years before retirement. Those six years have stretched to more than 20. When Norton joined the company as senior vice president of sales and marketing in 1981, La-Z-Boy was the best-known brand in the furniture industry, but its reputation was built on one product—the reclining chair. Its sales were stagnant, and it had a fledgling network of proprietary stores.

Norton went to work positioning the company competitively for the future. He developed the next generation of gallery stores—La-Z-Boy Furniture Galleries—and he updated and expanded the company's product line to include stationary furniture. He also spearheaded a series of acquisitions. La-Z-Boy sales increased from $158 million in 1981 to more than $2 billion in 2000, when it became the largest furniture manufacturer in the country. Norton became La-Z-Boy chairman of the board in 1997 after Charles Knabusch's death.

Although Norton humbly avoided taking credit for La-Z-Boy's success, others named him as the force behind the company's growth since 1981. La-Z-Boy Vice President of Administration Richard Micka said, "He knows more *communities. So the landscape is changing now. You have to make those hard decisions in order to stay in business these days. So I see that changing and probably a little bit . . . some of the close-knit-family sense. You've got 20,000 employees. It's hard to keep that [family feeling] as the company gets bigger.*[38]

But the culture at La-Z-Boy is intact today, many claim. "Whether it be Pat Norton, the chairman of the board, or the janitor in one of the factories, everybody has that same mission and vision of building exceptional products and offering exceptional service every time," Arizona and Las Vegas sales representative Steve Matlock said. "That's the company's vision, and everybody understands it. Everybody knows it, and that's why the company

Pat Norton, shown on the cover of *Upholstery Design & Manufacturing*, worked hard to keep the La-Z-Boy legacy alive following the death of the founders.

about the furniture industry than anybody in the world, in history."[3]

"If there is a single, outstanding senior statesman in the furniture industry, Pat Norton is the man," *Furniture/Today* reported in 1996.[4]

In 1999, then COO Gerald Kiser said, "The initiative and drive he possesses have certainly been instrumental in the growth of La-Z-Boy over the past 18 years."[5] In a 2000 awards ceremony, Norton was called "one part businessman, one part superhero, one part generous, one part tough as nails."[6]

Norton has been honored for his contributions to the furniture industry and the community at large. In 1986, he received the National Conference of Christians and Jews National Brotherhood Award in the field of Human Relations. He also received the City of Hope Spirit of Life Award. In 1995, he was inducted into the American Furniture Manufacturers Association Hall of Fame. Norton has served on the board of the American Furniture Manufacturers Association (AFMA) and was the first chairman of the Home Furnishings Council.

In 1992, La-Z-Boy established the Patrick H. Norton Scholarship Fund at High Point University, High Point, North Carolina. The fund provides financial assistance to students who plan a career in the furniture industry. In 2000,

the university named a furniture school building Norton Hall in his honor and awarded him an honorary doctor of law degree. In 1995, he was granted the Distinguished Service Award from the AFMA.[7]

La-Z-Boy has changed significantly since Norton joined the company. But one thing remains the same. Norton has preserved the principles established by founders Edward Knabusch and Edwin Shoemaker and carried on by Charles Knabusch. "I've always said that the shadow of those two gentleman still stands over our board table, and I hope it always does," Norton said. "They made decisions for business reasons. They also made them for humane reasons, and there's just not that many companies that operate that way anymore."[8]

has been able to maintain such a hometown-type atmosphere. It's unbelievable."[39]

Larry LaPointe tries to remind his employees why they can be proud to work at La-Z-Boy.

It's a product that people enjoy. They spend their leisure time, their quality time, usually their family time in this furniture. So I've always liked that part of the business because we work on a product that people enjoy.

I've been very fortunate in that the people who work at La-Z-Boy, I think, want to work here, and they like working here, and I think that the culture has always been very positive here. I think the co-founders had such an influence on the company from the beginning, and that has carried on through the years, through Charles Knabusch, and then with his passing, with the new management. It's still that very same way. I see it every day, that same emphasis on quality.[40]

Onward and Upward

Under its new leadership, La-Z-Boy continued on its growth track. The company met its goal of growing at a faster pace than the overall furniture industry throughout the 1990s. Sales increased through existing operations and acquisitions. Just prior to Charles Knabusch's death in 1997, La-Z-Boy acquired Centurion Furniture PLC.

Earlier in 1998, La-Z-Boy acquired Sam Moore Furniture Industries Inc., and in 1999, La-Z-Boy purchased Bauhaus U.S.A. Inc. and Alexvale. Alexvale was operated as a division of Kincaid, and its upholstery was marketed under the name Kincaid Custom Upholstery.

Acquired companies often found themselves at an advantage after merging with La-Z-Boy. "I would make the same decision today that we did in 1987 to join La-Z-Boy," Kincaid President Steve Kincaid said.

I think one thing that has made La-Z-Boy so successful with the companies that they purchased is the autonomy that they give you to operate your own business. They entrust you with running the business on a day-to-day basis, and I think they give you enough rope to succeed or hang yourself. I think that's been a real attribute to them,

SAM MOORE

IN APRIL 1998, LA-Z-BOY ACQUIRED Sam Moore Furniture Industries Inc., a privately held manufacturer of upholstered chairs for the home and office. Sam Moore Furniture was founded in 1940 in Delaware, Ohio, by Sam Moore, a Pennsylvania native who chose furniture making over the family funeral business. Three years later, the company moved to Christianburg, Virginia. It moved again in 1950, this time to Greenville, Tennessee. The company became known for its Sam Moore Chair, a channel-back barrel chair with solid mahogany frame that retailed for $39. The chairs came in 12 styles, and between 1943 and 1973, nearly 4 million were sold.

In 1959, Sam Moore Furniture moved to Bedford, Virginia, and it built a modern plant in 1960. The company expanded the plant 12 times in the next 40 years. When Sam Moore died in 1980, John Boardman, Moore's son-in-law, continued as chairman and chief executive. Michael Moldenhauer was the company's president. Sam Moore marketed its products through upscale department stores, furniture stores, and mail-order catalogs.[1]

and that's why they've been able to hold on to a lot of their management team, because they do empower you, and they challenge you to do as well as you can do, but then they certainly give you all the tools you need to do the job.[41]

In 1999, Kincaid opened Kincaid Home Furnishings stores in Albany, New York, and Wilmington, Delaware. Kincaid planned to open 25 to 30 stores over the next three years. The stores ranged from 15,000 to 18,000 square feet and featured the full line of Kincaid bedroom, dining room, and occasional furniture and the Kincaid Custom Upholstery lines. The stores also carried a private-label line of mattresses from Serta.[42]

In 1998, Kincaid and La-Z-Boy Residential introduced a new product line licensed by painter Thomas Kinkade, America's most collected artist. The Thomas Kinkade Collection included upholstery by La-Z-Boy Residential and solid wood pieces by Kincaid. The collection was styled with a relaxed European cottage look popularized by Kinkade's light-infused paintings. It soon became the most successful collection in Kincaid's history.[43]

Kincaid introduced another innovative product in 1999: a patented television armoire featuring a two-way mirror on its door. When the TV was on, it could be viewed and operated with the door closed. When the TV was off, the inside of the armoire was dark, leaving the mirror fully functional.[44]

Setting Trends

One of La-Z-Boy Residential's most unique and fun new products in 1999 was a chair nicknamed "The Coolest Recliner in America®." It was equipped with a cup holder and an electric cooler located under the arm pad. The exclusive cooler held six 12-ounce beverage cans. Under the other arm, the chair stored an optional telephone with caller ID. Finally, the chair featured a 10-speed motor and heated massager with hand-held controls. "For years, we've heard all the ideas for the perfect 'sports fan' chair—you know, the kind you can just hunker down in without having to get up between plays," said Gregory White, vice president of

The Thomas Kinkade Collection included upholstery from La-Z-Boy Residential and tables from Kincaid. The collection became the the most successful in Kincaid's history.

merchandising. "So we figured, why not? Let's make it. This chair has it all for the sports fan who doesn't want to miss a moment of the action."[45]

White said creative products are a must for the International Home Furnishings Market, held in April and October in High Point, North Carolina.

It is quite a show, and that's what we gear our plans around. Part of our mission statement and core values has always been, in the recliner area, to continue to be the leader and be innovative. So we have introduced before the rest of the markets some pretty innovative product in the last couple of years.

The chair, which was kind of tongue-in-cheek, was the first chair that had a cooler in it or refrigerator in it. Then we came out and worked with Microsoft and Sony on the [Web TV Plus Recliner].[46]

Also in 1999, La-Z-Boy went back in time and introduced a commemorative reproduction of its original wood slat reclining chair. The chair was crafted of solid European beech with brass-plated hardware. Each chair had a brass plate bearing a limited edition number verifying its authenticity. The chairs retailed for $399.[47]

Innovative and creative products like these were not just earning La-Z-Boy and its subsidiaries added sales. They were attracting the attention of the industry as well. In 1998 and 1999, La-Z-Boy Residential, Hammary, and Kincaid earned Pinnacle Awards from the American Society of Furniture Designers. The awards recognized furniture manufacturers

ALEXVALE

ALEXVALE, PRODUCER OF STYLISH, medium-priced upholstered furniture and occasional items, was acquired in 1999. Sold primarily through department stores and independent furniture retailers, Alexvale was marketed under the Alexvale and Hickory-Fry brands. It received the prestigious Pinnacle Design Achievement award in 1998.

Alexvale was headquartered in Taylorsville, North Carolina, and operated four factories. Its annual sales were approximately $60 million at the time of acquisition. The company was founded in 1976 by Ron Roseman, F. P. Wright, and Charles Bolick, who served as president at the time of the acquisition.

La-Z-Boy operated Alexvale as a division of Kincaid, which used Alexvale upholstery to complement its solid wood products. Alexvale upholstery was marketed under the name Kincaid Custom Upholstery. Kincaid could then sell its furniture in nearly 200 in-store galleries that previously purchased upholstered furniture from the manufacturers of their choice. Kincaid President Steve Kincaid called the partnership a "perfect fit" and said Kincaid galleries would gain a more uniform look that could be advertised and marketed cohesively.[1]

This recliner was nicknamed "The Coolest Recliner in America®." It came with built-in refrigerator, optional telephone, and massage.

for beautiful designs that met the needs of consumers, provided good value, and made the best use of materials and production technology.[48] La-Z-Boy Residential was recognized for its Metro motion sofa. Kincaid won its Pinnacle for a LeBistro casual dining group, and Hammary won for its Cadence collection of occasional furniture. La-Z-Boy Residential also received the Better by Design Award from the editors of *Better Homes and Gardens* magazine for its Carlyle reclining chair. The art deco chair was a high-leg lounger with wide maple-veneer arms.[49]

La-Z-Boy Business Furniture® was also recognized. The division's Sequel® Seating Series won a silver award for outstanding design, comfort, and value at NEOCON, the country's largest office furnishings trade show.[50]

Reinforcing La-Z-Boy Residential

La-Z-Boy strengthened and reorganized its La-Z-Boy Residential Division in 1999. The division had been managed by La-Z-Boy's corporate staff, but in 1999, La-Z-Boy Residential was established as a separate division with a dedicated management team. "Based on the accelerated growth of our residential business, which accounts for more than 50

Top right: The Carlyle chair, a high-leg lounger, won a Better by Design Award from *Better Homes & Gardens* in 1998.

Right: La-Z-Boy's Metro sofa won a Pinnacle Award from the American Society of Furniture Designers.

BAUHAUS U.S.A. INC.

IN 1999, LA-Z-BOY PURCHASED BAUHAUS U.S.A. Inc., of Saltillo, Mississippi, maker of medium-priced transitional and contemporary upholstered furniture and sleep sofas. Bauhaus designed its furniture for urban lifestyles.

Founded in 1989 in Saltillo, Bauhaus had 875 employees and four plants. La-Z-Boy was better able to access department stores with this acquisition because Bauhaus garnered most of its sales through this market. "Bauhaus has distribution strength in channels that we currently impact only slightly," Pat Norton said. "Like La-Z-Boy, Bauhaus's reputation for product style and quality is unmatched in its price category."[1]

At the time of acquisition, Marty Silver was CEO and Bauhaus was an $85 million company.

percent of our corporate sales, we felt the time was right to separate the day-to-day management of this division from the corporate management function," Kiser said.[51]

John Case was named president of the Residential Division. He had begun working at La-Z-Boy in 1977 and had held a variety of sales and marketing positions. In 1989, he left the company to join an advertising agency in Michigan. A year later, he formed Case Communications, an advertising and marketing consulting firm. Case rejoined La-Z-Boy in 1992 to take on retail development and services and the next year became vice president of marketing.[52]

At the same time, La-Z-Boy made other appointments to the Residential Division. Kurt Darrow was named senior vice president of sales and marketing. Darrow joined La-Z-Boy in 1979 and held various management positions, including regional sales manager and national accounts sales manager. Darrow had been vice president of sales since 1987, during the major growth years of the division.[53] David A. Layman became senior vice president of residential and contract operations. Layman had started his career with La-Z-Boy in 1971 as an upholsterer at La-Z-Boy Midwest, in Neosho, Missouri. He rose to plant superintendent, then vice president/plant manager before coming back to Monroe as vice president of manufacturing. Together, Case, Darrow, and Layman drew from more than 70 years of La-Z-Boy experience to function as a solid, stable leadership team.

La-Z-Boy also took steps to refine the Residential Division's product development and production. In 1998, the division's product development department moved from Monroe to Dayton, Tennessee, where it could work side-by-side with the Dayton manufacturing plant, the company's largest facility. The move eliminated about 20 positions, and 20 employees relocated to Tennessee.[54]

La-Z-Boy Residential also streamlined production. Since La-Z-Boy's expansion during the 1960s and 1970s, all plants had been self-sufficient, producing frames, metal finishing, upholstery, etc. During the 1990s, La-Z-Boy consolidated some of these operations and developed supply centers for wood, plywood, and metal parts. Frame construction, which had been han-

dled by 18 plants, was consolidated into two plants by 1998. When this consolidation took place, La-Z-Boy converted its rocker recliner production to UniBody® construction, which featured solid interior panels, allowing for stronger frames at a lower cost.[55] Similar consolidations occurred with metal operations. The consolidation helped La-Z-Boy cut costs without eliminating jobs.[56]

Broadening La-Z-Boy's Presence

Internal changes had strengthened La-Z-Boy and cut costs. Its acquisitions had helped the company grow. In 1999, La-Z-Boy was ranked the third-largest furniture manufacturer in the United States, behind Furniture Brands International and Lifestyle Furnishings.[57] All of the top companies were conglomerates of smaller furniture makers acquired during the 1980s and 1990s. Furniture Brands International included Broyhill, Lane, and

CENTURION

IN 1997, LA-Z-BOY ACQUIRED ITS BRITISH licensee, Centurion Furniture PLC. Based in Lancashire, England, Centurion had been a La-Z-Boy licensee since 1992. In addition to making La-Z-Boy® motion furniture for the European market, Centurion made traditional leather furniture, which it exported to 30 countries in Europe and the Far East.

In its early days, Centurion specialized in the English chesterfield design, which originated in 1770. The classic design remained a part of Centurion's product line. The company operated two manufacturing divisions and served more than 150 distributors in the European marketplace.

The merger with Centurion stimulated the development of the recliner market in the United Kingdom and Ireland and worked to increase awareness and acceptance of motion furniture. It also reflected La-Z-Boy's corporate vision to be regarded globally as a premier furniture provider.[1]

Thomasville. Lifestyle Furnishings International represented Berkline, Drexel Heritage, and Henredon.

La-Z-Boy had taken a friendly approach to its acquisitions. Industry publication *HFN* reported, "La-Z-Boy's acquisitions strategy could be described as 'If we build it, they will come.'" La-Z-Boy never went after a company; its hands-off management style made it attractive to smaller companies seeking to become part of a conglomerate.[58]

"We have never targeted—and I hope we never will," Norton told *HFN* in 1999.[59]

"If somebody wants to sell their business and they would like to be associated with us, then we'll make that judgment," Kiser added. "At the same time, they have to fit into the sense of where we're going as a company. One of our strategic initiatives is to look at companies that are available that could broaden our distribution." Alexvale, for instance, gave La-Z-Boy a greater presence in department stores.[60]

Companies that merged with La-Z-Boy gained a great deal. Being associated with the La-Z-Boy name boosted their image in the marketplace. In turn, La-Z-Boy gained new products, markets, and distribution.

Once a company was under its umbrella, La-Z-Boy had a hands-off management style. "As far as distribution, that's their business, not ours. As far as the product they bring out, they always show it to us and we talk about it, but the decision is theirs," Norton said.[61]

Kiser stressed uniqueness in the marketplace.

We want to give these companies the opportunity to continue to display their individual entrepreneurship. We don't want to transform these companies to where they're just a clone of another company that we own, because most of them have some uniqueness, and that contributed to the reason that we acquired the company.

So it's a fine line that we walk between running a decentralized operation and a centralized operation. But we think it serves us well to continue to capitalize on the niches that these companies fill.[62]

Norton told *HFN* that acquisitions would continue to be an integral part of La-Z-Boy's future. Even as Norton and Kiser discussed their acquisition strategy with *HFN*, the company was negotiating for its largest acquisition to date—one that would make it the country's largest furniture manufacturer.

Ladd Furniture

In March 1999, Fred Schuermann, chief executive officer of Ladd, approached La-Z-Boy about the possibility of merging the two furniture giants. Ladd, with sales of $571.1 million, was the seventh-largest furniture manufacturer in the United States.[63] The Greensboro, North Carolina, company comprised seven manufacturers, employed 6,500 workers, and operated 20 plants in eight states. It exported its product to more than 50 countries.[64]

Ladd produced wooden beds, dressers, dining sets, tables, and some upholstery. But what really attracted La-Z-Boy were Ladd's youth and contract furniture subsidiaries. Ladd's Lea brand included youth beds, dressers, and other pieces aimed at 3- to 18-year-olds. Its American of Martinsville line held 25 percent of the hospitality furnishings market, including hotels, motels, dormitories, and assisted living centers. La-Z-Boy had little presence in these markets.[65]

"In addition to reinforcing our leading market positions in upholstery and casegoods, Ladd immediately establishes us as a market leader in contract and youth furniture sales," Norton said.[66]

It was "a marriage made in merger heaven," Fred Schuermann said.[67] "The fit of Ladd and La-Z-Boy productwise was just natural. They're about 75 percent upholstery and 25 percent wood, and we're just the opposite. The combined product line is so deep and so strong, it creates a huge company that's financially powerful. The management cultures were very, very compatible."[68]

Ladd was formed in 1981 when Don Hunziker, Richard Allen, and seven other executives of the Sperry & Hutchinson Company bought the three divisions they led—Lea Industries, American Drew, and Daystrom—for $70 million.[69] The company went public in 1983.[70]

Ladd expanded rapidly during the 1980s, when it acquired Clayton Marcus, Barclay Furniture, and American of Martinsville.[71] In 1990, Ladd acquired Maytag Corporation's furniture group, which included Kittinger, Pennsylvania House, McGuire,

THE LADD MERGER

WHEN THE LADD FURNITURE ACQUI-sition was finalized in January 2000, La-Z-Boy had added several companies, representing eight brands, to its family.

American Drew

American Drew was a leading producer of quality medium- to upper-medium-price bedroom, dining room, and occasional wood furniture.

Founded in 1927, American Drew was a well-established company with collections that ranged from its 18th century traditional "Cherry Grove," which was still going strong after 42 years in production, to the popular Bob Mackie Home Collection, which debuted in October 1997, and the Jessica McClintock Home—The Romance Collection, which debuted in October 2000.

American Drew's headquarters were located in Greensboro, North Carolina, and the company operated manufacturing facilities in North Wilkesboro, North Carolina. Its products were distributed through thousands of independently owned retailers.

American of Martinsville

American of Martinsville was a leader in supplying contract furniture to the hospitality, assisted-living, and governmental markets domestically and abroad. The company was founded in 1906 by tobacco producers A. D. Witten and C. B. Keesee to manufacture quality bedroom furniture. In 1956, it entered the commercial furniture manufacturing business. Ladd bought it in 1986.

American of Martinsville operated manufacturing facilities in southern and southwestern Virginia, including at its headquarters in Martinsville, and employed approximately 1,300 skilled craftspeople with an average employment tenure of nearly 20 years. Products were sold to leading hotel chains and resorts as well as to smaller, family-owned guest room properties.

Clayton Marcus

Clayton Marcus was founded in Hickory, North Carolina, in 1960 and acquired by Ladd in 1984. It produced quality upholstered furniture featuring hardwood frames and eight-way, hand-tied construction. Its mid-price line of fabric and leather sofas, loveseats, and ottomans came in traditional, casual, and transitional styles.

La-Z-Boy finalized a merger with furniture giant Ladd in 2000. Comprising seven furniture manufacturers, Ladd brought names such as American Drew, Clayton Marcus, and Lea into the La-Z-Boy family.

Clayton Marcus's headquarters and manufacturing facilities were located in Hickory, North Carolina. The company distributed its products through thousands of independently owned retailers.

Lea

Lea was the leading producer of moderately priced correlated youth bedroom furniture. It also made adult bedroom furniture in a wide variety of styles and finishes. The company had celebrity collections with National Basketball Association star Grant Hill, America's Cup Yachtsman Dennis Conner, and fashion designer Jessica McClintock.

Lea's youth furniture offered styles for both girls and boys, including four-poster canopy beds, bunk beds, storage beds, dual sleep beds, student desks, and computer desks. Founded in 1869, Lea operated headquarters and manufacturing facilities in Greensboro, North Carolina, and Morristown, Tennessee.

Pennsylvania House

Pennsylvania House was one of the country's best-known and most respected furniture manufacturers. It produced top-quality, solid wood bedroom, dining room, and occasional furniture and custom upholstery. The company marketed its products through a network of in-store retail galleries. Pennsylvania House was founded in 1887 and acquired by Ladd in 1989.

Pennsylvania House manufactured upholstery in Monroe, North Carolina, and produced furniture in Lewisburg, Pennsylvania, a few miles from one of the world's richest stands of virgin cherry. Pennsylvania House produced classic American traditional designs with timeless appeal as well as less formal designs and was committed to uncompromising heirloom-quality construction.

Brown Jordan, Gunlocke, and Charter Group.[72] Two other acquisitions followed: Fournier (1992) and Pilliod (1994). Ladd's strategy was to cover all the bases and build strength in each of its major categories: bedroom, casegoods, casual dining, upholstery, hospitality and contract, and metal.

The acquisitions made Ladd one of the top furniture manufacturers in the country. But Ladd's debt caught up with it when a recession in the early 1990s slowed industry sales.[73] By 1995, Ladd was losing $25 million.[74] It was deeply in debt and had stopped paying a dividend on its shares. Its stock plummeted.[75] To recover, it sold some of its divisions and restructured its management team. Fred Schuermann, a vice president with operating responsibility for six of Ladd's 12 operating companies, was named president and chief executive officer.[76]

"The company had grown very rapidly through acquisitions," Schuermann said. "Some of those pieces either weren't making money or strategically were just not good fits."

Schuermann worked to reduce debt and improve profitability. He concentrated on Ladd's core businesses—upholstery and casegoods—selling three divisions and liquidating another. He then reorganized Ladd into three segments: residential casegoods, residential upholstered furniture, and institutional furniture.[77] By 1999, the companies were performing well, although there was room for improvement in profitability. La-Z-Boy management expressed admiration for Schuermann's leadership in turning the company around.[78]

With combined sales of $2 billion, La-Z-Boy was now the largest furniture manufacturer in the United States. The company produced 17 brands, employed 21,500 people, and operated 56 plants.[79]

La-Z-Boy used a series of illustrations in magazine advertising and calendars during the early 1970s to appeal to middle America. This August drawing came with the tag line, "La-Z-Boy—the chair for every generation in the family."

CHAPTER NINE

BUILDING THE BRAND

La-Z-Boy has a 98 percent brand awareness. Sometimes it measures 100 percent. No one comes close to that in the industry. And it drives a lot of what we do.
—John Case, President, La-Z-Boy Upholstery Group

Helping Put
Monroe on the Map—

The La-Z-Boy Chair

A patent of the Floral City Furniture Company, manufactured and distributed in the United States by the Michigan Chair Company of Grand Rapids, Michigan.

In Canada it is manufactured and distributed by the De Luxe Upholstering Company of Kitchener, Ontario.

Patents on this chair have also been applied for in Germany, England, France and Australia.

The La-Z-Boy is made and distributed in Monroe County by the designers.

For Genuine Comfort in Your Home Get a La-Z-Boy.

FLORAL CITY FURNITURE CO.
Telegraph Road —————— Monroe, Michigan

THE SUCCESS OF LA-Z-BOY IS largely rooted in the strength of its brand name. Catchy as it is, the La-Z-Boy name didn't become the industry's best-known brand through cleverness alone. The strength of the La-Z-Boy brand grew out of aggressive marketing and advertising. Co-founders Edward Knabusch and Edwin Shoemaker recognized the importance of advertising La-Z-Boy® chairs from the beginning. Soon after inventing the reclining chair, Floral City Furniture Company began advertising it in the local newspaper.

The chair's first advertising slogan, "Recline, Relax, Recuperate," was developed by a supplier who produced La-Z-Boy chairs for Floral City Furniture Company during the 1930s. A pamphlet explained the benefits of reclining in a La-Z-Boy chair.

Recline, relax and immediately you begin to recuperate—to get back the energy, the 'pep,' you've used up. All your tiredness disappears; you feel new strength, new energy, tingling through your body. Come in and experience for yourself what it means to Recline-Relax-Recuperate.[1]

1940s

After Floral City opened its own manufacturing facility in 1941, the founders began marketing

La-Z-Boy chairs outside the immediate area. They installed 10-by-12-foot billboards across the Eastern United States. The signs pictured a woman reclining in a La-Z-Boy chair. The billboards read "Relax with La-Z-Boy Chair" and included a local dealer's name. La-Z-Boy had planted 100 of these signs along roadsides east of the Mississippi River by 1942, when the company stopped making recliners and converted its factories for the war effort.[2]

La-Z-Boy's First National Campaign

La-Z-Boy Chair Company returned to manufacturing recliners after World War II and launched its first national advertising campaign in 1947. The company spent $27,000 on one-quarter-page, black-and-white ads in the *Saturday Evening Post, House Beautiful, Better Homes and Gardens, Holiday*, and several trade magazines. The results were difficult to measure, but Knabusch believed the ads raised awareness of La-Z-Boy® recliners among consumers and dealers.

Floral City Furniture Company advertised the La-Z-Boy chair soon after it was invented.

The 1948 annual stockholders meeting report stated that the ads resulted in "many inquiries." Knabusch told stockholders that "inasmuch as many furniture dealers throughout the country gave preference to nationally advertised products, we should continue to build up our reputation and prestige with them in some form with a program of either national or pinpoint advertising."[3]

The first ads featured women reclining in the chairs. In June 1949, a La-Z-Boy Father's Day ad pictured a man for the first time. La-Z-Boy provided dealers with free ad mats in unlimited quantities. Five hundred dealers took advantage of the advertising opportunity.

Local advertising by dealers was considered a key element in the chair's marketing, and it helped strengthen the brand name nationally. La-Z-Boy also provided dealers with point-of-sale materials, including circulars, decals, framed copies of newspaper ads, cutaway models of chairs, and a motorized unit that continually moved, demonstrating the chair's reclining action. La-Z-Boy used every opportunity to put its name in the customer's mind. Protective plastic covers on the chairs' backs were printed with the La-Z-Boy logo. Often, the covers stayed on in the customers' homes as a fabric protector.[4]

La-Z-Boy's magazine ads always pictured women reclining in La-Z-Boy® chairs until a Father's Day ad, similar to this one from 1955, appeared in 1949.

John Case said those early sales and advertising aids helped strengthen the La-Z-Boy brand. "The one thing that La-Z-Boy did from day one and continues to do better than anyone is the quality and quantity of retail advertising materials they supply to their dealers. We have always put in the hands of our retailers quality materials to help generate local advertising in support of the brand," he said.[5]

La-Z-Boy's First Color Magazine Ad

Competition increased during the 1950s, and La-Z-Boy stepped up its advertising. By 1952, it was spending $68,000 on advertising and ranked fourth in advertising expenditures in the furniture industry.[6] In 1955, La-Z-Boy produced its first color magazine ad.[7] In addition to its usual magazine mix, La-Z-Boy began advertising in *Successful Farming*. La-Z-Boy chairs were very popular in rural areas, and the company wanted to reach those customers through a farm magazine.[8]

Many La-Z-Boy magazine ads included a coupon or a phone number and an invitation to call or write for more information. Inquiries to La-Z-Boy headquarters were referred to a La-Z-Boy salesman, who directed the customer to a local dealer. In 1958, Knabusch reported that La-Z-Boy had received some 4,000 inquiries from its national advertising, including inquiries from 25 countries after an ad appeared in *National Geographic*.[9]

Into Suburbia

The 1950s saw tremendous changes in the lifestyles of middle-class Americans. Many people in rural and urban areas moved to new homes in the suburbs. Two cars in the driveway and a television in the living room grew more and more common. TV was becoming a source of news, entertainment, and escape; it also served as a new advertising medium, allowing viewers (who generally trusted advertisers) to see a product in use. La-Z-Boy chairs first appeared on television in 1958, when the company gave away 13 Hi-Lo-Matic chairs as prizes on the *Big Payoff* game show.[10] La-Z-Boy continued game show promotions during the 1960s.

America's new suburban lifestyle was reflected in La-Z-Boy magazine ads during the 1950s and early 1960s. Family togetherness pervaded.[11] A 1958 ad pictured a man relaxing in his La-Z-Boy chair and his wife and young daughter trying to lever him out of it under a headline that read, " . . . can't PRY him out of his La-Z-Boy."[12]

"...can't PRY him out of his *La-Z-Boy*"

1960s

Advertising in the first part of the next decade continued to showcase men enjoying well-deserved relaxation in a family context. One ad during the 1960s pictured a father reclining in a La-Z-Boy chair with his briefcase and hat beside him. The copy read, "All day you've been on the go. It's been an up-hill struggle and you're beat. You want time to enjoy your family, to relax and take it easy. You sit in your favorite chair, your La-Z-Boy Reclina-Rocker®. The tough part of the day melts away quickly as you relax." The ad went on to describe the chair's features.[13]

La-Z-Boy sales skyrocketed following the introduction of the Reclina-Rocker in 1961. La-Z-Boy increased its production capacity and promoted the chair heavily. Advertising budgets doubled from $250,000 in 1963 to $500,000 just three years later.

Then in 1967, La-Z-Boy's advertising took a new turn. Bing Crosby began appearing as a spokesperson for La-Z-Boy in magazine, newspaper, and trade

magazine ads. The magazine ads pictured Crosby and his wife, Kathryn, relaxing in La-Z-Boy chairs. Some of the ads featured a disposable recording of Crosby talking about La-Z-Boy chairs. Dealers received a life-size cutout of Crosby for store display. They also handed customers a Crosby album titled *Songs of Christmas*.[14]

Crosby was the first of many celebrity spokespersons La-Z-Boy worked with during the 1960s and 1970s. Betsy Palmer and Bess Myerson recorded radio commercials for NBC and CBS radio, respectively.[15]

La-Z-Boy's First Television Commercial

In fall 1969, La-Z-Boy aired its first television commercials: Ed McMahon demonstrating La-Z-Boy® recliners during 60-second spots on *The Tonight Show*.[16] Appearing with McMahon was Nauga, a character representing Uniroyal's Naugahyde vinyl, which was used as a cover on La-Z-Boy chairs. McMahon demonstrated the recliners' multiple positions and discussed the chairs' comfort and style.[17] Some 12 million people watched.[18]

La-Z-Boy emphasized its chairs' quality construction in a magazine ad campaign during the late 1960s. Headlined "Beauty Is More Than Skin Deep with La-Z-Boy," the ads contained detailed information about the construction of La-Z-Boy chairs. They pictured a stripped-down chair frame and discussed various quality components, such as wood, bushings, glue, shoulder bolts, and spring clips.[19]

Some of the ads featured animals. For instance, a photograph of a sleeping dog was accompanied by text that read, "Ever notice how natural it is for a dog to relax? Instinctively, he knows just how to go about it. He doesn't fuss or fidget, just takes it easy. La-Z-Boy has a parallel to that. Our chairs are built to respond easily to any relaxing mood, and to hold firm in any position." The ad went on to describe quality construction.[20]

Above: The headline of this 1958 ad read, " . . . can't PRY him out of his La-Z-Boy."

Right: In 1967, La-Z-Boy hired its first advertising spokesperson, Bing Crosby. He was the first of many celebrities to boost the company's name recognition.

Bing Crosby says,
"My LA-Z-BOY gives me that relaxed feelin' after a day of golf."

The campaign was well suited to La-Z-Boy, which had always emphasized its chairs' quality construction. The ads also promoted the recliners' lifetime warranty.

1970s

Family scenes returned in 1972, when La-Z-Boy commissioned two popular artists to illustrate homespun scenes featuring La-Z-Boy® recliners. Magazine illustrators Howard Terpning and Joseph Bowler created a series of paintings that many people compared to Norman Rockwell's *Saturday Evening Post* covers. The scenes, which were used in magazine advertising and calendars during the early 1970s, were meant to appeal to middle America, a major part of La-Z-Boy's market. One pictured a man sleeping in a recliner while his toddler daughter sits on his lap looking at a book. In another illustration, a boy brings flowers to his mother, who relaxes in a La-Z-Boy® chair.[21]

In 1970, La-Z-Boy increased its advertising impact by contracting with popular television, movie, and stage personality Jim Backus to serve as spokesman for the company. Backus and his alter ego, Mr. Magoo, appeared in radio, television, and magazine ads, dealer tie-ins, and point-of-purchase materials. In the 10 years that Backus served as La-Z-Boy spokesman, he recorded more than 15,000 radio spots. Most of the spots were recorded

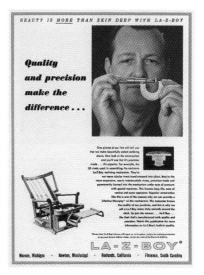

for dealers who participated in La-Z-Boy's advertising program. The recordings earned Backus a place in *The Guinness Book of Records* for most spots recorded.

Television advertising increased during the 1970s. La-Z-Boy aired commercials on daytime game shows such as *Let's Make a Deal, The Newlywed Game, Concentration, Sale of the Century,* and *Beat the Clock* and talk shows starring Steve Allen, Merv Griffin, and Dinah Shore.[22]

In 1972, La-Z-Boy signed up New York Jets quarterback and actor Joe Namath to serve as advertising spokesman. La-Z-Boy ads featuring Namath appeared on prime-time shows including *Man Trap, Monday Night Football,* and other college and pro football broadcasts, as well as during evening news, late night entertainment, and morning news.[23]

Namath was one of many sports personalities who appeared in La-Z-Boy advertising. Others included football coaches Rick Forzano, Bo Schembechler, and Don Shula.[24] "The target audience for the ads was definitely men," John Case said. "The inherent belief was that this is a male product."[25]

1980s

La-Z-Boy and its dealers had reinforced the image of the man's recliner with its advertising schedule as well. La-Z-Boy's national advertising

Clockwise from left: Jim Backus was one of the most frequently featured celebrities in La-Z-Boy ads; a 1970s magazine advertising campaign inspired by the consumerism movement discussed the quality and workmanship of La-Z-Boy recliners; football player and actor Joe Namath was a La-Z-Boy spokesperson during the 1970s.

Clockwise from top right: A 1973 ad emphasized La-Z-Boy chairs' comfort and style; illustrations reminiscent of Norman Rockwell's appeared in magazines; this April illustration for an early 1970s calendar was captioned, "How refreshing, a La-Z-Boy and spring flowers."

targeted Father's Day and Christmas almost exclusively. During the early 1980s, however, La-Z-Boy encouraged retailers to advertise during other times of the year. The company began running four two-week periods of advertising per year. Promotions ran in February, June, September, and December, coinciding with national sales events in stores.[26]

The June and December advertising schedule had become a self-fulfilling prophecy, Kurt Darrow said.

We finally demonstrated, to ourselves and to the rest of the retail world, that recliners were anything but seasonal. They were absolutely a year-round product and could support sales 12 months of the year.[27]

The company created national promotions that ran for many years in *Parade* magazine. "We would heavily incentivize the retailers to participate," Case said. "If you signed on and bought product, you got advertising materials, you got your name listed in a national ad. You may have received additional finance terms. The incentives were such that you almost couldn't *not* participate. That began turning our business into a year-round business."[28]

A Woman's Chair

In 1982, a new pair of spokespersons began representing La-Z-Boy Chair Company: actor and former Detroit Lions player Alex Karras and his actor wife, Susan Clark. The ad campaign was a major turning point for La-Z-Boy.

"That campaign marked a total transition to a female target," Case said.

We didn't hire Alex Karras because he was a sports personality. We hired Alex Karras and his wife because they were a couple and they played up the fact that giving a La-Z-Boy® recliner to each other was a couples thing. That was all based on research that the end user of recliners was no longer predominantly male. Even though we'd been targeting men all that time, the [people] who actually used the chair [were] women as [often as] men. A major decision here was that by simply promoting recliners and La-Z-Boy recliners in general, we had attempted to convince people that La-Z-Boy recliners could go in any room in the home and were beautiful and didn't have to look like quote-unquote recliners. All that was doing was benefiting the entire category for us and for our competitors.

Our research also told us that a man may say he wanted to buy a recliner, but when it came down to the style, brand, and cover, the wife was a major part of the decision. He could get his recliner, but she was going to be the one who made the final decision as to [which] recliner. *We felt that targeting women and differentiating La-Z-Boy recliners [would cause women to] gravitate to La-Z-Boy. We made that switch, and we've targeted females ever since.*[29]

Karras and Clark urged consumers to insist on a genuine La-Z-Boy® product and emphasized La-Z-Boy's lifetime warranty. La-Z-Boy fastened hangtags to every recliner to identify the chair as a "Genuine La-Z-Boy" recliner and to inform shoppers of the warranty protection.[30]

"'Genuine La-Z-Boy' became the center point of the campaign," Case said. "We moved to absolutely differentiate La-Z-Boy from a quality standpoint. It was a key message, and it was targeted toward women." There was strong retail support. "That campaign probably had the most comprehensive

An ad campaign featuring Alex Karras and Susan Clark targeted women for the first time and encouraged customers to buy genuine La-Z-Boy recliners.

tie-in between national ads and what we provided retailers," Case said.[31]

La-Z-Boy expanded its prime-time television advertising in 1983.[32] Previously ads were concentrated on daytime drama and game shows.

By the mid-1980s, La-Z-Boy was manufacturing and marketing a variety of products besides recliners. It launched a six-month, half-million-dollar advertising campaign in 1984 to promote its new Signature II® sleep sofa. The campaign featured a one-page, four-color magazine ad showing the stylish sofa. It was the first time La-Z-Boy had featured a product other than a recliner in national advertising. The ad represented another first: It prominently displayed the Signature II logo and downplayed the La-Z-Boy name.[33]

"La-Z-Boy meant recliners so much in those days," Case said. "We wanted to come up with a name for our nonreclining upholstery line, which at that point was mainly sleep sofas. We came up with Signature II by La-Z-Boy. We kept the reference to La-Z-Boy as part of the name, but we really didn't want to emphasize La-Z-Boy because it was so aligned with recliners."[34] Over the next couple of years, La-Z-Boy added stationary sofas and nonreclining chairs to its magazine advertisements.

La-Z-Boy turned to a softer approach when the Alex Karras and Susan Clark ads ended in 1988. The campaign had been extremely successful. In addition to shifting the target from men to women, the Karras-Clark campaign had introduced an emotional element into La-Z-Boy advertising. La-Z-Boy built on that emotion with its next ad campaign, which focused on the theme "La-Z-Boy, The name America's comfortable with." The commercials showed warm, emotional, everyday scenes meant to illustrate that La-Z-Boy had long been a part of America's home life. In one of four 15-second spots, a father sits in a chair, rocking a baby to sleep. The announcer says, "Nobody has rocked more babies to sleep than we have."[35]

One of the campaign's ads won a CLIO, advertising's most prestigious award. The ad features a dog lying on a La-Z-Boy® chair. The dog quickly moves to the floor when the front door opens. The announcer says, "For more than 60 years, we've been everybody's favorite chair." Then a woman's voice says, "Good boy!"[36] The ad was the best in

This 1991 ad targeted baby boomers and discussed La-Z-Boy's longevity in the furniture industry.

its category, from among 27,000 entries from 70 countries.[37]

The ads emphasized La-Z-Boy's longevity in the furniture industry and appealed to the country's baby boomer population. La-Z-Boy's largest market had always been people 60 and older. As baby boomers aged, La-Z-Boy hoped to appeal to a new generation of buyers whose parents had owned La-Z-Boy products.[38]

Shifting Gears in the 1990s

During the early 1990s, La-Z-Boy cut back on television advertising in favor of magazine and radio ads. In 1992, La-Z-Boy's radio advertising included a series of spots on the syndicated *Paul Harvey News*. Paul Harvey was a veteran radio commentator whose folksy style lent itself to testimonial ads. The Paul Harvey ads ran through 1993.[39]

La-Z-Boy began to position itself as a full-line furniture manufacturer during the 1990s. A $2.5 million magazine ad campaign in 1993 fea-

Starting August 26, Paul Harvey's going to help you sell La-Z-Boy® products.

tured an eight-page, four-color insert that ran in *Family Circle, Good Housekeeping, People,* and *American Home Style* magazines. The ads promoted La-Z-Boy's full line of upholstery. Another series of ads promoted the American Home Collection® of stationary furniture.[40]

In 1994, La-Z-Boy developed a new campaign to position La-Z-Boy as America's premier family room and living room fur-niture resource. The campaign was based on consumer research that revealed that consumers associated quality, durability, and com-fort with the La-Z-Boy name but were generally unaware that La-Z-Boy manufactured other furni-ture. La-Z-Boy accordingly launched a massive television campaign on highly rated prime-time national network shows and select cable networks.

The campaign goal was to get consumers to transfer their perceptions about the quality and comfort of La-Z-Boy® recliners to the company's other products. The ads highlighted the wide vari-ety of furniture La-Z-Boy made and featured slice-of-life scenes and the tag line "We make the rooms that make a home®." The ads pictured typical fam-ily scenes such as a teenager doing her homework on a La-Z-Boy® sofa or a mature couple dancing in the living room. Like previous La-Z-Boy ad cam-paigns, the Make-A-Home campaign associated La-Z-Boy® furniture with warm family feelings.

The ads also attempted to create a relation-ship between consumers and La-Z-Boy dealers by offering a free, 20-page decorating guide to view-ers who called 1-800-Make-A-Home. The guide included the name of the consumer's nearest La-Z-Boy dealer, who in turn received the name and address of the consumer and was encouraged to ini-tiate contact by a personal letter.[41] La-Z-Boy received 300,000 calls to its 800 number in the campaign's first year.[42]

Talking Raccoons

La-Z-Boy continued to use television advertis-ing throughout the 1990s. Since 1992, La-Z-Boy had been working with W. B. Doner Advertising to think outside the box and advertise in a way atypical of the furniture industry. The result in 1996 was a playful television commercial unlike any other ad La-Z-Boy had produced. It featured two talking raccoons named Wendall and Al, who sneak through a win-dow into a family room full of La-Z-Boy furniture. Wendall and Al lounged around on sofas, chairs, and recliners, watched television, and marveled at the style and selection of La-Z-Boy furniture. The ads used real animals, computer imaging, and anima-tronics to make the raccoons look as if they were talking. The techniques had been employed by producers of the Academy Award winning movie *Babe,* in which farm animals appeared to talk.[43]

"This is a much more fun and direct approach than we've taken in the past," said Kevin R. Wixted, then director of advertising and public relations for La-Z-Boy. "We've employed the highest forms of technology available, not to mention the best people in the business, to create commercials that define a contemporary, friendly, all-American personality for La-Z-Boy."[44]

The duo returned in 1999 in a commercial in which they sat outside peeking into the window of a room outfitted with La-Z-Boy furniture. The rac-coons enviously watched the family dog curl up on a La-Z-Boy recliner and, moved to song, belted out "Wouldn't It Be Loverly" from the musical *My Fair Lady.* It was the first time an advertiser was granted a license to use a Lerner & Lowe show tune.[45]

"The strategy behind the commercials is to com-municate to consumers in a delightful, charming, and memorable way that La-Z-Boy produces more than recliners," Wixted added. "So far it's proven extremely successful. Consumers absolutely love Wendall and Al and identify them with La-Z-Boy."[46]

Above: Paul Harvey advertised La-Z-Boy recliners on his radio show in the early 1990s.

Opposite: Magazine ads during 1997 featured families using La-Z-Boy furniture.

The company produced plush versions of Wendall and Al and sold them at La-Z-Boy dealers. Store owners and salespeople displayed the spokes-animals creatively. At a Jackson, Tennessee, store, raccoons peeked out at customers from holes cut in the ceiling. In a Memphis store, Wendall and Al hid in storage ottomans. Some stores used Wendall and Al in community relations activities, such as a zoo membership drive or as donations to a children's hospital.

La-Z-Boy also broke new ground with print advertising during the late 1990s. In 1997, the

Right: Clever headlines and stylish, silhouetted furniture pieces were spotlighted in The New Look of Comfort ad campaign, which debuted in 2000. The ads targeted young consumers and showed off La-Z-Boy's more contemporary pieces.

Below: Playful raccoons Wendall and Al lounged around on La-Z-Boy® furniture in this popular 1996 commercial.

Perfect for the rugged, indoorsy type.

The Mackenzie Sofa

LA-Z-BOY
The new look of comfort

company introduced a print campaign designed to show how La-Z-Boy fits into families' lifestyles. Each ad pictured a family living with La-Z-Boy furniture. One ad read, "Anyone can make furniture that goes with your carpeting. We make furniture that goes with your life."[47]

A 1999 print advertising campaign invited consumers to submit pictures of themselves in their new La-Z-Boy® chairs. Participants qualified for $25 rebates and opportunities to appear in ads. The ads pictured people of different ages, races, and genders in various styles of La-Z-Boy chairs, dispelling the myth that La-Z-Boy customers were middle-aged male couch potatoes.[48]

Kurt Darrow, then vice president of sales and marketing, recognized the need for a campaign that emphasized style.

"We have long been famous for the comfort and quality of our furniture, but as we continue to expand our product line with dramatic and contemporary new designs, word is spreading that

La-Z-Boy has style as well," Darrow said. "This new ad campaign promotes absolute style and elevates our product and brand to a whole new level."[49]

2000 and Beyond

In fall 2000, La-Z-Boy debuted a print ad campaign aimed at young consumers and women. Ads in fashion and shelter magazines told consumers that La-Z-Boy offered stylish furniture for the living room or family room. Each ad pictured a single sofa or chair and a clever headline. One ad pictured the contemporary Catalina sofa, which was distinguished by its rolled arms and curvaceous frame. It was upholstered in an animal print. The headline read, "Your Other Furniture Will Fear For Its Life." The ads featured a new tag line, "The New Look of Comfort®," and a redesigned logo.[50]

Television ads with the same theme aired beginning in 2002. Twelve 15-second television ads ran on targeted cable TV channels. Each spot pictured a La-Z-Boy® sofa or chair upholstered in a unique way. Voice-over emphasized the furniture's style and included the new tag line.[51]

John Case said the ads have always been based on research and focused on a single message, which has evolved over the years.

Every campaign was created for a reason, and, for the most part, they were very successful at either changing the perception or adding to it. I look at the current campaign as just one of [many] that have evolved. And at some point, we will feel that we really have made huge progress on the style side, and we'll do some more research and say, "OK, what is it now that we need to represent?"

The good news is that it has not been a stagnant message. It has evolved as our customer has evolved.[52]

La-Z-Boy and its subsidiaries produce furniture for every room in the home. Lea Industries manufactures this bedroom suite.

CHAPTER TEN

75 YEARS OF COMFORT

2000–2002

We have never been stronger or better positioned.

—Pat Norton, chairman, 2000

LA-Z-BOY ENTERED THE NEW millennium as the country's largest furniture maker. The recent acquisitions of Ladd, Alexvale, and Bauhaus boosted the company's sales to $2 billion and strengthened its product mix and distribution.

But in spring 2000, the U.S. economy and La-Z-Boy's growth slowed. The country's 8-year economic expansion ceased, and sales in many industries slumped.

The faltering economy hit the furniture industry hard. In 2000-2001, three major retailers went out of business. The first to go was Heilig-Meyers, in August 2000. Heilig-Meyers had started out in small towns in the Southeastern United States. During the 1990s, it had expanded into other markets and regions. From 1997 until its demise, it was ranked the largest furniture retailer in the United States.[1]

In December 2000, Montgomery Ward closed its doors after struggling for many years. The 128-year-old department store had 252 stores that sold an estimated $577 million in furniture during 2000. Its bankruptcy affected many furniture manufacturers.[2] Ward's had long been La-Z-Boy's largest customer.

Then in July 2001, HomeLife called it quits. The former Sears furniture retailer had never grown as fast as its owners hoped. At the time of its demise, HomeLife was the country's eighth-largest furniture retailer.[3]

"I think the real problem for our industry when these businesses close is not necessarily losing the dollars that they owe us, although that certainly hurts and impacts [us]," said Gregory White, vice president of merchandising.

It's that when you close 2,000 retail locations, you can't pick those up overnight. So not only are you missing the sales that you would have had in the immediate sense, but you somehow have to make up all that ground. It's not like you can say, 'Well, we're no longer going to sell HomeLife. We're going to sell somebody else.' There really is nobody else, and you've got to really start to go in and think about it. There's certainly a lot fewer places for the consumer to purchase furniture than there were. That's why the sooner we can get all of these Furniture Galleries stores open, the better off we're going to be.[4]

For La-Z-Boy, the slowdown's immediate effect was to reduce work schedules, freeze hiring, and close some facilities. Heilig-Meyers' closure severely impacted Pilliod, a promotionally priced casegoods

La-Z-Boy Chairman Pat Norton (seated) and CEO Gerald Kiser led the company into the new millennium.

maker acquired with Ladd. The chain had been Pilliod's largest customer. In September 2000, Pilliod closed its Swanton, Ohio, manufacturing plant, which employed 130 people.[5] A few months later, Pilliod closed its Selma, Alabama, plant, leaving the company with only one manufacturing plant, in Nichols, South Carolina. La-Z-Boy also closed Lea's Marion, Virginia, plant.[6]

Slowdowns in hotel, health care, and senior-living-facility remodeling resulted in declining sales in La-Z-Boy's contract business. In April 2001, La-Z-Boy discontinued production of contract casegoods at its Lincolnton, North Carolina, plant. The facility continued producing upholstered furniture. "Our Contract Division is refocusing its manufacturing and marketing strategy and placing greater emphasis on its historical strength in office and commercial seating," Gerald Kiser said.[7]

Kiser said the hardships are just part of the business cycle. "Every six to eight years, it seems like we have to go through one of these tightening-up periods. From a competitive standpoint, it's healthy, occasionally, to take a step back and to take a hard look. If there are some excesses out there, it gives you a chance to clean those up. When everything is going extremely well, and you're selling a lot of product, that covers a lot of sin.

"Most of the folks who are strong get stronger during these periods," Kiser continued. "It gives you an opportunity to gain both some competitive advantage and some market share when you come out of a downturn like this. We have to face that it's the nature of our business. During times like these, our product is a postponable purchase, and you've got to be flexible enough to deal with the downturns just like the upswings in business."[8]

Creative Flow

For 20 years, La-Z-Boy had grown faster than the rest of the furniture industry. Despite its hardships, the company was determined to stick to fundamentals. Pat Norton told investors, "If we tinker with our program and introduce gimmicks out of

desperation, we'll likely stay in our slump longer because we will confuse our consumer. In fact, we might just make things worse long-term, with only limited immediate benefit."[9]

New product introductions boosted La-Z-Boy's presence in the marketplace. In 2000, La-Z-Boy attracted a lot of media attention with its E-Cliner, a recliner equipped with a wireless keyboard used for surfing the Internet, sending e-mail, and interacting with Web TV.[10]

"We continually focus on adding innovative features to our recliners to enhance the La-Z-Boy comfort experience," said Gregory White. "This chair is the next step in our effort to be on the cutting edge of our industry without sacrificing our signature comfort." The chair came with a Sony Web TV Plus Internet Receiver keyboard and two free months of Web TV Plus interactive service.[11]

A more popular innovative product was introduced in the sleep sofa line. Called the SlumberAir mattress, the La-Z-Boy® exclusive product consisted of a 5-inch air mattress attached to the sofa bed's 4-inch innerspring mattress. The mattress inflated and deflated in 45 seconds, added extra comfort to the bed, and eliminated crossbar

The E-Cliner®, designed to be used with a laptop computer or Web TV, brought lots of media attention to La-Z-Boy.

discomfort. SlumberAir was offered as an option on all La-Z-Boy® sleep sofas.[12]

Catering to Women

In April 2001, La-Z-Boy teamed up with trend forecaster Faith Popcorn to market a line of recliners for women. Faith Popcorn Cocooning Chairs were designed specifically to fit women's lifestyles, bodies, and style preferences. Popcorn identified the concept of cocooning in 1981. It was defined as the desire to protect oneself from the harsh, unpredictable realities of the outside world by surrounding oneself with warmth, comfort, and tranquility at home.[13]

Cocooning Chairs came in two styles and featured an optional attached worktable with built-in bud vase, a tailored storage pocket on the outside of the chair, and a chenille throw. The collection was accompanied by the first La-Z-Boy® stationary chairs for children. The children's chairs matched Mom's and came with a storage ottoman and a plush throw. A portion of the proceeds from sales of the Faith Popcorn line went to charity.[14]

Teaming up with artists, designers, or pop-culture figures remained a popular trend in the furniture industry. Kincaid introduced Laura Ashley Home in April 2001. The 200-piece collection featured bedroom, dining room upholstery, and occasional pieces. American Drew introduced the Jessica McClintock Collection. McClintock was a fashion designer known for her wedding dresses and special-occasion ladies' wear. Her collection had a romantic feel and featured a wealth of carved shapes.

By 2001, American Drew had completely revised its product line. The overriding theme was to "offer a lot of look at reasonable prices," American Drew President Jack Richardson told investment analysts at a spring 2001 meeting. "Now that sounds pretty simple, but we've been able to accomplish this by going out and finding some dynamic designers to bring designs and new products to us."[15]

In October 2002, La-Z-Boy took massage to a new level when it introduced the AirSpa Massage System®. AirSpa used an air pillow system that supported the back and relieved strain on muscles, ligaments, and discs. The chair's back had two inflatable cushions, one in the lower back region and one in the middle back region. As one cushion inflated, the other deflated, providing continuous passive motion that relaxed the spine and nourished the discs.[16]

Role Changes

In July 2001, La-Z-Boy reorganized into two operating groups: Residential Upholstery and

---

Above: La-Z-Boy sleep sofas were outfitted with SlumberAir mattresses, pairing an innerspring mattress with an air mattress.

Below: Faith Popcorn Cocooning Chairs were designed for women and paired with matching children's chairs.

Residential Casegoods. John Case, president of La-Z-Boy Residential since 1999, was named president of the Upholstery Group, which included Bauhaus, Centurion, Clayton Marcus, England, HickoryMark, La-Z-Boy Residential, and Sam Moore. The La-Z-Boy Contract Furniture Group also reported to Case.[17]

Kurt Darrow was promoted to president of La-Z-Boy Residential, replacing Case. Since Darrow's appointment to vice president of sales in 1987, the annual volume of La-Z-Boy Residential had more than doubled.[18]

The transition was a comfortable one, said Case. "Residential is in very capable hands, and now I'm going to be freed up to explore how to bring this group of companies together. Part of my responsibility now is International, and I see that as a great opportunity."[19]

The acceleration of changes caused by acquisitions brought a need for new talent, Case added.

We led sales and marketing for so long. I was the marketing; Kurt was the sales. Pat gave it the overall direction. We built the store system. It was fun. It was quite a ride. But unfortunately, when you have people in place that long, you're not building. You're not bringing in new talent.

Now we've got the challenge on the residential side of bringing in some fresh, young talent. We have to be the mentors now. We have got to stop thinking of ourselves as young men, and we've got to be the ones who look and find that 27-year-old or 30-year-old down there who we can build on, just as we were given that opportunity.[20]

Don Mitchell was named president of the Casegoods Group. Mitchell had been president of the Casegoods Group of Ladd since 1996 and had more than 32 years of experience in the casegoods segment of the industry.[21] La-Z-Boy's Casegoods Group included Alexvale, American Drew, Hammary, Kincaid, Lea, Pennsylvania House, and Pilliod. American of Martinsville also reported to Mitchell.[22]

Kiser said, "The new organizational structure will allow us to capitalize on the many synergistic opportunities that exist between our companies and brands and the broad areas of marketing, manufacturing and logistics. The new management structure will also hasten the recognition and selective implementation of best practices among our companies . . . and will streamline and improve the management decision-making process throughout our entire company."[23]

Kiser cited some of the benefits of the new management structure: England had implemented systems at HickoryMark to improve scheduling, manufacturing, and delivery. American Drew and Lea had consolidated lumber handling operations. In addition, La-Z-Boy overall was working to reduce import freight and brokerage fees and leveraging purchases of raw materials to reduce costs.[24]

The companies were also cross marketing some of their products. HickoryMark produced a signature line of starting-price leather upholstery that was sold at La-Z-Boy Furniture Galleries. The Galleries also sold Kincaid and Hammary occasional tables. Sam Moore produced some Laura Ashley accent upholstery pieces for Kincaid and Alexvale and accent chairs for American of Martinsville contract

England produces stylish, affordable upholstered furniture. The company is well known for its on-time delivery.

sales. Alexvale manufactured upholstery for Kincaid and Hammary. Lea produced a La-Z-Boy Youth Collection® that was marketed at La-Z-Boy dealers.[25]

Retirements prompted additional management changes at La-Z-Boy. Secretary-Treasurer Gene Hardy retired in 2000 after 30 years with the company. Mark Stegeman was named his replacement as treasurer. He had worked as a senior audit accountant at PricewaterhouseCoopers public accounting firm, in the commercial loan area of KeyBank, and as an account vice president at Paine Webber and Salomon Smith Barney.[26]

Fritz Jackson retired in 2001 after 32 years with the company. He was succeeded by David Risley, former vice president of finance and CFO of Aeroquip-Vickers, Inc.[27]

La-Z-Boy completed the transition set in motion following Charles Knabusch's death when it named Gerald Kiser CEO in July 2001. In making the announcement, Norton said, "We are confident the experience Jerry has gained during his tenure as chief operating officer, which built on his prior successful career on the operations side of our industry, will serve him well in the future."[28]

Stegeman's confidence in La-Z-Boy's future was tied to the skill of executives past and present. "When Fritz Jackson and Gene Hardy joined the company, it was a fraction of what it is today. Those two gentlemen really provided the financial discipline and principles that enabled us to be an acquirer and not an acquiree.[29]

"I think Jerry [Kiser] is a quick study," Stegeman added. "He understands the manufacturing and distribution sides extremely well and has assembled a great team to lead us forward."[30]

La-Z-Boy gained its first woman board member in 2000 when Helen Petrauskas was elected to the board. Petrauskas had been vice president of environmental and safety engineering at Ford Motor Company. She sat on the boards of the Sherwin-Williams Company and MCN Energy Inc. and was also a member of the advisory board of the Center for Risk Analysis at the Harvard School of Public Health.[31]

New Generation of Stores

In June 2001, La-Z-Boy unveiled the next generation of La-Z-Boy Furniture Galleries. Dubbed the "New Generation" format, the stores measured 15,500 square feet, about 2,000 square feet larger than La-Z-Boy's earlier Furniture Galleries. The stores' new layout encouraged customers to follow a circular pathway around the sales floor. In the center was an updated design center with a 13-foot skylighted ceiling. The centers featured the Screen Test® video catalog and an interactive and educational play area for children. Interior signage and graphics throughout the store called attention to product categories and gave meaningful information to customers.[32]

Another notable difference was the stores' emphasis on decorative accessories, including

Above: Gerald Kiser was promoted from COO to CEO in 2001.

Below: La-Z-Boy debuted its New Generation stores in 2001. The new format boosted sales and included decorative accessories.

lamps, area rugs, and wall art. The large selection of home accents contributed to greater sales. Average sales per square foot were significantly higher in the New Generation stores. Sixteen percent of sales came from lamps, tables, and home accents, as opposed to 12 percent in the rest of the chain.[33]

"The [new] stores speak more to room environments and completing-the-whole-room sales," Darrow said. "Although we were moving in that direction already, the [older] stores still appeal to more of an item shopper."[34]

Six New Generation stores opened during the second half of 2001. Eight stores opened in Canada during 2002. "We still believe we can locate 425 to 450 stores in North America," Darrow said. Much of the growth was expected in areas where La-Z-Boy already had stores.[35]

September 11, 2001

The economy, the furniture industry, and La-Z-Boy had been in a slowdown for more than a year when the world was rocked by the devastating terrorist attacks of September 11. Americans were shocked by the events; the future now seemed even more uncertain. The economy went from bad to worse as corporate earnings, sales warnings, and job cuts increased.

Attendance was down 25 to 30 percent at the October furniture market that year. Surprisingly, La-Z-Boy collected more orders than expected at the market.[36]

Ed Breunig Jr. was an independent dealer with La-Z-Boy for nearly 20 years before selling the business to his son, Ed Breunig III. "People are spending more time at home," Breunig Jr. said. "And they are fixing up their home so that it's a better quality of life when they come home from work. They're spending more time with their neighbors. So business has been growing for Ed [III]."[37]

John Weaver, a board member since 1971, also noticed the surprising outcome. "It has been pretty solid, and I think people, as they give up travel and tend to stay home a little more, are taking a little better care of their homes. I think the future looks bright for La-Z-Boy over the coming years."[38]

Sales representative Steve Matlock called the dynamics since the attacks "truly amazing."

Due to the economic conditions, our first six months of 2001 were pretty flat. After the attacks, we had a significantly higher second half.

A couple things happened. In the last couple of years, we introduced some new concepts, and they've really been doing well. At the same time, over the last couple of years, with the tough economy, a lot of the majors, Montgomery Ward, the HomeLife stores, the Heilig-Meyers stores—that whole retail program—imploded. It evaporated. It's gone. So all of a sudden, there were [fewer] storefronts in America. Then after the September 11 tragedy, people moved back into their homes. They became more conscious of being a family, and as a result, they have spent money on a tried and true product like La-Z-Boy.[39]

On the International Front

One group of buyers noticeably absent from the October market was foreign buyers. La-Z-Boy appreciated the potential of the overseas market. It had been licensing foreign manufacturers since the 1930s. In December 2001, La-Z-Boy announced a joint venture with Steinhoff Group, one of the largest household goods manufacturers in Europe, Australia, and South Africa. Steinhoff was founded in 1964 and had more than 90 production facilities and 21,000 employees worldwide. It produced and distributed household goods in 15 countries and exported to several others.[40]

The new venture, called La-Z-Boy Europe, designed, manufactured, marketed, and distributed motion furniture in Europe. Headquartered in the Netherlands, the company was led by Steinhoff's Ralph Rengshausen and La-Z-Boy's Thomas F. Zollar.[41]

La-Z-Boy Europe produced a line of recliners specifically for the European market. Europeans preferred smaller-scale upholstery than North Americans. Their tastes were generally more contemporary. La-Z-Boy Europe accommodated different preferences in different countries. The group's first product line was introduced at the International Furniture Fair in Cologne, Germany, in January 2002.[42]

John Case was eager to look abroad.

AMERICA'S LOVE-HATE RELATIONSHIP WITH THE RECLINER

YOU WON'T FIND A LA-Z-BOY® CHAIR IN *Landmarks of Twentieth Century Design*, a pictorial handbook of 400 objects considered to be the century's best designs. But you will find it in Jane and Michael Stern's 1990 book, *The Encyclopedia of Bad Taste*, subtitled "A Celebration of American Pop Culture at Its Most Joyfully Outrageous." Yes, right there along with Hamburger Helper® and professional wrestling is the reclining chair.

What is it about reclining chairs that some people hate and others love? Designers always disliked reclining chairs, Edwin Shoemaker said in a 1986 interview.[1] Their bulky size and shape didn't fit into fashionable homes. New York interior designer Mario Buatta described them as "puffy and awful" in a 1996 *Washington Post* article.[2]

The Sterns wrote, "Their image problem was inevitable: With their heavy padding and big, blocky frames [to conceal the mechanism], recliners look oafish—suitable, at best, for the rumpus room in the basement, certainly not for company. Besides, etiquette demands that polite people sit upright while in the company of others. Lying flat on one's back in the living room, or even tilted forty-five degrees with one's feet raised in the direction of everyone else present, is good form only for invalids or babies."[3]

Recliner fans would argue that the comfy chairs are not just another piece in a tastefully decorated room. They're more than just a place to cradle your buttocks. Recliners serve a higher purpose. A recliner, those who love them will tell you, is a refuge.

Lovers of recliners speak reverently about them. Patrick Beach, of the *Austin* (Texas) *American-Statesman*, says, "To have a La-Z-Boy® recliner, preferably one of those with the side pocket for magazines and the remote, is to have a beach house in the middle of your living room—to have within walking distance a retreat. You don't sit in a La-Z-Boy . . . so much as succumb to it. To sit in a La-Z-Boy is to sit with your essence."[4]

Is there any other piece of furniture that evokes so much emotion? President of La-Z-Boy Upholstery Group John Case says, "It's not just a chair. It's someone's space. There's a great deal of emotion attached to a recliner. You can recognize it when you walk into a room and you have to ask permission to sit in that chair."[5]

Since the early 1980s, La-Z-Boy has encouraged this emotional bond with warm, homey advertising that illustrates a relationship between families and their furniture. "We wanted the consumer to make the emotional connection between La-Z-Boy and themselves," Case explained. The chair has become more than just a hunk of furniture, he added. "It's a part of their lives."[6]

Research tells us that consumers associate La-Z-Boy recliners with comfort—but not with style. Despite the fact that La-Z-Boy® furniture styles have evolved over the years and have even earned awards, the image of the stodgy recliner often persists.

"We are in a fashion business," Case concedes.[7] In 2000, La-Z-Boy took on the challenge of changing the perception that La-Z-Boy furniture is unfashionable. A television and magazine ad campaign featured hip furniture and catchy headlines that just may help La-Z-Boy overcome its stodgy image—and earn it a place as a landmark of 21st century design.

Mexico is a very undeveloped market for us. With NAFTA and everything else, we could and should have been there much stronger with the chairs.

If there's an exporting opportunity, the recliner is the primary one. When you export a sofa to other countries, it gets a little more difficult. You've got styling, cover, and cost considerations. You've got local or national manufacturers. We're going to try to sell other products from the other divisions wherever we can, but the strength will be in getting a recliner into a given marketplace. It's not as cover specific. It's not a fashion statement by most stretches, and there are some countries where there's not

that many recliners, so this is a huge opportunity for us.[43]

Case said La-Z-Boy's best international opportunity lies in manufacturing independently or with joint ventures. The company was producing recliners in Thailand by 2000. "We're exploring other joint venture opportunities with other major players," Case said.[44]

Kiser agreed. "We can't go out there and do this on our own without knowing the local market and the local culture. It would prevent us from making a successful attempt. So we think our best chance for success is to identify those parties that we would most like to join forces with us to attack some

REMARKABLE REPS

MAKING A GREAT PRODUCT IS HALF the battle. The other half is getting it out the door. The men and women who have sold La-Z-Boy® products during the last 75 years are an invaluable part of La-Z-Boy's history.

Although the brand is well known today, it wasn't always so, said retired sales representative Bill Gallagher, who started with La-Z-Boy in 1952 and worked his way up from the shipping dock. "La-Z-Boy was not well known in the 1950s," Gallagher said. "In fact, I would go into a store and say, 'I'm Bill Gallagher from La-Z-Boy,' and people would say, 'Is that a mattress line?' I could travel for a week and not sell a single piece of merchandise. It was a very hard sell. It was a very good product, but I remember selling chairs at cost for what our competitors were retailing their chairs for."[1]

The sales representatives of the past have paved the way for today's representatives. "La-Z-Boy sales representatives are among the best," said John Quinn, who retired from sales in 1998. "They are the most professional and the highest paid in the industry, which is why when somebody leaves, La-Z-Boy can go into an area and hire the absolute best rep

available . . . he's going to make more money working for La-Z-Boy."[2]

Sales reps were skeptical when Pat Norton joined the La-Z-Boy team. He had come from Ethan Allen, where commission had been replaced by salary, Quinn said. "[La-Z-Boy] sales reps are all still on commission."[3]

In 1973, Steve Matlock joined, right out of college, as an associate representative. A college football player, he was hired by one of his fans—an Arizona La-Z-Boy sales representative. Today Matlock is a top sales rep at La-Z-Boy, covering more than 30 storefronts in Arizona and Nevada. He praised Pat Norton's restructuring of La-Z-Boy's distribution system.

"Mr. Norton spent his first 20 years with Ethan Allen developing a totally exclusive retail program," Matlock said. "When he came to La-Z-Boy, he realized that our name was a more accepted name with a broader client base, and to tie it up with just an exclusive distribution didn't make much sense."[4]

The company's products are sold through La-Z-Boy Furniture Galleries (proprietary stores); general dealers, who often dedicate space within their store called a La-Z-Boy In-Store Gallery; and national accounts.

of these markets and these opportunities."[45] Competition will be high, Kiser added.

To play in the international arena, products will probably have to be manufactured in other areas of the world. With the strength of the dollar and with the labor rates in the United States today, there are countries we would find it hard to compete in.

As Asia and China and Europe and the Eastern bloc countries continue to develop, those are going to be huge market opportunities. Our direction should be finding partners in these parts of the world that would allow us to manufacture, capitalizing on local resources, and yet carrying what La-Z-Boy is known for today, which is the strength of our brand name and the strength of our marketing and proprietary programs. Seeing how that might fit in some form in these developing markets presents huge opportunities for us.[46]

Conversions and Closings

In late October 2001, La-Z-Boy closed three plants and converted two others to warehousing, subassembly, and import services. Two of the shuttered plants were casegoods facilities: American Drew's North Wilkesboro, North Carolina, plant and Lea's Waynesville, North Carolina, plant.[47]

The casegoods plants closed because La-Z-Boy and its subsidiaries, like the rest of the industry, were forced to import more and more furniture and components. Hammary, for example, once proud to be a 100 percent American-made furniture manufacturer, had begun to import most of its products. La-Z-Boy's imported casegoods tripled during 2000–2001 and were expected to increase another 50 percent during the next year. The company expected imports to make up 30 to 35 percent of total casegoods volume during 2003.[48]

"As our casegoods companies continue to increase the ratio of imported components and finished products, our manufacturing space requirements can be reduced," Kiser said. Manufacturing operations from the closed casegoods plants were shifted to other plants that were operating below capacity.[49]

The third plant to close was La-Z-Boy's Florence, South Carolina, upholstery plant. The adjacent Fabric Processing Center remained open. La-Z-Boy's

efforts to minimize redundancy in its upholstery manufacturing plants had been successful. Wood and metal operations, plywood supply, and leather cutting had been centralized. These consolidations freed up manufacturing space at other plants and brought about the closure of the Florence plant. The upholstery produced at the Florence plant was absorbed by plants in Newton, Mississippi; Lincolnton, North Carolina; and Dayton, Tennessee.[50]

Shortly after the plant closures, La-Z-Boy sold Pilliod. The subsidiary had been hit hard by the large retailer bankruptcies and weaknesses in the industry's promotional end. "The product line produced by Pilliod did not strategically align with our other product lines," Kiser said.[51] Pilliod never fit La-Z-Boy's product strategy or its image.[52]

Adding the Jazz Section

One area of La-Z-Boy's business that remained constant during the economic downturn was its advertising. "When consumers come back to the furniture stores in earnest, we want them to be

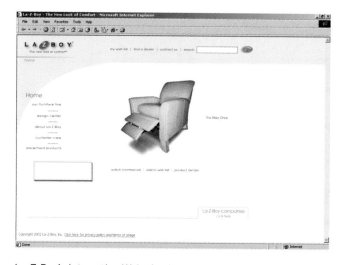

La-Z-Boy's interactive Web site (above) debuted in 2001. It allowed clients to view pieces in a variety of fabrics. La-Z-Boy launched a stylish ad campaign in 2000 that featured the tagline "The new look of comfort®" and a redesigned logo (top).

thinking of La-Z-Boy and La-Z-Boy brands," Kiser underscored.[53]

La-Z-Boy launched a bold print advertising campaign in fall 2000 that emphasized its furniture's style and appealed to younger customers, particularly women. The ads, which appeared in fashion and shelter magazines, told consumers that La-Z-Boy offered stylish furniture and more than recliners. Each ad featured a single sofa or chair and a clever headline. One ad pictured the Panache sofa upholstered in plum chenille with bold-patterned pillows. The headline read, "We thought it was about time furniture had a jazz section." The ads also featured a redesigned logo.[54]

The campaign extended to television in 2001. Twelve 15- and 30-second television ads ran on targeted cable TV channels. Each spot pictured a La-Z-Boy® sofa or chair upholstered in a unique way. Voice-over emphasized the furniture's style and included the new tagline, "The New Look of Comfort.®"[55]

La-Z-Boy's marketing also included a redesigned Web site that allowed customers to view furniture in the fabric of their choice. Using technology similar to the in-store Screen Test® video catalog system, the Web site allowed consumers to pair a chair or sofa frame with a fabric. During the interactive site's first four months, 100,000 unique visitors logged on to the site per month, versus 40,000 in previous months. The average customer stayed on the site 15 minutes, versus 4 minutes on the previous site.[56] The site also included an improved dealer locator.

La-Z-Boy is developing plans to use Internet technology to create an even closer one-on-one relationship with its customers. According to

THE INDEPENDENT DEALER

LA-Z-BOY® FURNITURE HAS FOUND ITS WAY into people's homes all around the world. But not everyone goes into a La-Z-Boy Furniture Galleries store to find it. Independent dealers have been marketing La-Z-Boy® goods for decades.

Irv Blumkin, president of Nebraska Furniture, said his store had done business with La-Z-Boy for nearly 50 years, since his father, Louie, led the company. Most independent dealers choose to sell the brand for the same reason: name recognition. "I've grown up in the furniture business, and La-Z-Boy has certainly been the most influential name brand," Blumkin said.[1]

"La-Z-Boy is always way, way far ahead of anybody else when it comes to name recognition," said Ken Larson, president of Slumberland Furniture. "There really isn't someone even close. La-Z-Boy has clearly emerged, especially over the last decade, as the leader in the whole furniture business."[2]

Most dealers sell the breadth of La-Z-Boy® home products: recliners, motion upholstery, leather, stationary sofas, and sleepers, and they say the popularity and variety of the brand draw customers from across the board. "La-Z-Boy has a tremendous reputation," Blumkin said. "We try to devote a lot of space to the brand because of its value and because it satisfies customers."[3]

But selling La-Z-Boy is also satisfying to the dealers themselves. "The thing that comes to mind when I think about La-Z-Boy is the tremendous integrity and honesty in dealing with the people," Blumkin said. "We closed many deals on handshakes. It's really a pleasure when you can talk in terms of doing business with a company for 30, 40, 50 years and still have that personal relationship and feel confident. As big a company as it is, you still have the relationships with the people who still understand and have the drive and the passion for the business."[4]

Bill Child, chairman of the board at R. C. Willey Home Furnishings, said his company, with 11 stores in Salt Lake City, Boise, and Las Vegas, had dealt with La-Z-Boy for at least 45 of his 49 years, with 11 stores in. "They're just wonderful friends," Child said, "and they're one of our very best vendors."[5]

Doug Collier, vice president of marketing for the Residential Division since April 2002, "When a customer buys a product from a La-Z-Boy dealer, we want to begin, literally, a lifelong relationship and dialogue with that consumer."[57]

The Next Generation

The recession took its toll on La-Z-Boy sales, although the company continued to outpace the industry. Fiscal 2001 sales were down about 1 percent, still stronger than the rest of the industry. Casegoods were down about 8 percent, residential upholstery was up about 1 percent, and contract sales declined 11 percent.[58]

Throughout the recession, La-Z-Boy Furniture Galleries produced greater sales gains than the rest of the industry. The Galleries' 2000 sales increased

Like its parent company, Kincaid markets its furniture through proprietary stores. Kincaid Home Furnishings stores debuted in 1999.

Operator and franchiser of nearly 75 stores in eight states, Larson said Slumberland Furniture started in 1967 as a sleep shop. A weak winter business cycle pushed the company to look for a strong product to add to its floors. "We knew after researching it that the product cycle for reclining chairs was very strong during that time," Larson said. "Back then it didn't take a lot of space to show reclining chairs. So our small store format worked very well with that."[6]

La-Z-Boy, of course, was the best-known name in recliners, and thus began the relationship between the two companies. It was a perfect match. "Our values and our culture line up very, very well with La-Z-Boy's," Larson said.[7]

Larson was not the only one who boosted profits by adding La-Z-Boy® products to his showrooms. "The La-Z-Boy line of products is definitely one of our top lines in the furniture area and one of our most profitable lines overall," Child said. "We were lucky to get the line."[8]

Art Van Elslander, president and CEO of Art Van Furniture, oversaw 30 stores across Michigan. The company began carrying La-Z-Boy in the late 1960s. "We felt the name La-Z-Boy, which was so very, very strong, particularly here in Michigan, was necessary to have," Van Elslander said. "We have enjoyed the sales and the line ever since."[9]

There are many benefits to being an independent dealer of La-Z-Boy products, Van Elslander added. "It has been a tremendous relationship. They're a real quality line. Also, it's a line that people recognize very quickly. And the relationship with Pat has been really one that I cherish very deeply."[10]

It is common for dealers to mention La-Z-Boy Chairman Pat Norton. "Pat Norton is a great teacher, and if you listen well, there are a lot of lessons and knowledge in all of what he tells you," Blumkin said.[11]

"La-Z-Boy has been very instrumental in our success, and we count Pat Norton as one of our best friends," Child said. "La-Z-Boy has far-sightedness—I suspect that Pat had something to do with that. He is a very visionary man.

"When we first met him, I think we were a little intimidated," Child added. "But he became a mentor. He was a sounding board for us. We always seemed to go to him for advice. And it was free—much better than a consultant. He can read people extremely well. He'll tell you in a hurry who's going to be successful and who isn't. He's got a knack. He's kind of the Warren Buffett of the furniture industry."[12]

4.7 percent.[59] With $743.7 million in annual sales, La-Z-Boy Furniture Galleries were the second-largest single-source furniture network in the country, behind only Ethan Allen's $1.19 billion network.[60] The 287 La-Z-Boy Furniture Galleries represented 4 million square feet of space.

In-store galleries accounted for another 2 million square feet.[61] La-Z-Boy upgraded its in-store galleries in 2000, offering its dealers improved graphics and signage as well as layout assistance to maximize floor space. La-Z-Boy's 319 in-store galleries generated 16 percent of La-Z-Boy's revenues.[62]

La-Z-Boy subsidiaries also experimented with stores and in-store galleries. Kincaid had 172 in-store galleries and eight Kincaid Home Furnishings stores. Pennsylvania House had 262 in-store galleries and 12 freestanding stores. Clayton Marcus had 243 in-store galleries. England/Corsair, which shortened its name to England in 2001, had 51 in-store galleries, called Custom Comfort Centers, and was beginning to open gallery stores. Lea had 315 Kids Generation in-store galleries and was test marketing a La-Z-Boy Youth Collection® in La-Z-Boy dealers. Sam Moore also opened in-store galleries.[63]

By spring 2002, evidence began to hint that the economic slump had bottomed out and furniture industry sales would improve, especially in the upholstery area. Casegoods, it seemed, were still lagging and faced increasing competition from imports. Layoffs from the plant closures, combined with attrition and a hiring freeze, resulted in reductions of 3,200 jobs and 2.5 million square feet of floor space between October 2000 and February 2002.[64]

Looking to the Future

Gallery owner Paul Opfermann saw tremendous opportunity ahead. "I think the momentum, particularly in the recent past, has shown that the potential of the Furniture Galleries program is starting to be realized. The program itself is a much higher profile—more people are interested in getting involved and investing—and La-Z-Boy corporate seems to be concentrating more and more of [its] resources internally in developing the Furniture Galleries program to a higher level. I think things are going to happen."[65]

John Quinn said the company's depth of research has laid a strong foundation for its future.

La-Z-Boy has obviously done a good job of determining the ultimate consumer's needs. I can tell you that there are not a lot of firms that do this. La-Z-Boy has always tried to figure out what the consumer wants and let us make it. Then, through our proprietary stores, let us display it well, sell it well, and price it well, and we'll be successful.

I guess it was Franklin Roosevelt who said the only thing to fear is fear itself, and in La-Z-Boy's case, the only thing they have to fear is becoming complacent and not getting the job done, because no one is going to take it away from them.[66]

Gallery owner Ed Breunig III looked forward to converting his stores to the latest format.

"The style and the look of the new store is just fantastic, and the increase in sales has been unbelievable," he said. Breunig recalled his family's relationship with the La-Z-Boy team.

One thing that La-Z-Boy has done is work on not just product but people. As we do competitive research, we know that our people have to be the best educated and the sharpest in the business if we're going to win the consumer. So commitment to training and keeping our people on top of their game is the other difference outside of the fact that La-Z-Boy has done such a great job with the product.

It's an absolute pleasure to be involved with a company that is constantly looking at the business for improvement in every area. They are always looking for the areas of weakness and the areas of strength and trying to improve on them. We've had an incredible experience with all the people from La-Z-Boy. It's obviously worked hard—or maybe it's the people they've got in the organization. It has a small community feel even though it's grown to the size it is today.[67]

Darrow looks forward to navigating the company through changes without losing the principles sown by the founders. "The shadow that Mr. Knabusch and Mr. Shoemaker cast over this company is pretty large," Darrow said. "They put doing things right and treating people fairly above profit. There's a culture here that I hope we don't lose. Pat was the first non-family-member chairman ever at La-Z-Boy, and he takes that very seriously. He works to keep the culture and the integrity of the company in place."[68]

Sales representative Steve Matlock recalled a day when La-Z-Boy was a product-driven company. "We spent most of our time learning and selling product, whereas today, it's a marketing-driven company," he said. "We're more of a consultant to the retailer than a liaison to La-Z-Boy. When I started, we were product salesmen. It's as different as night and day."[69]

The biggest change came in 1981, when Pat Norton came aboard, Matlock recalled.

He started to build our proprietary retail system. I still remember his speech to the sales force in March 1981. He said, "Look to the left and look to the right because not everybody is going to make this journey. We'd like everybody to go, but unfortunately, not everybody is going to be able to adapt to the changes that need to take place in order to build a strong, proprietary retail system. And in that system, you have to become a partner with your retailer, and that's going to include a lot more work and attention to things."

Now we've developed a retail furniture gallery system that's the best retail furniture chain in America. It's growing like crazy. Pat has an unbelievable leadership quality—one I've never seen in any man. At 80, he exudes integrity. But at the same time, he's just Pat. He's just a great guy.[70]

But Pat Norton passed the credit on to what he calls the heart and soul of La-Z-Boy: founders Knabusch and Shoemaker. "It's just fortunate that I came in long enough ago that I got to know these men and what made them tick. A lot of people don't understand the difference between this company and [others in the industry]. It's the charisma and the principles that these men laid down on the table."[71]

Norton added that the goodness of the company deserves as much credit as its marketing and manufacturing abilities. "Everybody in the industry respects us. All the vendors want to sell La-Z-Boy because La-Z-Boy is honest in the way they deal."[72]

And Norton feels it is important to maintain the historical values of the company as the team builds for the future.

We have all kinds of people out there building chairs and dressers, and unfortunately, they don't really understand, and it's a shame. At one time, most of the people here worked 10 or 15 years with [Shoemaker and Knabusch]. They took that message out to the field, and you could feel it in the plants. There was a pride, and it's hard to maintain that same pride today.

When Ed Shoemaker was 80 and living in Phoenix, he would go in some of the local stores and look at the chairs and see if they were OK. He'd tell the man in the back room how to fix them if they weren't. It was his life. Those are the things that make this company great, and I've always said that to be able to spend 20 years at La-Z-Boy—one of the greatest companies in the industry—that's a blessing. It's been a hell of a trip.[73]

President and CEO Gerald Kiser, left, and Chairman of the Board Pat Norton guide the La-Z-Boy team into the future and predict many more years of success.

THE NEXT CHAPTER

TODAY, THE MEN AND WOMEN OF LA-Z-BOY are writing the next chapter in an extraordinary story that began 75 years ago, when cousins Edwin Shoemaker and Edward Knabusch introduced what would become an American icon: the La-Z-Boy® recliner.

The Monroe, Michigan, men gave birth to an enterprise that today circles the globe. In fact, no matter where you go—whether in the United States, Canada, Mexico, Europe, Asia, New Zealand, South Africa, or even Thailand—there's a good chance La-Z-Boy will be there too.

Through years of ingenuity, hard work, and strategic acquisitions, the company now offers furniture for every room of the home, as well as business, healthcare, and hospitality settings— all with the comfort, quality, and style synonymous with the La-Z-Boy name.

By marshaling the powers of imagination and hard work, successive generations of La-Z-Boy people have pushed the frontiers of furniture with innovative designs. The same ingenuity that drove its founders to make and market the recliner later inspired the company to build a network of La-Z-Boy Furniture Galleries, helping to make La-Z-Boy a household name.

In the years to come, La-Z-Boy will continue to strive toward its goal of bringing La-Z-Boy comfort, quality, and style to as many people as possible by introducing exciting new furniture and expanding its distribution—both domestically and abroad. Soon much more of the world will be able to enjoy the unparalleled comfort of La-Z-Boy® furniture.

Yes, a lot has changed at La-Z-Boy over the years. The little furniture company started in a garage by "two guys named Ed" has grown into the nation's largest manufacturer of upholstered furniture, as well as the world's leading producer of reclining chairs, selling twice as many recliners as its closest competitor. And the company has no plans to kick its feet up and relax.

As outstanding as La-Z-Boy's achievements have been in the last 75 years, its prospects today are even brighter. The greatness of its past is exceeded only by the promise of the future. The pioneering spirit that has characterized the company for so many years will go on, as new furniture is developed and evaluated to meet the changing needs of consumers.

But don't expect La-Z-Boy to stray too far from its roots. Growth and success in the future will continue to be driven by the same values that made the first chair possible—a passion for innovation and a dedication to producing quality, comfortable, stylish furniture.

La-Z-Boy is more than a furniture company; it is a living force in American culture, and its history of products reflects the evolution of our lifestyles. It has mastered the art of making homes out of our houses and bringing comfort into our lives.

NOTES TO SOURCES

Chapter One

1. Thomas E. O'Neil and Alice A. O'Neil, "The Custers of Monroe," Monroe County Library System, 1991 (accessed at http://monroe.lib.mi.us, 10 October 2001).
2. Edwin Shoemaker, interviewed by Charlotte Kumler, 1970, La-Z-Boy archive.
3. Suzy Farbman and Stuart Hanger, "From Little Wood Slats to Fashion Giant," *Home Furnishings Daily*, 26 October 1967, 6.
4. "The Growth of An Empire," *Monroe Evening News*, 27 May 1974.
5. "They Work to Make You Lazy," *Inside Michigan*, July 1952, 30.
6. Ibid.
7. Edwin Shoemaker, interview, Kumler.
8. "They Work to Make You Lazy," 30.
9. Edwin Shoemaker, interview, Kumler.
10. Ibid.
11. "From a Cornfield in 1927 . . . ," *La-Z-News*, October/November 1970.
12. Edwin Shoemaker, interview, Kumler.
13. Farbman and Hanger, "From Little Wood Slats," 6.
14. "Off the Farm, into Fame: It Takes Hard Work To Make a Career out of Relaxing," *The La-Z-Boy Golden Times*, 1979, 2.
15. Dale Shoemaker, interviewed by Richard F. Hubbard, tape recording, 6 February 2002, Write Stuff Enterprises.
16. "They Work to Make You Lazy," 30.
17. "How International Furniture Empire Grew," *Monroe Evening News*, 27 May 1974.
18. "From a Cornfield."
19. *La-Z-Boy: Making History Since 1927*, (La-Z-Boy Inc., 1999), 4.
20. Edwin Shoemaker, interviewed by Dennis M. Au, 22 June 94, transcript, 18, La-Z-Boy archive.
21. Notes of Edwin Shoemaker, La-Z-Boy archive.
22. Edwin Shoemaker, interview, Kumler.
23. "Built It with Own Hands," *Monroe Evening News*, 31 December 1927.
24. Ibid.
25. Farbman and Hanger, "From Little Wood Slats," 6.
26. "Did You Know?" Floral City Furniture Company advertisement, *Monroe Evening News*, 1928.
27. Farbman and Hanger, "From Little Wood Slats," 6.
28. "La-Z-Boy Chair Sales Force Local Plant Expansion," *Monroe Evening News*, 1940.
29. "It Takes Hard Work," *The La-Z-Boy Golden Times*, 2.
30. Ray Helmers, "Builders of the Industry: Knabusch & Shoemaker," *Upholstering Today*, August 1984, 6, La-Z-Boy archive.
31. Edwin Shoemaker, interviewed by Judith Carr, transcript, September 1986.
32. Helmers, "Builders of the Industry," 6.
33. "How International Furniture Empire Grew."
34. "Furniture Company Expanding Rapidly in Local Factory," *Monroe Evening News*, 31 December 1928; and notes of Edwin Shoemaker.
35. "A Beautiful Present for Your Little Girl," Floral City Furniture Company advertisement, *Monroe Evening News*, n.d.
36. Helmers, "Builders of the Industry," 6.
37. Edwin Shoemaker, interview, Carr.
38. Ibid.
39. "Furniture Company Expanding Rapidly."
40. Ibid.
41. Ibid.
42. Edwin Shoemaker, interview, Au, 151.
43. "They Work to Make You Lazy," 31.
44. Fall Price List, July 1929.
45. "Furniture Company Expanding Rapidly."
46. "Floral Concern Reorganized Here," *Monroe Evening News*, 9 April 1929; and Meeting Minutes of the Floral City Furniture Company Board of Directors, 3 April 1929.

47. "Howard M. Comstock, City Pharmacist, Dies," *Monroe Evening News,* 24 March 1949.
48. Edwin Shoemaker, interview, Au, 27.
49. "They Work to Make You Lazy," 31.
50. "New La-Z-Boy Chair Is a Real Sensation in the Market," Market newsletter, Grand Rapids, July 1930.
51. "Built It with Own Hands."

Chapter Two

1. "The First Decade and the Big Decision," *La-Z-News,* January/February 1971.
2. Edwin Shoemaker, interview, Carr.
3. "Kroehler Buys Luce Company," *Furniture World,* 16 January 1930, 97.
4. Edwin Shoemaker, interview, Au, 213–214.
5. "La-Z-Boy Specialist in Reclining Comfort," *Furniture South,* March 1956.
6. "The First Decade."
7. Remarks by E. M. Knabusch to John Blair of Harness, Dickey & Pierce, 25 January 1980.
8. Edwin Shoemaker, interview, Au, 30–31.
9. Edwin Shoemaker, interview, Carr.
10. Remarks by E. M. Knabusch to John Blair.
11. Special Meeting Minutes of the Floral City Furniture Company Board of Directors, 13 September 1930.
12. Edwin Shoemaker, interview, Carr.
13. Ibid.
14. Ibid.
15. "La-Z-Boy Chair Sales Force Local Plant Expansion."
16. Edwin Shoemaker, interview, Au, 111.
17. Ibid., 31.
18. E. M. Knabusch, "History of Our Retail Business," *La-Z-News & Floral Views,* November 1943.
19. Edward Knabusch, interviewed by Charlotte Kumler, 1970.
20. "How International Furniture Empire Grew."
21. *La-Z-News & Floral Views,* June 1945.
22. Floral City Furniture Company advertisement, *Monroe Evening News,* 11 May 1933.
23. E. M. Knabusch, "History of Our Retail Business."
24. Ibid.
25. "They Work to Make You Lazy," 33.
26. "The First Decade."
27. Floral City Furniture Income Tax Forms, 1932, 1933, 1934.
28. "The First Decade."
29. "Floral City Co. Enlarges Plant," *Monroe Evening News,* 1935.
30. "The First Decade."
31. Helmers, "Builders of the Industry," 6.
32. Herman Gertz, interviewed by Judith Carr, transcript, September 1986, La-Z-Boy archive.
33. Betty Lou White, interviewed by Richard F. Hubbard, tape recording, 14 February 2002, Write Stuff Enterprises.
34. "Monroe Concern Makes Progress," *Monroe Evening News,* 14 December 1937.
35. Edwin Shoemaker, interview, Carr.
36. "La-Z-Boy Chair Sales Force Local Plant Expansion."
37. "Floral City Will Manufacture Here," *Monroe Evening News,* January 1940.
38. "La-Z-Boy Chair Sales Force Local Plant Expansion."
39. *La-Z-News & Floral Views,* June 1945.
40. "President's Annual Report to Stockholders," Floral City Furniture Company Annual Report, 1939.
41. "Floral City Firm Votes Expansion," *Monroe Evening News,* 22 January 1941.
42. "Growth of An Empire."
43. "New Chair Plant Holds Open House," *Monroe Evening News,* 25 November 1941.
44. Ibid.
45. "Bigger La-Z-Boy Plant Called 'Most Modern,'" source unknown, 7 January 1942.
46. "Popularity of Chair Creates Large Back Log of Orders," *La-Z-News & Floral Views,* 2 December 1941.
47. Employee newsletter.
48. La-Z-Boy Annual Report, 26 January 1942.

Chapter Three

1. "January Furniture Market," *La-Z-News & Floral Views,* 16 January 1942.
2. La-Z-Boy Annual Report, 26 January 1942.
3. La-Z-Boy Annual Report, 23 June 1943.
4. "Present Situation at La-Z-Boy Factory," *La-Z-News & Floral Views,* March 1943.
5. "Continual Changes in War Work," *La-Z-News & Floral Views,* June 1943.
6. "La-Z-Boy Making Post-War Plans," *Monroe Evening News,* 16 May 1944.
7. "Changes in War Work," *La-Z-News & Floral Views.*
8. Gertz, interview.
9. "'Production Is Our Motto,'" *La-Z-News & Floral Views,* July 1943.
10. "Victory Gardens," *La-Z-News and Floral Views,* April 1943.
11. "New Government Rulings Make a Few Articles Available," *La-Z-News & Floral Views,* 26 June 1942.
12. Minutes of the Annual Meeting of Stockholders of the La-Z-Boy Chair Company, 21 May 1945.
13. "Chicago Furniture Market," *La-Z-News & Floral Views,* July 1943.
14. Gertz, interview.
15. Ibid.
16. Ibid.
17. Ibid.
18. Edwin Shoemaker, interview, Au, 52–55.
19. Minutes of the Board of Directors of La-Z-Boy Chair Company, 21 May 1945.
20. Ibid.
21. Minutes of the Board of Directors of La-Z-Boy Chair Company, 24 May 1948.
22. "Furniture Firm Has Open House After Enlarging," *Monroe Evening News,* 9 October 1946.
23. "Giant Roadside Store," *Lighting & Lamps,* January 1950.
24. Edwin Shoemaker, interview, Au, 27.
25. "La-Z-Boy Adds a New Department," *La-Z-News & Floral Views,* October 1946.
26. Ibid.

27. "A Visit with La-Z-Boy,"
La-Z-Brochure sales aid, 1952.
28. Minutes of the Board of Directors
of La-Z-Boy Chair Company,
22 May 1950.
29. "Two Decades of Chair-Making
Produce 80,000 La-Z-Boys,"
Monroe Evening News,
10 April 1948.
30. Jim Waltz, interviewed by
Richard F. Hubbard,
tape recording,
18 June 2002,
Write Stuff Enterprises.
31. Ibid.
32. Minutes of the Board of Directors
of La-Z-Boy Chair Company,
19 May 1947.
33. Betty Lou White, interview.
34. Minutes of the Board of Directors
of La-Z-Boy Chair Company,
25 May 1953.
35. Minutes, Board of Directors,
La-Z-Boy, 21 May 1945.
36. Minutes, Board of Directors,
La-Z-Boy, 28 May 1956.
37. Minutes, Board of Directors,
La-Z-Boy, 25 May 1959.
38. Minutes, Board of Directors,
La-Z-Boy, 24 May 1948.
39. Gertz, interview.
40. "Otto C. Uecker, 46,
Dies in Home,"
Monroe Evening News, 1950.
41. Minutes of the Board of Directors
of La-Z-Boy Chair Company,
26 May 1952.
42. Minutes, Board of Directors,
La-Z-Boy, 25 May 1953.
43. Minutes of the Board of Directors
of La-Z-Boy Chair Company,
27 May 1957.
44. "Big Profit News . . . La-Z-Boy
Vibrator Chairs!" Letter from
Walter S. Marder to La-Z-Boy
dealers, 16 April 1957.
45. Dale Shoemaker, interview.
46. Minutes, Board of Directors,
La-Z-Boy, 24 May 1948.
47. "Nadeau Named
Advertising Official,"
Monroe Evening News, n.d.
48. Minutes, Board of Directors,
La-Z-Boy, 25 May 1953.
49. Minutes, Board of Directors,
La-Z-Boy, 24 May 1948.
50. "Don't Dream Money . . . Make It!,"
sales training aid, La-Z-Boy Chair
Company, 1950.

51. Minutes of the Board of Directors
of La-Z-Boy Chair Company,
23 May 1955.
52. "La-Z-Boy on Club 60 TV Show,"
La-Z-Boy Market News,
September 1957.
53. "La-Z-Boy on 'Big Payoff' TV
Program Starting Feb. 17,"
La-Z-Boy Sales Tales,
February 1958.
54. "La-Z-Boy Officials Will Auction
Mink-Upholstered, $600 Chair,"
Monroe Evening News,
10 January 1959.
55. Minutes, Board of Directors,
La-Z-Boy, 25 May 1959.
56. "Visit with La-Z-Boy."
57. Minutes, Board of Directors,
La-Z-Boy, 27 May 1957.
58. Minutes, Board of Directors,
La-Z-Boy, 23 May 1955.
59. Minutes, Board of Directors,
La-Z-Boy, 28 May 1956.
60. Minutes of the Board of Directors
of La-Z-Boy Chair Company,
23 May 1960.
61. "Brueckner Quits La-Z-Boy Post,"
Monroe Evening News,
16 December 1969.

Chapter Four

1. "The Story of Newton," Supplement
to *La-Z-News,* n.d.
2. Edwin Shoemaker, interview,
Au, 218.
3. Ibid.
4. Minutes of the Board of Directors
of La-Z-Boy Chair Company,
12 June 1961.
5. Richard Micka, interviewed by
Jeffrey L. Rodengen, tape
recording, 17 August 2001,
Write Stuff Enterprises.
6. "Story of Newton."
7. Ibid.
8. Minutes, Board of Directors,
La-Z-Boy, 12 June 1961.
9. Ibid.
10. "McLeod, 91,
Former La-Z-Boy Foreman, Dies,"
Monroe Evening News,
3 November 1997.
11. "La-Z-Boy Chair Makes Shifts,"
Monroe Evening News, n.d.
12. "The Man at the Helm, Dewey
Turner," in "The Story of Newton,"
n.d., 6.
13. Dale Shoemaker, interview.

14. Minutes of the Board of Directors
of La-Z-Boy Chair Company,
4 June 1962.
15. La-Z-Boy Annual Report, 1964.
16. La-Z-Boy Annual Report, 1963.
17. Ibid.
18. La-Z-Boy Annual Report, 1964.
19. "La-Z-Boy President Announces
New Appointments,"
Newton Record,
25 August 1965.
20. "Key Men Sent to Train Work
Force," *Redlands Daily Facts,*
19 September 1966.
21. Ibid.
22. Courtney Leckler, interviewed by
Richard F. Hubbard,
tape recording, 26 June 2002,
Write Stuff Enterprises.
23. Kathi Stiefel, interviewed by
Jeffrey L. Rodengen,
tape recording, 12 June 2002,
Write Stuff Enterprises.
24. Edwin Shoemaker, interview,
Au, 232.
25. "La-Z-Boy Takes Over
Furniture Industries Today,"
Florence Morning News,
12 August 1966.
26. "Portrait of Florence," *La-Z-News,*
fall/winter 1971–72.
27. Minutes of the Board of Directors
of La-Z-Boy Chair Company,
7 June 1965.
28. La-Z-Boy Annual Report, 1967.
29. Gene Hardy, interviewed by
Richard F. Hubbard, tape
recording, 21 June 2002,
Write Stuff Enterprises.
30. Ibid.
31. La-Z-Boy Annual Report, 1967.
32. "La-Z-Boy Lists New Executives,"
Monroe Evening News, n.d.
33. Ibid.
34. "Betsy Palmer Joins Forces with
La-Z-Boy for Television
Advertising," *Furniture World,*
14 August 1969; and La-Z-Boy
Annual Report, 1969.
35. "La-Z-Boy Sets Spot for 'Tonight'
Show," *Home Furnishings Daily,*
26 September 1968.
36. "La-Z-Boy Chair Company
Specialists in Action Seating,"
Furniture World, 1 July 1969.
37. Ibid.
38. La-Z-Boy Annual Report, 1966.
39. Alfred DeBat, "La-Z-Boy Chair
Succeeds as Rocker-Recliner

Specialist," *Furniture Design & Manufacturing,* July 1968, 39.

40. Micka, interview.
41. "La-Z-Boy Announces the New 'Mini-Pak' Carton . . . A Packaging Breakthrough," *American Furniture Mart Daily,* 19 June 1968, 17; and DeBat, "La-Z-Boy Chair Succeeds," 39.
42. La-Z-Boy Annual Report, 1969.
43. "'The Sofette' . . . Created by Public Demand," La-Z-Boy promotional brochure, n.d.
44. Floral City Furniture Company Annual Report, 1967.
45. Floral City Furniture Company Annual Report, 1969.
46. Alice Vagt, interviewed by Richard F. Hubbard, tape recording, 1 July 2002, Write Stuff Enterprises.
47. Hardy, interview.
48. Ibid.
49. Rita Van Pelt, "'The Good Life' Is Evident in Show's Recliner Sales," *Home Furnishings Daily,* 17 July 1969; and "La-Z-Boy Contracts in Mobile Home Field," *Monroe Evening News,* n.d.
50. La-Z-Boy Annual Report, 1969.
51. "5,350 Companies = A Mixed-up Furniture Industry," *Fortune,* February 1967, 145.
52. La-Z-Boy Annual Report, 1964.
53. La-Z-Boy Annual Report, 1969.
54. "La-Z-Boy Contracts in Mobile Home Field."

Chapter Five

1. Judith Carr, interviewed by Jeffrey L. Rodengen, tape recording, 17 August 2001, Write Stuff Enterprises.
2. Ibid.
3. Ibid.
4. Betty Lou White, interview.
5. Carr, interview, Rodengen.
6. Ibid.
7. La-Z-Boy Annual Report, 1970.
8. La-Z-Boy Annual Report, 1971.
9. La-Z-Boy Annual Report, 1973.
10. Fritz Jackson, interviewed by Richard F. Hubbard, tape recording, 4 February 2002, Write Stuff Enterprises.
11. La-Z-Boy Annual Reports, 1972 and 1970.
12. La-Z-Boy Annual Report, 1970.

13. La-Z-Boy Annual Report, 1972.
14. La-Z-Boy Annual Report, 1970.
15. La-Z-Boy Annual Report, 1972.
16. "La-Z-Boy Strengthens Bid for Greater Contract Sales," *Contract,* June 1972, 1.
17. "Doctors, Patients Cheer Special Recliners," *The La-Z-Boy Golden Times,* 1978.
18. "La-Z-Boy Markets New Mobile Base," *La-Z-News,* winter/spring 1974.
19. "La-Z-Boy Adds New Low-Style Chairs to Line: Hi-Lo and Swivel Rocker in Production," *La-Z-News,* fall 1973.
20. Ibid.
21. Ibid.
22. "La-Z-Boy Lists News Appointees," *Monroe Evening News,* n.d.
23. Letter from W. C. Knake to United Furniture Workers of America, AFL-CIO, Monroe Local 416, 8 April 1971.
24. Minutes of the Board of Directors of La-Z-Boy Chair Company, 29 September 1971.
25. "Return to Work at La-Z-Boy Chair Is Scheduled Friday," *Monroe Evening News,* 5 October 1971.
26. "Dateline Dayton," *La-Z-News,* winter 1973; and " La-Z-Boy Tennessee," *La-Z-News,* winter/spring 1974.
27. "La-Z-Boy Tennessee," *La-Z-News,* spring/summer 1972.
28. Ibid.
29. "New Plant Acquired in Siloam Springs for Production of La-Z-Rocker," *La-Z-News,* fall 1973.
30. "La-Z-Boy Dedicates Siloam Springs, Arkansas, Plant," *La-Z-News,* September/October 1974.
31. La-Z-Boy Annual Report, 1971.
32. "Welcome to La-Z-Boy Chair Company," script for plant tour, 4 April 1972.
33. La-Z-Boy Annual Reports, 1971 and 1973.
34. La-Z-Boy Annual Report, 1973.
35. "Investments in Conservation Paying Quick Dividends in Factory Savings," *La-Z-Boy Golden Times,* 1973.
36. La-Z-Boy Annual Report, 1975.
37. La-Z-Boy Annual Report, 1978.
38. "La-Z-Boy Saves on Fabric Cost with Computer-Controlled Central Warehousing & Distribution,"

Furniture Production Magazine, July 1976, 16.
39. "La-Z-Boy Dedicates Fabric Processing Center," *La-Z-News,* March 1975.
40. Ibid.
41. Floral City Furniture Company Annual Report, 1973.
42. "Floral City Furniture Co. Nearing End of Liquidation Sale," *La-Z-News,* September/October 1974.
43. Lloyd White, interviewed by Jeffrey L. Rodengen, tape recording, 7 June 2002, Write Stuff Enterprises.
44. Vagt, interview.
45. Ibid.
46. "Motion Chair Makers Compete in Billion $ Retail Market," *Furniture/Today,* 25 July–1 August, 1977.
47. "Sleeper Joins La-Z-Boy Line," *Monroe Evening News,* 14 February 1977.
48. La-Z-Boy Annual Report, 1978.
49. "La-Z-Boy Doesn't Always Speak for Itself," *The La-Z-Boy Golden Times,* 1978.
50. La-Z-Boy Annual Report, 1977.
51. "More Independent Stores Add La-Z-Boy Name to Logo," *Home Furnishings Daily,* 9 December 1975.
52. John Case, interviewed by Jeffrey L. Rodengen, tape recording, 17 August 2001, Write Stuff Enterprises.
53. La-Z-Boy Annual Report, 1976.
54. "La-Z-Boy Shoppe Has Last Laugh," *Retailing Home Furnishings,* 9 August 1976.
55. "La-Z-Sleeper, 'Super Chair' to Debut at Market," *Furniture/Today,* 19–26 September 1977.
56. "La-Z-Boy Shoppe Has Last Laugh."
57. Ibid.
58. Paul Opfermann, interviewed by Richard F. Hubbard, tape recording, 14 February 2002, Write Stuff Enterprises.
59. "Not an Easy Decision," *La-Z-News,* November 1978.
60. Ibid.
61. "'Big Red' Schroeder," *Retailing Home Furnishings.*

62. Ibid.
63. Carr, interview, Rodengen.
64. Ibid.
65. La-Z-Boy News Release,
17 May 1978.
66. Bill Gallagher, interviewed by
Richard F. Hubbard,
tape recording,
26 February 2002,
Write Stuff Enterprises.
67. "Welcome Aboard La-Z-Boy
Canada Ltd.," *La-Z-News*,
March 1979.
68. La-Z-Boy Annual Report, 1979.
69. Ibid.
70. "Manor Death Stuns La-Z-Boy,"
La-Z-News, December 1979.
71. "Recliners Come of Age,"
Furniture/Today 20th Anniversary
Edition, 9 September 1996, 51.

Chapter Six

1. "Top Players Sitting Taller in
Reclining Chair Arena,"
Furniture/Today, 4 August 1986.
2. "Furniture Wizard to Guide
La-Z-Boy," *Furniture/Today*,
7–28 December 1981, 25.
3. "New Sofette Introduced,"
La-Z-News, June 1980.
4. La-Z-Boy Annual Report, 1981.
5. Larry LaPointe, interviewed by
Jeffrey L. Rodengen,
tape recording,
18 August 2002,
Write Stuff Enterprises.
6. La-Z-Boy Annual Report, 1982.
7. "La-Z-Boy Sets Plan in Motion for
New Products, New Customers,"
HFD Retailing Home Furnishings,
11 August 1980, 8.
8. La-Z-Boy Annual Report, 1981.
9. Memo from C. T. Knabusch to
La-Z-Boy management,
16 March 1981.
10. Joyce Earnhardt, "Norton Sets 2nd
Career in Motion with La-Z-Boy,"
Furniture/Today,
26 April–11 May 1981, 26.
11. "La-Z-Boy Is Straightening Up,"
HFD Retailing Home Furnishings,
28 February 1983, 10.
12. Rocque Lipford, interviewed by
Richard F. Hubbard,
tape recording, 1 July 2002,
Write Stuff Enterprises.
13. John Quinn, interviewed by
Richard F. Hubbard,

tape recording,
5 February 2002,
Write Stuff Enterprises.
14. "Furniture Wizard to Guide
La-Z-Boy," 25.
15. Kim D. Shaver, "La-Z-Boy Halfway
with Milestone," *Furniture/Today*,
23 February 1987; La-Z-Boy
Annual Report, 1982.
16. Quinn, interview.
17. La-Z-Boy Annual Report, 1987.
18. Quinn, interview.
19. "Norton Stresses Good Partnership
Between Manufacturing, Retail,"
*Upholstery Manufacturing
Management*, October 1985, 10;
and Earnhardt, "Norton Sets 2nd
Career in Motion," 26.
20. La-Z-Boy Annual Report, 1983.
21. "The New Motion-Modulars
from La-Z-Boy," La-Z-Boy
advertisement, n.d.
22. Case, interview, Rodengen.
23. "Top Players."
24. Quinn, interview.
25. Ibid.
26. La-Z-Boy Annual Report, 1983.
27. La-Z-Boy Annual Report, 1984.
28. Ibid.
29. La-Z-Boy Annual Report, 1985.
30. La-Z-Boy Annual Report, 1986.
31. "Karras' TV Ads for La-Z-Boy Bring
Raves From Movie Critics,"
Furniture/Today, 8 July 1985.
32. La-Z-Boy Annual Report, 1985.
33. Ibid.
34. "Gertz Quits La-Z-Boy Post,"
Monroe Evening News,
12 October 1982.
35. Bruce Vernyi, "New La-Z-Boy
Chief Is Another Knabusch,"
Toledo Blade, 30 July 1985.
36. La-Z-Boy Annual Report, 1989.
37. La-Z-Boy Annual Report, 1981.
38. La-Z-Boy Annual Report, 1983.
39. La-Z-Boy Annual Report, 1981.
40. LaPointe, interview.
41. La-Z-Boy Annual Report, 1985.
42. LaPointe, interview.
43. La-Z-Boy Annual Report, 1983.
44. Carr, interview, Rodengen.
45. Mark True, "La-Z-Boy Continues
Role as Innovator in Materials
Handling," *Upholstery
Manufacturing Management*,
September 1985, 29.
46. "La-Z-Boy Expanding at Five Plant
Sites," *Toledo Blade*,
31 July 1984.

47. Bill Wellborn, "Casegoods by La-Z-
Boy," *Furniture Manufacturing
Management*, March 1985, 22.
48. La-Z-Boy Annual Report, 1985.
49. La-Z-Boy Annual Report, 1984.
50. La-Z-Boy Annual Report, 1985.
51. La-Z-Boy Annual Report, 1984.
52. La-Z-Boy Annual Report, 1986.
53. Jackson, interview.
54. La-Z-Boy Annual Report, 1987.
55. Ibid.
56. Ibid.
57. LaPointe, interview.
58. La-Z-Boy Annual Report, 1989.
59. Ibid.
60. "La-Z-Boy: Correlites
Designed to Fit Shoppes' Mix,"
Furniture/Today,
7 September 1987; and
La-Z-Boy Annual Report, 1987.
61. La-Z-Boy Annual Report, 1987.
62. Kurt Darrow, interviewed by
Jeffrey L. Rodengen,
tape recording,
18 August 2001,
Write Stuff Enterprises.
63. La-Z-Boy Annual Report, 1987.
64. Ibid.
65. Case, interview, Rodengen.
66. "La-Z-Boy Cited as Social
Investment in Lear Report,"
Furniture/Today,
6 February 1989.
67. "La-Z-Boy Drops Use of CFCs,"
Monroe Evening News, n.d.;
and "La-Z-Boy Takes Action
against Chlorofluorocarbons,"
La-Z-News, July 1989.
68. "La-Z-Boy Cited as Social
Investment."
69. "La-Z-Boy Ranked among *Fortune*
500 Companies," *La-Z-News*,
April 1991, 3.
70. Matthew Schifrin,
"Rocking the Recliners,"
Forbes, 16 October 1989, 194.
71. Ed Breunig Jr., interviewed by
Richard F. Hubbard,
tape recording,
17 June 2002,
Write Stuff Enterprises.
72. Ibid.
73. "Gallery Openings Announced,"
La-Z-News, October 1991, 5.
74. Pat Norton, interviewed by
Jeffrey L. Rodengen,
tape recording,
17 August 2001,
Write Stuff Enterprises.

Chapter Six Sidebar:
If Walls Could Talk

1. Judith Carr, interviewed by Barbara Koch, tape recording, 27 March 2002, Write Stuff Enterprises.

Chapter Six Sidebar:
RoseJohnson

1. "RoseJohnson," La-Z-Boy Annual Report, 1986.
2. "RoseJohnson, Incorporated," La-Z-News, December 1986.
3. Ibid.
4. Ibid.
5. La-Z-Boy Annual Report, 1987.
6. Ibid.
7. Ibid.
8. La-Z-Boy Annual Report, 1984.

Chapter Six Sidebar:
Burris Industries

1. "Burris Industries, Inc.," La-Z-News, October 1987.
2. "Burris," La-Z-Boy Annual Report, 1986.
3. Ibid.
4. Ibid.

Chapter Six Sidebar:
Hammary Furniture

1. "Hammary Furniture Co., Inc." La-Z-News, December 1986; and "Celebrating 50 Years of Excellence!" Hammary Headliner, November 1992.
2. www.hammary.com/history.html, accessed October 2002.
3. La-Z-Boy Annual Report, 1987.

Chapter Six Sidebar:
Kincaid Furniture Company

1. "Kincaid Moves La-Z-Boy into New Areas of the Home," La-Z-Boy Annual Report, 1988.
2. Steve Kincaid, interviewed by Richard F. Hubbard, tape recording, 11 February 2002, Write Stuff Enterprises.
3. Ibid.

Chapter Six Sidebar:
The Beloved Mr. K.

1. Gertz, interview.
2. Edwin Shoemaker, interview, Au, 27.
3. Carr, interview, Rodengen.
4. Betty Lou White, interview; and Carr, interview, Rodengen.
5. "In Memory of Edward M. Knabusch," La-Z-News, March 1988.
6. Ibid.

Chapter Six Sidebar:
Miss America's Throne

1. Kaye Lani Wilson, interviewed by Richard F. Hubbard, tape recording, 5 February 2002, Write Stuff Enterprises.

Chapter Seven

1. La-Z-Boy Annual Report, 1990.
2. La-Z-Boy Annual Report, 1991.
3. La-Z-Boy Annual Report, 1990.
4. Case, interview, Rodengen.
5. Ed Breunig III, interviewed by Richard F. Hubbard, tape recording, 7 February 2002, Write Stuff Enterprises.
6. Case, interview, Rodengen.
7. La-Z-Boy Annual Report, 1990.
8. La-Z-Boy Annual Report, 1991.
9. La-Z-Boy Annual Report, 1990.
10. Ivan S. Cutler, "La-Z-Boy Plans Broader Scope for Gallery Units," Furniture/Today, 27 November 1989, 20.
11. Michael Chazin, "Survival Lessons," Upholstery Design & Manufacturing, January 1997.
12. Cutler, "La-Z-Boy Plans Broader Scope," 20.
13. Ivan S. Cutler, "La-Z-Boy Unveils Prototype Gallery Store," Furniture/Today, 16 March 1992, 54.
14. "La-Z-Boy Opens 60th Gallery; Expanded Offerings, Broad Ad Campaign Yield Total Furniture Resource," HFD—The Weekly Home Furnishings Newspaper, 28 December 1992, 16, www.galenet.galegroup.com, accessed 28 September 2001.
15. Cutler, "La-Z-Boy Unveils Prototype Gallery Store," 54.

16. Chazin, "Survival Lessons," 16.
17. Cutler, "La-Z-Boy Unveils Prototype Gallery Store," 54.
18. Lee Buchanan, "La-Z-Boy Readying Computer Link," Furniture/Today, 26 October 1992.
19. Cutler, "La-Z-Boy Plans Broader Scope," 20.
20. "What You See Is What You Get With New Video Cataloging," Shoppe Talk, October 1993, 4.
21. "$299 Remains Center of Activity as Function Bumps Up Margins," Furniture/Today, 2 November 1992, 8.
22. "La-Z-Boy Phases Out Burris," Furniture/Today, 15 February 1993.
23. Lee Buchanan, "La-Z-Boy Enters $299 Arena With La-Z-Rest Recliner Line," Furniture/Today, 28 October 1991.
24. Ibid.
25. La-Z-Boy Annual Report, 1992.
26. Lee Buchanan, "La-Z-Boy Transforming Itself From Chair Maker to Complete Living Room Resource," Furniture/Today, 26 July 1993. 28.
27. Norton, interview.
28. "New Chair Rubs Executives the Right Way," Monroe Evening News, 24 August 1994, 6A.
29. La-Z-Boy Annual Report, 1990, 6.
30. Michael S. McCahey, "Hammary Revamps Upholstery Lineup for Better Fit With Tables," Furniture Today, 13 August 1990.
31. La-Z-Boy Annual Report, 1991.
32. "Kincaid Appoints Kiser Senior VP, Operations," Furniture/Today, 30 April 1990.
33. The American Furniture Hall of Fame Induction Ceremony program, 1992.
34. "Industry Recognizes La-Z-Boy's Norton," Monroe Evening News, 8 November 1995, 1A.
35. Sharon Stangenes, "Furniture Firms Join in Ad Push," Chicago Tribune, 29 May 1990, 10C, accessed via Lexis/Nexis, 31 August 2001.
36. Ibid.
37. Kim D. Shaver, "La-Z-Boy Campaign Combines Theory and Practice," Furniture/Today, 26 June 1995, 12.

38. Case, interview, Rodengen.
39. La-Z-Boy Annual Report, 1994.
40. La-Z-Boy Annual Report, 1995.
41. La-Z-Boy Annual Report, 1994.
42. Barbara Garet, "Revisions Puts La-Z-Boy in High Gear," *Wood & Wood Products,* February 1993, 3, galenet.galegroup.com, accessed 21 January 2002.
43. Ibid.
44. La-Z-Boy Annual Report, 1995.
45. Ibid.
46. "Plant to Boost Stationary Mfg." *Furniture/Today,* 23 January 1995, 64.
47. Rodney England, interviewed by Richard F. Hubbard, tape recording, 28 February 2002, Write Stuff Enterprises.
48. Ibid.
49. Norton, interview.
50. England, interview.
51. "La-Z-Boy Strengthens Independent Ties," *Furniture/Today,* 23 January 1995, 64.
52. Lee Buchanan, "La-Z-Boy Sets Big Buy," *Furniture/Today,* 23 January 1995, 1.
53. La-Z-Boy Annual Report, 1993.
54. Tahree Lane, "'Happy Chair' Heading for the Far East," *Toledo Blade,* 26 July 1994, via Business NewsBank, www.infoweb3.newsbank.com, accessed 21 January 2002.
55. La-Z-Boy Annual Reports, 1995 and 1996.
56. "Gertz Quits La-Z-Boy Post," *Monroe Evening News,* 12 October 1982; and "Civic Leader Herman Gertz Dead at 85," *Monroe Evening News,* 13 November 1995.

Chapter Seven Sidebar: England Inc.

1. La-Z-Boy Annual Report, 1995; and "Plant to Boost Stationary Mfg." *Furniture/Today,* 23 January 1995, 64.

Chapter Eight

1. Charles Slat, "La-Z-Boy Dropping the 'Chair,'" *Monroe Evening News,* 30 July 1996.
2. La-Z-Boy Annual Report, 1996.
3. Ibid.

4. Ibid.
5. Ibid.
6. Ibid.
7. "Top 25 News Stories: HomeLife," *Furniture/Today* 25 Years, September 2001, 14.
8. Nancy Butler, "Sears Adding La-Z-Boy to All HomeLife Stores," *Furniture/Today,* n.d.
9. Ibid.
10. "La-Z-Boy Wins 'Quality Source of Year' Award From Sears," *The Newton* (Mississippi) *Record,* 6 May 1998, 5A.
11. "Top 25 News Stories: HomeLife," 14.
12. Charles Slat, "La-Z-Boy Takes $3.1 Million Hit From Montgomery Ward Bankruptcy," *Monroe Evening News,* 6 August 1997.
13. La-Z-Boy Annual Reports, 1996 and 1997.
14. "Kincaid, Hammary and Ducks Unlimited . . . It's a Natural," La-Z-Boy News Release, n.d.
15. Ibid.
16. La-Z-Boy Annual Reports, 1996 and 1997.
17. Ibid.
18. Charles Slat, "Kiser to Lead La-Z-Boy," *Monroe Evening News,* 30 October 1997; and Gary T. Pakulski, "Lounging Around," *Pittsburgh Post-Gazette,* 24 March 1998.
19. Rebecca Garau, "Energetic La-Z-Boy," *HFN—The Weekly Newspaper for the Home Furnishings Network,* 8 December 1997, 1.
20. Hardy, interview.
21. Darrow, interview.
22. Jerry Epperson, "Remembering Charles Knabusch, Quiet Industry Giant," *Furniture/Today,* 27 October 1997.
23. Vanessa Gezari, "La-Z-Boy's Chief a Leader in Community," *Toledo Blade,* 15 October 1997.
24. Ben Klayman, "La-Z-Boy Goes on Without Knabusch," *Toledo Blade,* 16 October 1997.
25. Sheila Long, "La-Z-Boy CEO Dies," *Furniture/Today,* 17 October 1999.
26. Norton, interview.
27. Lipford, interview.
28. Leckler, interview.
29. Case, interview, Rodengen.

30. Waltz, interview.
31. Ibid.
32. Lipford, interview.
33. Dale Shoemaker, interview.
34. John Weaver, interviewed by Richard F. Hubbard, tape recording, 22 February 2002, Write Stuff Enterprises.
35. Lipford, interview.
36. Stiefel, interview.
37. Norton, interview.
38. Hardy, interview.
39. Steve Matlock, interviewed by Jeffrey L. Rodengen, tape recording, 7 June 2002, Write Stuff Enterprises.
40. LaPointe, interview.
41. Kincaid, interview.
42. La-Z-Boy Annual Report, 1999.
43. Ibid.
44. Ibid.
45. Gregory White, interviewed by Jeffrey L. Rodengen, tape recording, 18 August 2001, Write Stuff Enterprises.
46. Ibid.
47. Donald W. Patterson, "Say Hello Again to Original La-Z-Boy," *News & Record* (Greensboro, North Carolina), 11 September 1999, 1D, accessed via Lexis-Nexis, 31 August 2001.
48. "About the Pinnacle Design Achievement Awards," www.asfd.com/pinnacle.htm, accessed 11 February 2002.
49. "La-Z-Boy Furniture Gets Industry Recognition," *Monroe Evening News,* 25 November 1998.
50. Ibid.
51. Gerald Kiser, interviewed by Jeffrey L. Rodengen, tape recording, 18 August 2001, Write Stuff Enterprises.
52. "La-Z-Boy Division Gets Management Team," *Monroe Evening News,* 15 September 1999.
53. Ibid.
54. La-Z-Boy Annual Report, 1999.
55. Ibid. and La-Z-Boy Annual Report, 2000.
56. Doug Donnelly, "La-Z-Boy Cuts, Moves Jobs," *Monroe Evening News,* 2 September 1998.
57. Jennifer Bott, "La-Z-Boy Leap to Records," *Detroit Free Press,*

23 July 1999; and "Top 25 U.S. Furniture Manufacturers," *Furniture/Today,* 10 May 1999, 9.

58. Angel Schroeder, "La-Z-Boy Flexes Muscle; Acquisition of Ladd Should Please Investors," *HFN— The Weekly Newspaper for the Home Furnishing Network,* 11 October 1999, 46, galenet.galegroup.com, accessed 13 February 2002.

59. Ibid.

60. Kiser, interview.

61. Angel Schroeder, "Nothing Idle about La-Z-Boy; Acquisitions, Sales Growth Give La-Z-Boy Plenty of Exercise," *HFN The Weekly Newspaper for the Home Furnishing Network,* 23 August 1999, 17, galenet.galegroup.com, accessed 19 February 2002.

62. Kiser, interview.

63. Schroeder, "Nothing Idle," 17.

64. "La-Z-Boy Incorporated Agrees to Strategic Combination With Ladd Furniture Inc.," La-Z-Boy News Release, 28 September 1999.

65. Jennifer Bott, "Deal Has La-Z-Boy Sitting Pretty," *Detroit Free Press,* 30 September 1999, 1C.

66. Charles Slat, "La-Z-Boy Acquires Ladd," *Monroe Evening News,* 29 September 1999.

67. Richard Craver, "Furniture Analysts Praise Pact," *High Point Enterprise,* 30 September 1999, www.hpe.com, accessed 30 September 1999.

68. Schroeder, "La-Z-Boy Flexes Muscle," 46.

69. Richard Craver, "Merger Creates No. 1," *High Point Enterprise,* 30 September 1999, www.dpe.com, accessed September 1999.

70. "Playing to Win," *HFN—The Weekly Newspaper for the Home Furnishings Network,* 11 October 1993, 18, galenet.galegroup.com, accessed 13 February 2002.

71. *LADD: Diversity & Distinction,* company booklet, 1999; and Craver, "Merger Creates No. 1."

72. Robert Marks, "Buys of 6 Firms Make Ladd 3rd Biggest Furniture Maker," *HFN—The Weekly Newspaper for the Home*

Furnishings Network, 12 June 1989, 1, galenet.galegroup.com, accessed 13 February 2002.

73. Slat, "La-Z-Boy Acquires LADD."

74. Amy Joyner, "La-Z-Boy Set to Merge With City's Ladd," *News & Record,* 30 September 1999, A1.

75. Dale Gibson, "Moving Furniture Makes Ladd Look a Lot Better," *Business North Carolina,* April 1999, 20, galenet.galegroup.com, accessed 13 February 2002.

76. "Schuermann Named CEO at Ladd," *HFN—The Weekly Newspaper for the Home Furnishing Network,* 25 December 1995, 22, galenet.galegroup.com, accessed 13 February 2002.

77. Gibson, "Moving Furniture."

78. Bott, "Deal Has La-Z-Boy Sitting Pretty."

79. La-Z-Boy Annual Report, 2000; and "La-Z-Boy Incorporated Agrees to Strategic Combination with Ladd Furniture Inc.," La-Z-Boy News Release, 28 September 1999.

**Chapter Eight Sidebar:
A Mechanical Genius**

1. Steve Matlock, interviewed by Barbara Koch, 22 March 2002.

2. "La-Z-Boy Co-founder Remains Active in Firm," *Monroe Evening News,* 18 August 1991.

3. LaPointe, interview.

4. Carr, interview, Rodengen.

5. Judy Tarjanyi, "Gothic Chapel Adds Heavenly Piece to Home," *Toledo Blade,* 10 December 1994, 16.

6. Charles Slat, "La-Z-Boy's Shoemaker Dies at 90," *Monroe Evening News,* 17 March 1998.

7. Ibid.

**Chapter Eight Sidebar:
Caretaker of the La-Z-Boy Legacy**

1. "Anticipating War Kept Him in the Air, Not on Ground," *Furniture/Today,* 19 February 2001.

2. "Norton Stresses Good Partnership Between Manufacturing, Retail," 9.

3. Micka, interview.

4. "Movers Shape the Industry," *Furniture/Today* 20th Anniversary Edition, 9 September 1996, 11.

5. Ibid.

6. Kim D. Shaver, "HPU Honors Norton With Building, Degree," *Furniture/Today,* 17 April 2000.

7. "Furniture School Honors La-Z-Boy Chairman," *Monroe Evening News,* n.d.

8. Norton, interview.

Chapter Eight Sidebar: Sam Moore

1. La-Z-Boy Annual Report, 1998.

Chapter Eight Sidebar: Alexvale

1. "Alexvale Good Fit, Says Kincaid," *Furniture/Today,* 26 April 1999.

**Chapter Eight Sidebar:
Bauhaus U.S.A. Inc.**

1. "La-Z-Boy Incorporated to Acquire Bauhaus USA," PR Newswire, 10 March 1999, via Lexis-Nexis, accessed 31 August 2001; and "Monroe-Based La-Z-Boy to Buy Furniture Maker," *Detroit Free Press,* 11 March 1999, 3F.

Chapter Eight Sidebar: Centurion

1. La-Z-Boy Annual Report, 2000; and information provided by John Ong, La-Z-Boy director of investor relations, to Heather Deeley, October 2002.

**Chapter Eight Sidebar:
The Ladd Merger**

1. La-Z-Boy Annual Report, 2000; and information provided by John Ong, La-Z-Boy director of investor relations, to Heather Deeley, October 2002.

Chapter Nine

1. "Recline Relax Recuperate," promotional brochure (1931).

2. "National Advertising," *La-Z-News & Floral Views,* March 1943.

3. Minutes, Board of Directors, La-Z-Boy, 24 May 1948.

4. Minutes, Board of Directors, La-Z-Boy, 22 May 1950.
5. John Case, interviewed by Barbara Koch, 6 May 2002.
6. Minutes, Board of Directors, La-Z-Boy, 26 May 1952.
7. Minutes, Board of Directors, La-Z-Boy, 23 May 1955.
8. Minutes of the Board of Directors of La-Z-Boy Chair Company, 24 May 1954.
9. Minutes of the Board of Directors of La-Z-Boy Chair Company, 26 May 1958.
10. Ibid.
11. La-Z-Boy Annual Report, 1969.
12. "Can't Pry Him Out of His La-Z-Boy Chair," La-Z-Boy advertisement, 1958.
13. "The Most Comfortable Part of Your Day..." La-Z-Boy advertisement, 1968.
14. La-Z-Boy Annual Report, 1967.
15. "Betsy Palmer Joins Forces with La-Z-Boy," *Furniture World*; and La-Z-Boy Annual Report, 1969.
16. "La-Z-Boy Sets Spot for 'Tonight' Show."
17. Gary Schroeder, Memo to sales representatives, 6 September 1968.
18. La-Z-Boy Annual Report, 1969.
19. "Beauty Is More Than Skin Deep With La-Z-Boy: Comfort Experts," La-Z-Boy advertisement, 1969.
20. "La-Z-Boy Chair Company Specialists in Action Seating," *Furniture World*, 1 July 1969.
21. "Family Life Paintings Commissioned by La-Z-Boy," *La-Z-News*, spring/summer 1972.
22. La-Z-Boy Annual Report, 1971.
23. "La-Z-Boy Proves It in Every Media: It Really Does Pay to Advertise," *La-Z-Boy Golden Times*, 1978.
24. "La-Z-Boy Doesn't Always Speak for Itself."
25. Case, interview, Koch.
26. "Savvy Segment Accelerates, Refines Consumer Advertising," *Furniture/Today*, 4 August 1986.
27. Darrow, interview.
28. Case, interview, Koch.
29. Ibid.
30. "La-Z-Boy Plans $2 Million Ad Program," *Furniture/Today*, 14 April 1983.
31. Case, interview, Koch.

32. "La-Z-Boy Plans $2 Million Ad Program."
33. "La-Z-Boy Plans Autumn Blitz to Tout New Sofa-Sleeper Line," *Furniture/Today*, 9 July 1984.
34. Case, interview, Koch.
35. James Cox and Stuart Elliott, "La-Z-Boy's Soft Rock," *USA Today*, 17 November 1988, 48.
36. "La-Z-Boy Television Spot Receives CLIO Ad Award," *Furniture/Today*, 19 June 1989, 12.
37. La-Z-Boy Annual Report, 1990.
38. "Players Poised for Era of Progress," *Furniture/Today*, 4 August 1986, 8.
39. "La-Z-Boy Advertising on Nationally Syndicated Radio Show," *La-Z-News*, December 1992.
40. "La-Z-Boy Ads Emphasize Full Upholstery Line," *Furniture/Today*, 6 December 1993.
41. "Ads Designed to Tap into Home-Related Values," *Furniture/Today*, 26 June 1995, 12.
42. Christine Wray Carnett, "The Consumer Connection: Manufacturers Reach Out Directly to Consumers Through Advertising," *HFN—The Weekly Newspaper for the Home Furnishing Network*, 16 October 1995, 32, galenet.galegroup.com, accessed 21 January 2002.
43. Ibid.
44. Information provided by La-Z-Boy to Heather Deeley.
45. "'Loverly' Singing Raccoons," *La-Z-World*, fall 1999, 2.
46. Information provided by La-Z-Boy to Heather Deeley.
47. Gary T. Pakulski, "Raccoon Duo Gets Song Gig as La-Z-Boy Revamps Ads," *Toledo Blade*, 16 February 1999.
48. Cutler, "La-Z-Boy Plans Broader Scope," 20.
49. Darrow, interview.
50. Tanya Irwin, "La-Z-Boy Targets Younger Buyers," *Adweek*, 20 November 2000, 6, galenet.galegroup.com, accessed 13 February 2002.
51. Ibid., 10.
52. Case, interview, Koch.

Chapter Ten

1. "Top 25 News Stories: Heilig-Meyers," *Furniture/Today* 25 Years, September 2001, 8.
2. Ibid., 10.
3. "La-Z-Boy Announces Plant Restructuring Plans," La-Z-Boy News Release, 25 April 2001.
4. Gregory White, interview.
5. "La-Z-Boy Announces Plant Restructuring Plans."
6. Pat Norton, La-Z-Boy Second Quarter 2000 Conference Call, 9 November 2000, transcript, 3.
7. Kiser, interview.
8. Ibid.
9. Norton, La-Z-Boy Second Quarter 2000 Conference Call, 3, 10.
10. "La-Z-Boy and WebTV Networks Team Up on New 'E-Cliner,'" La-Z-Boy News Release, n.d.
11. Ibid.
12. La-Z-Boy Investor Analyst Meeting, 20 April 2001, transcript, 34.
13. "Partnership Formed to Produce Line of Recliners for Women," *La-Z-World*, fall 2001, 2.
14. Ibid.
15. Steve Kincaid and Jack Richardson, La-Z-Boy Investor Analyst Meeting, 20 April 2001, transcript, 12–15.
16. Michael Chazin, "Recliners Get More Respect," *Upholstery Design & Management*, December 2000, proquest.umi.com, accessed 28 December 2001.
17. "La-Z-Boy Incorporated Announces Corporate Structure and Management Changes," La-Z-Boy News Release, 23 July 2001.
18. "Darrow Named President of La-Z-Boy Residential," *Furniture/Today*, 20 August 2001.
19. Case, interview, Koch.
20. Ibid.
21. "La-Z-Boy Changes Corporate Structure," *Monroe Evening News*, 25 July 2001.
22. "La-Z-Boy Incorporated Announces Corporate Structure."
23. Gerald Kiser, Second Quarter Conference Call, 16 August 2001, transcript, 7.
24. Ibid.

25. Gerald Kiser,
   La-Z-Boy Investor Analyst
   Meeting, 20 April 2001,
   transcript, 13; and La-Z-Boy
   Third Quarter Conference Call,
   14 February 2002.
26. "Finance Department Expands at
   La-Z-Boy," *Monroe Evening News,*
   14 June 2000.
27. "La-Z-Boy Incorporated Names
   New CFO," La-Z-Boy News
   Release, 29 March 2001.
28. "La-Z-Boy Incorporated Appoints
   CEO," La-Z-Boy News Release, 16
   July 2001.
29. Mark Stegeman, interviewed by
   Richard F. Hubbard,
   tape recording,
   22 February 2002,
   Write Stuff Enterprises.
30. Ibid.
31. "First Woman Elected to Board
   of Directors," *La-Z-World,*
   winter 2000.
32. Gerald Kiser, Second Quarter
   Conference Call,
   15 November 2001, transcript, 4.
33. Ibid.
34. Darrow, interview.
35. Ibid.
36. Ed Breunig Jr., interview.
37. Ibid.
38. Weaver, interview.
39. Matlock, interview, Rodengen.
40. "La-Z-Boy Incorporated and
   Steinhoff International Holdings
   Limited Announce Joint Venture
   in Europe; La-Z-Boy Europe
   Formed," La-Z-Boy News Release,
   4 December 2001.
41. Ibid.
42. Ibid.
43. Case, interview, Koch.
44. Ibid.
45. Kiser, interview.
46. Ibid.
47. "La-Z-Boy to Close 3 Plants,
   Convert 2 to Support Imports,
   Furniture/Today,
   5 November 2001.
48. Dave Risley, Third Quarter
   Conference Call,
   14 February 2002.
49. Kiser, interview.

50. "La-Z-Boy to Close 3 Plants."
51. Kiser, interview.
52. "La-Z-Boy Incorporated Sells
   Pilliod Division," La-Z-Boy
   News Release, 3 December 2001.
53. Kiser, Second Quarter Conference
   Call, 15 November 2001, 4.
54. Irwin, "La-Z-Boy Targets Younger
   Buyers."
55. Tanya Irwin, *Adweek,* 16 July
   2001, 10, galenet.galegroup.com,
   accessed 13 February 2002.
56. John Case, La-Z-Boy Investor
   Analyst Meeting, 20 April 2001,
   Transcript, 32.
57. Doug Collier, interviewed by
   Jeffrey L. Rodengen, tape
   recording, 11 September 2002,
   Write Stuff Enterprises.
58. Gerald Kiser, La-Z-Boy Investor
   Analyst Meeting, 20 April 2001,
   Transcript, 13.
59. Pat Norton, La-Z-Boy Third
   Quarter 2000 Conference Call,
   8 February 2001, Transcript, 5.
60. David Perry, "La-Z-Boy's Gallery
   Push," *Furniture/Today,*
   23 July 2001.
61. Norton, La-Z-Boy Third Quarter
   2000 Conference Call,
   8 February 2001, 5.
62. Case, La-Z-Boy Investor Analyst
   Meeting, 20 April 2001, 36.
63. Pat Norton, La-Z-Boy Third
   Quarter 2000 Conference Call,
   8 February 2001, Transcript, 5.
64. Gerald Kiser, La-Z-Boy Third
   Quarter Conference Call,
   14 February 2002.
65. Opfermann, interview.
66. Quinn, interview.
67. Ed Breunig III, interview.
68. Darrow, interview.
69. Matlock, interview, Rodengen.
70. Ibid.
71. Norton, interview.
72. Ibid.
73. Ibid.

**Chapter Ten Sidebar:
America's Love-Hate Relationship
with the Recliner**

1. Edwin Shoemaker, interview, Carr.

2. "Recliners in the Comfort Zone;
   America's Favorite Chair Doesn't
   Have to be Clunky Anymore,"
   Washington Post,
   25 January 1996, T12.
3. Jane and Michael Stern,
   The Encyclopedia of Bad Taste
   (New York: HarperCollins, 1990),
   263.
4. Patrick Beach, "The Recline of
   Western Civilization," *Des Moines
   Register,* 26 December 1998.
5. Case, interview, Koch.
6. Ibid.
7. Ibid.

**Chapter Ten Sidebar:
Remarkable Reps**

1. Gallagher, interview.
2. Quinn, interview.
3. Ibid.
4. Matlock, interview, Rodengen.

**Chapter Ten Sidebar:
The Independent Dealer**

1. Irving Blumkin, interviewed by
   Richard F. Hubbard,
   tape recording,
   3 January 2003,
   Write Stuff Enterprises.
2. Ken Larson, interviewed by Richard
   F. Hubbard, tape recording,
   21 November 2002,
   Write Stuff Enterprises.
3. Blumkin, interview.
4. Ibid.
5. Bill Child, interviewed by
   Richard F. Hubbard,
   tape recording,
   30 December 2002,
   Write Stuff Enterprises.
6. Larson, interview.
7. Ibid.
8. Child, interview.
9. Art Van Elslander, interviewed by
   Richard F. Hubbard,
   tape recording,
   22 January 2003,
   Write Stuff Enterprises.
10. Ibid.
11. Blumkin, interview.
12. Child, interview.

INDEX

Page numbers in italics indicate photographs.